THE Shining Cloth

VICTORIA Z. RIVERS

THE Shining Cloth

Dress and Adornment that Glitter

With 287 color illustrations

Thames & Hudson

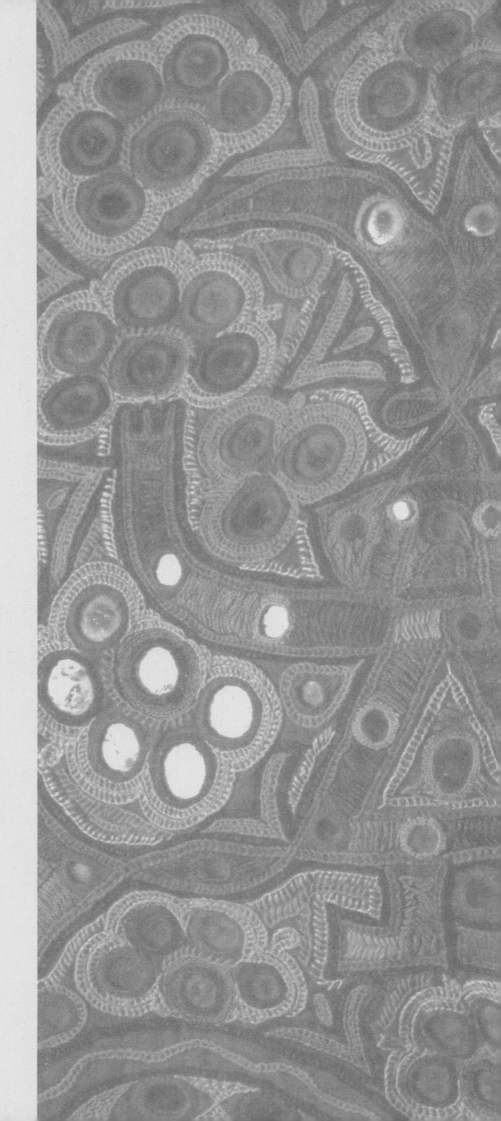

Design by Avril Broadley

First published in hardcover in the United States of America in 1999 by Thames & Hudson Inc., 500 Fifth Avenue, New York, New York 10110

Library of Congress Catalog Card Number 99-70843
ISBN 0-500-01951-7

Printed and bound in Singapore

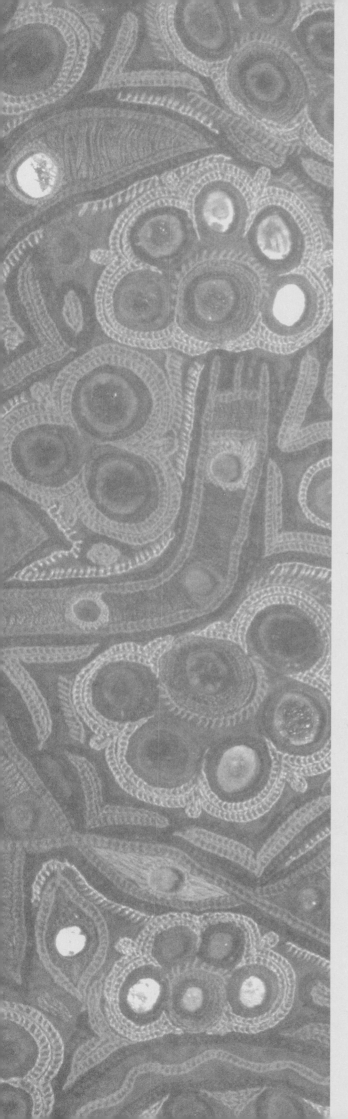

Contents

Glittering Journeys *through* Time

The cultural context of shining cloth

Embellishment with glittering substances is a worldwide and ancient practice. Traces of textiles and other artifacts embroidered and decorated with gold were depicted in Assyrian bas-reliefs, frozen in the tombs of Scythian nomads, unearthed with the treasures of the Pharaohs, and preserved with the burial goods of the Andean cultures' high priests and nobles. The quest for lustrous, seemingly magical silk and other valuable goods resulted in interaction between different cultures and civilizations, and brought new-found wealth which created cities, empires, and fortunes.

In antiquity, many peoples worshipped the sun. Synonymous with light, fire, and fertility, the sun was, and still is, inextricably linked with shimmering, light-reflecting substances. Male and female solar gods were covered with ornaments made of gold. Later, golden-dressed rulers—those of the Scythians, Sakas, and Incas for example—claimed divine origins from the sun.[1] Polished metal mirrors, which may have originated in Siberia or China, were also identified with the sun because of their reflecting and illuminating properties, restoring darkness to light and banishing evil blackness to the purity of day.[2] That so many light-reflecting materials— mirrors, beads, sequins, and white shells—are still associated with protection, with the ability to ward off evil and thereby to preserve fertility, attests to the power of these primal beliefs.

Textiles that people use in their daily and ritual lives convey complex concepts of cultural identity, social status, and spirituality. Abundance, fertility, and continuity through rites of passage are all expressed by shining cloth. Rich and poor alike define their sense of themselves and their positions within their communities through light-reflecting materials. Sumptuous silks and special dyeing techniques make shimmering surfaces. Creative manipulations of gold, silver, and other metals imbue cloth with wealth, power, and opulence. Applications and massed accretions of sequins, beads, shells, and mirrors sparkle with glinting, vibrant light. The flashing energy from these encapsulates soul-force, attracts or deflects spirits in unseen worlds, and provides protection. Natural materials, cleverly manipulated into shapes and pieces, include beetle elytra, minerals such as hematite, mica, and pyrite, shells, and iridescent feathers.

Civilizations all around the world assign great value to cloths and items of personal adornment which use light-reflecting materials. Prized shining textiles and articles of adornment were often buried with the deceased, a reflection of the high regard in which such items were held. The messages inherent in embellished cloth serve many purposes beyond simple adornment or an expression of the obvious preciousness of the materials. Much human endeavor, energy, and expense are devoted to the creation of stunning, lavish, and imaginative light-reflecting textiles, although they are hardly essential to survival.

But from prehistory onwards, the ability to perceive shining, glossy surfaces has been essential to human survival: humankind's first mirrors were probably pools of life-sustaining water. As they drank, our ancestors may have understood their reflections to be physical manifestations of their souls. Interestingly, embroidery incorporating mirrors is found in the desert regions of Afghanistan, Pakistan, and India; perhaps such mirrored surfaces express the desire for water, as well as reflecting sunlight. The use of mirrors, rich in symbolism, serves magical, restorative, and evil-banishing functions. Although the appeal of light-reflecting substances may lie deep within the human psyche, other reasons exist closer to the surface for people's incorporation of light-reflecting materials into their material culture.

Wealth, power, and leadership

Shining materials have always been highly valued because of their beauty, allure, and rarity. Gold is probably the most ancient valuable material used for personal adornment: its seductive glowing warmth, the ease with which it can be fashioned, and its non-corrosive, malleable, and heat-conducting properties all made it appealing, and its seeming indestructibility lent it magical associations. Wealth, and consequently power and leadership, are manifested visually by the possession and wearing of gold in numerous societies. The display of wealth to elevate and secure social position has been widespread for millennia. Ceremonial occasions, such as weddings, are times when ornate dress and wealth are displayed to enhance individual and family status. In Indonesia, for example, people of Chinese cultural heritage often wear dress heavily gilded with gold leaf, called *perada*, which is applied over batiked or Indian-made imported cloth.

Large amounts of precious, expensive materials in dress establish and reinforce financial and social standing within a group and boost the self-esteem of the wearer. Sometimes, protective spirits are believed to manifest themselves through an abundance of precious materials. The approval of ancestors is also believed to result in the accumulation of objects of wealth. An extraordinary appearance deliberately sets someone apart. Rulers, whether of supposed divine or human descent, and their entourages "dress the part" to maintain powerful roles.

The skill, labor, novelty and innovation involved in the creation of garments also help to elevate the wearer's appearance, indicating the income necessary to pay for such work. Competition among rival groups pushed artisans to new artistic heights. Among the royal courts of India, for example, competition for unique, artistic designs led to the use of innovative and unusual materials, which contributed to a greater perceived value. Iridescent elytra from wood-boring buprestid beetles reflect brilliant metallic greens and blue-violets, which, from a distance, resemble the glint and color of emeralds.

Trade

Materials which reflect light—silk, iridescent feathers, and beads fashioned from amber, agate, glass, shell, and pearl—were among the most highly prized trade items. Throughout history, humans have obtained and exchanged desirable goods which have eventually become symbols of wealth.

Faience, glass, and amber beads were traded as early as 2500 BC, and shell beads were highly prized by the North American Indians for centuries before outsiders brought imported beads.[3] Glass beads from Bohemia and Venice were distributed throughout the world by traders. In Cameroon, Africa, elephant masks were worn as symbols of a society of élite leaders which had close contact with the ruler, who controlled the distribution of beads. These masks were considered emblems of high status because of the value and exclusivity of the glass beads with which they were thickly covered.[4]

The male–female metaphor

Additions of beads, shells, or metal often increase the value of textiles significantly. Throughout areas of the Pacific and Southeast Asia the symbolic value of embellished textiles is enhanced through combinations of traditionally associated male elements with female. Beads and shells, along with ivory, metal jewelry, and weapons, are classified as "hard" or male, and textiles as "soft" or female.[5] The manufacture of textiles embellished with these substances often involved labor from both sexes, so that the product became a metaphor for the duality and balance of life. Among several cultural groups in the Mindanao area of the Philippines, for example, hard-shell sequins were created by men and stitched to the soft fabric by women.

The ritual and spirit worlds

People express their spiritual beliefs, as well as their wealth, when presenting precious cloths and objects to deities as symbols of sacrifice and devotion, and to earn merit for good karma. In Japan, wealthy merchants frequently donated sumptuous kimonos woven in silk and precious metals to Buddhist temples. After a death, a favorite robe of the deceased was given in exchange for prayers. These robes were cut up and made into *kesa*, large rectangular priests' mantles consisting of multiple pieces which hung over the shoulder and were partially wrapped around the body. High-ranking priests wore splendidly rich vestments as symbols of their status, and often *kesa* were handed down to indicate a monk's lineage of training.[6] These rich robes were transformed into elements of dress with religious significance. In some areas, religious shrines and altars are still hung with exquisitely worked gold and silver curtains, and images of gods are dressed in far finer clothes than their human worshippers. Lustrous and expensive costumes, when worn in dances and dramas, symbolize the presence of a deity or a demigod.

Dazzling, glinting light reflected from moving sequinned flags or banners (*drapo*) in Haitian Vodou ceremonies catches the attention of deities and summons their presence. Stitched sequins cover the cloth with symbolic images of the deities and magical diagrams called *veves*. In fire-lit rituals, the flags are waved and embraced, and their shining movements honor and attract the powerful god to enter the ceremony and take possession of worshippers. Older banners contain cryptic images disguised in masses of sequins, while more recent examples represent the deities clearly. Often images are synthesized from those of Roman Catholic saints, from imagery associated with societies such as the Masons, and from West African spirits. Both sequins and mirrors symbolize the watery domain of the spirits, or supernatural forces in forest and bush.

Some light-reflecting objects are offered to ancestors, and others mark rites of passage such as puberty and marriage. Highly prized shining elements and feathers imbued with meaning elevate northern Californian Native American Pomo treasure baskets from the mundane to the extraordinary. Colorful, often iridescent feathers are a natural resource that embodies the spirit of the bird, and many cultural groups gather and incorporate plumes in their dress and ritual objects. Splendid feather artifacts from various Andean peoples' burial mounds were constructed from the plumage of tropical birds; feathers from these birds would have been traded over routes crossing the Andes. Among some peoples, supernatural or spiritual meanings were assigned to feathers, based upon observations of birds' behavior. The use or wearing of these feathers imbued a person with the same qualities.

Protection

Power from a malevolent gaze or stare, the so-called evil eye, can bring about misfortune or harm. Belief in the evil eye is widespread throughout Central America, the Middle East, parts of Asia, and in many other parts of the world. Natural substances, such as seeds, certain plants, animal eyes, eye-like beads and shells, and man-made objects fashioned from reflective metal into symbolic forms, have been employed to protect the wearer from the evil eye's malevolence. The ability of shiny objects to reflect light and thereby deflect negative forces associated with darkness is the ancient root of their protective powers. Shiny objects are worn as prophylactic forms of personal adornment, used as jewelry, or incorporated into dress. Amulets provide protection by association with their sources. For example, strength is derived from wearing a tiger's claw, a hat with tiger images, or eye-like shapes that can stare back at the evil eye. The scents of cloves and other aromatic plants repel evil and are incorporated into costume with beads and other reflective materials. Shiny amulets, such as metal coins, coin-shaped medallions with protective verses, and sequins, have the power to reflect or deflect the evil eye through dazzling, shimmering light which absorbs or distracts its attention.

Sequins, originally small rounds of flat gold money, serve a dual purpose in textiles: to display wealth and to ward off the evil eye. Later, they were made from metal wire that had been coiled around a cylinder, sliced into rings, and pounded flat. When in motion, garments and objects embellished with sequins create dazzling kinetic effects, as well as tinkling sounds which further distract the evil eye.

Coins and sequins are often combined with brightly colored beads in dress from the Near and Middle East. Sometimes shining mother-of-pearl or colorful plastic buttons are used with, or substituted for, coins. Nomads, who face many uncertainties in their wandering lives, wear silver or gold ornaments as a practical means of transporting a ready source of cash.

Sequins are frequently employed in some traditional Turkish dress. Since wedding couples are particularly vulnerable to the envious evil eye, they are protected with shiny substances and embroidery. Wedding clothes with attached amulets and talismans ensure the happiness, longevity, and fertility of the new couple: bridegrooms wear headscarves, shoulder cloths, and small purses decorated with metal spangles; and bridal costumes often contain shiny elements serving multiple purposes, as well as cloves, whose fragrance, as we have seen, has a powerful protective effect.

Cultural identity

In numerous societies, dress is worn according to prescribed social customs which embody community beliefs and identity. For the initiated, those who know how to read the clues, appearance functions as a complex language. Information about a person's origins, social and marital status, and even occupation can be communicated at a glance. Light-reflecting materials such as silk embroidery, metallic elements, beads, mirrors, beetle elytra, and iridescent feathers and dyes are important signposts in this system of communication.

Beautiful variations in textiles and costume elements can be seen within the many subgroups of Miao and Dong, two of China's large minority nations in southwest China. Separated by mountains and hills, distinct dress groups have evolved whose community styles are identifiable from one group to another. Rural costumes, echoes of ancient Chinese court dress, are lavishly embellished, and their images, shapes and proportions, motifs, and stitches compose part of the visual language of group identity.

The fabrics onto which complex embellishment is applied also reflect light. Cotton pounded with indigo, animal blood pounded into indigo to create a violet sheen, and indigo burnished with egg-white to create rich iridescent hues: these are all techniques practiced by Miao and Dong women for festive dress.[7] Perhaps these time-consuming techniques evolved to imitate the luster of silk. In Huangping county of Guizhou province, where sericulture burgeoned, Miao people dye silk rather than cotton. Instead of using indigo and steaming egg-white into the fabric, they pound it with gentian violet. The purple antiseptic creates an iridescent greenish-bronze color similar to the shine obtained from the use of older indigo-dyeing practices.

Hierarchical distinctions within groups are sometimes expressed through accumulations or accretions of certain light-reflecting materials, including beetle elytra, mother-of-pearl, cowrie shells, and beads. The Shuar of Amazonia, the Naga groups of northeast India, and the Bilaan and Bagobo of the Philippines were traditional headhunting cultures who wore certain kinds of shiny decorative elements. The chief aim of headhunting was to capture and harness life-force for the continued fertility and survival of the victor's group. The more a warrior succeeded in contributing to his society by taking heads or other meritorious acts, the more he rose in standing. The kinds of substances and the quantities of embellishment used depended on whether warriors had taken a required number of heads, given a prescribed number of feasts, or performed other ritual acts that benefitted the community. Many of these decorative embellishments were made of once-living things whose color or brilliance lasted beyond their demise. The colorful vitality of iridescent green beetle elytra, pearly shells, or bright yellow orchid straw was probably thought to possess an on-going life-force.

Innovation and invention

We all derive pleasure from glinting and shimmering light-reflecting materials, and this fascination has contributed to a widespread desire to use them in adornment. When surveying the broad spectrum of light-reflecting textiles and costumes worldwide, the amazing diversity and creativity that humans employ is evident. For countless centuries, resourceful hands have experimented with and developed artistic ways of using shiny materials. In areas where mineral deposits are found, people develop methods of incorporating ground particles of pyrite, hematite, and mica into their personal adornment.

People from several areas of Indonesia added small round mirrors and pieces of mica to their dress. Maybe this was a spontaneous invention, or perhaps an imitation of mirrored textiles from India. *Tapis* (tube skirts) from southern Sumatra, embellished with embroidery and mirror pieces, seem magically to capture the essence of stars twinkling in a night sky. Like many other glittering examples, they represent our human urge to use light-reflecting materials to express ourselves, our cultural values, and our place under the sun.

This book is dedicated to the anonymous makers of marvelous things whose opulent beauty, creativity, and innovation continue to delight and inspire us.

1 Noh robe, detail, Japan. *Nuihaku* (combined gold leaf and embroidery) was often used in Noh theater for female roles. The gold-leafed semicircular patterns represent water, while the Ryujin, dragon-god of the sea, indicated a character of great strength.

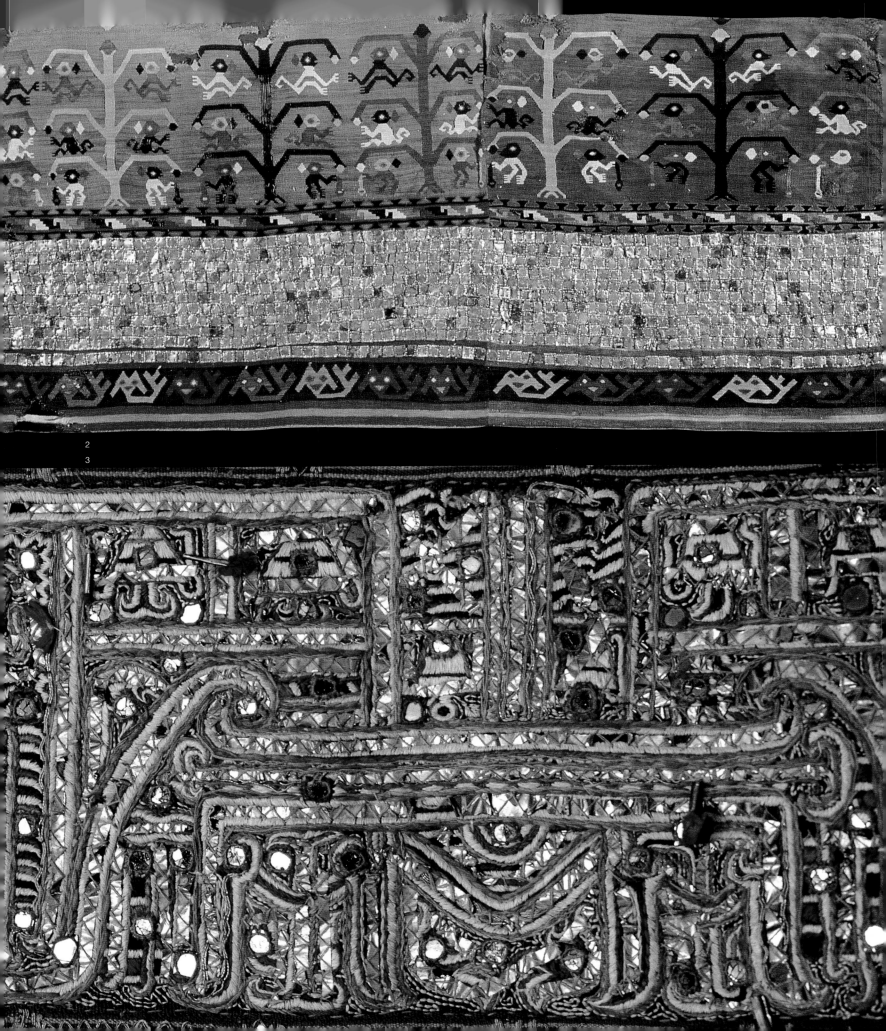

Glittering journeys through time

Over thousands of years, people have devoted great artistry and large proportions of their income to luxurious textiles and dress. The worldwide diversity of glittering surfaces promotes a timeless feeling of beauty and magic.

Ica mantle, detail, Peru. Tunics made for élite members of Ica society were frequently embellished with metal platelets. Some used thousands of gold and silver scales, and others were stamped with bird, feline, and geometric images.

Tapis, detail, Lampung, Sumatra. *Tapis* (tube skirts) with lavish amounts of gilded metal strips, silk-thread embroidery, and mirrors, obtained from trade with India, conveyed the wearer's wealth at festive times such as weddings, births, and funerals.

Dharaniyo, detail, Ahir people, India. On the *dharaniyo* (dowry quilt cover), myriad mirrors, interspersed with flower and mother-goddess images, reflect the sun's life-sustaining energy. This reflective vitality linked through shining surfaces expresses concepts of fertility and survival.

5 *Patka*, detail, Mughal India. A *patka* (man's sash) was frequently awarded for meritorious service. By the mid-seventeenth century, rich materials, such as iridescent beetle elytra and gold, were used to convey high status and favor.

6 Ebrie chiefs and notables wearing gold headdresses, Côte d'Ivoire. Almost universally, gold communicates powerful expressions of leadership. Ebrie golden ornaments relate to parables of wisdom, proclaim social and spiritual powers, and offer spiritual protection.

6

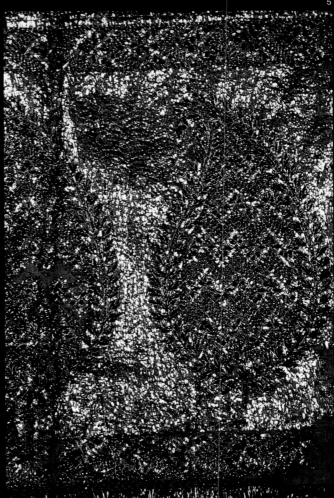

7

8

9

10

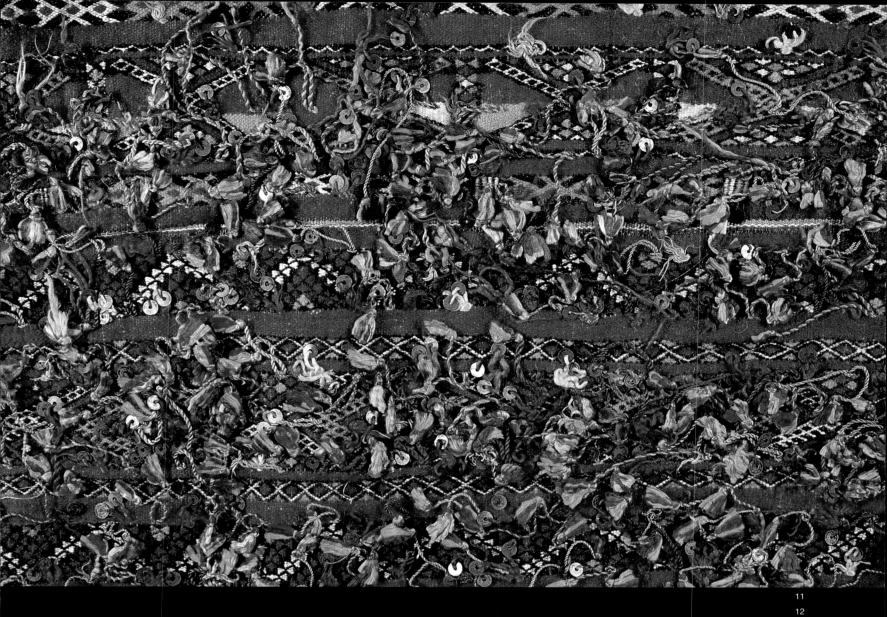

Beyond the surface: meanings in materials

From mirrors that allude to supernatural forces to metallic medallions that proclaim identity, glinting materials are usually intended to communicate as well as to embellish.

7 *Donson dlokiw* (shirt of a hunter's bard), West Africa. Powerful objects of the bush, representing the wild, untamed powers of nature, are attached to hunters' shirts, as well as to the shirts of the bards who sing their praises and exploits. Bards also attach mirrors as dramatic accents to accompany their tales.

8 Young Miao women of Shidong village in festive dress, southwestern China. Miao girls wear distinctive festival dress encrusted with their families' wealth in silver. Shiny satin-stitched silk-embroidered images, silver platelets, and certain types of silver ornaments, such as the horn-shaped headdress, constitute a specific language of identity.

9 *Yafus* (a ceremonial Hupa woman's dance apron and backwrap), detail, northern California. Native Americans of northern California measured wealth in trade objects like dentalium (tusk shell), beads, and coins. Dance regalia incorporated powerful natural materials and prized possessions to display family prestige.

10 Bridal dress, detail, Central Asia. Protective substances such as glinting coins exhibited wealth and fascinated the evil eye, while the scents of cloves and coral beads dangling from sachet tassels repelled malevolent forces from the bride.

11 *Tayttait* (Berber saddle blanket), Zemmour, Morocco. Tethered silver sequins and twisted silk tags sparkle in the sunlight to distract the attention of the evil eye. Protective snake and saw-edge patterns add to the cloth's protective properties.

12 Pomo treasure basket, detail, northern California. Such Pomo treasure baskets were frequently given at marriages; lustrous feathers were inserted into vegetable fiber coils, and further decoration was provided by abalone and clam shells obtained from trade.

Adaptation, ingenuity, and innovation

Glittering substances—sumptuous scraps of kimono; pieces of mirror glued to the soles of shoes; gleaming protective feline images—all add beauty to elements of dress.

13 *Kesa*, detail, Japan. Multiple-pieced mantles (*kesa*), sometimes made from cut and restructured rich kimono fabrics that had been donated to temples, were worn by monks. Some textiles were woven with gold foil applied to strips of mulberry paper.

14 Golden lily slippers, China. In Chinese villages, some young girls competed with one another to achieve the smallest bound foot or the most creative slipper. The fragility of the mirrors heightened the poignancy of the foot-binding practice, as the wearer could not put any pressure upon mirrored parts of the shoe without breaking the glass.

13

14

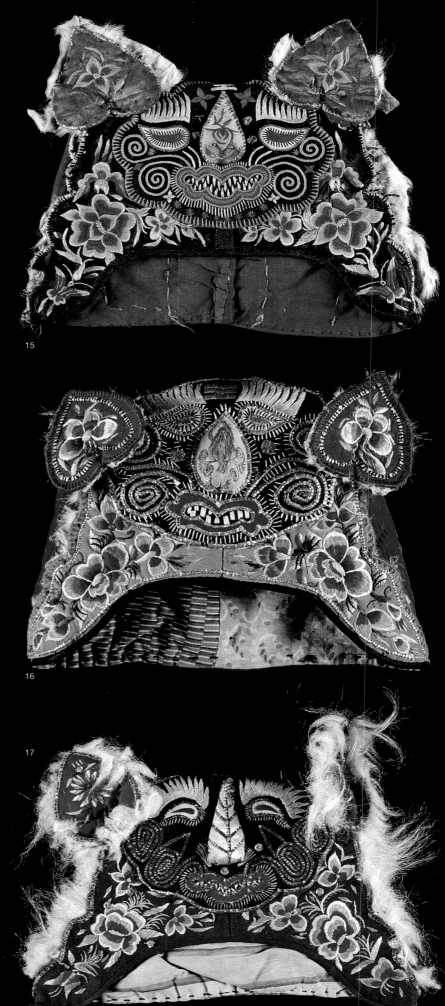

15, 16, 17 Children's hats, Bai people, Yunnan, China. At home and in small cottage industries, tiger hats were made to protect children from demons, ghosts, and malevolent spirits. The word for tiger, *hu*, sounds like the word for wealth. Opulent silk and metallic elements further reinforced hopes for prosperity.

15

16

17

Part One:
Silks and Surfaces

18 *Adras* ikat, detail, Bukhara, Uzbekistan. Central Asian ikat-weavers utilized novel techniques to maximize the glimmer potential of mixed fibers like *adras*, which were woven with cotton and silk. The fabric was often burnished with egg-white or pounded with a convex-faced wooden *kudung* (hammer) to produce a moiré effect.

Silk

Most people know that the soft, lustrous fiber we call silk is produced by certain species of insects. But many hundreds of years ago, the source of the smoothest, whitest silk and the knowledge of how to harvest and weave it were closely guarded secrets. China was the land of *Bombyx mori*, the silkworm that produced the shiniest silk fiber. Silk's sheen, which makes the fiber so desirable, is due to triangular-shaped, prism-like strands of animal protein spun from the insects' mouthparts. Today, the Chinese silk industry recognizes over three hundred varieties of silkworm. Wild silkworms occur throughout Southeast Asia and Africa and other peoples produced wild silk locally, but China was the first culture successfully to cultivate silkworms and to develop sericulture as an industry.[1]

Silk is produced by many types of insects. Spiders produce silk for their webs and to protect their eggs. They spin from fine papillae at the hinter part of the abdomen with five spinnerets compared to the silkworm's two; some species of spider even have six. In the spinnerets, minute fibers are united to make single strands, with the result that spider silk is both stronger and finer than that of the silkworm. Several attempts have been made to produce spider silk commercially, but all were doomed to failure. In the eighteenth century, a Frenchman named Monsieur Bon attempted to farm spider silk. Monsieur Bon made stockings and gloves from the arachnids' silk, but his chief problem lay in procuring enough to supply demand. A large number of spiders were required to produce just a small amount of silk, while silkworms produce many times their own body weight. Monsieur Bon's spiders had a bad habit of eating each other, too; silkworms are content with mulberry leaves.[2] In commercial cultivation silkworms consume processed diets of mulberry leaves and soya beans. The young larvae have voracious appetites and their body-size increases dramatically over a three- to four-week period. After several molts, the worms prepare to pupate by spinning a cocoon. Formed of protein spun from their spinnerets, these cocoons are made of the fiber we know as silk. If they are allowed to hatch, metamorphosed insects break out of their peanut-shaped cocoons as adult silkworm moths. In order to interrupt the life cycles and harvest the lustrous fibers, the cocoons are steamed and the silk strands are unravelled.

Some silk terms and geographical locations have entered the language, while others, once widely used, have been forgotten. The records of medieval merchants describe many diverse weaves and patterns, but it is difficult to know exactly what they looked like. A famous ancient textile produced in Egypt was called *abu qalamun*, or *buqalimun*, and was described as resembling "glowing opals or iridescent feathers." No one is sure what it was, but Patricia Baker has theorized that it was silk or a combination of silk and byssus (mollusk fibers from *Pinna marina*).[3] The word satin probably came from a place in China called Zatun; the cloth was introduced to Europe by Genghis Khan in the thirteenth century.[4] The multiplicity of

Islamic textile names attests to how widespread they were, having reached Europe via the Silk Road, an ancient caravan route which linked the Mediterranean to China. Muslin was described by Marco Polo as a cloth made of silk and gold. Today, muslin is a lightweight cloth made from cotton or silk; its name came from Mosul, the city in Iraq where it originated. Taffeta, another silk or silklike fabric, is associated with a distinctive rustle and shine; its name originated from the Persian *tafta*, to shine. Tabby was originally a striped taffeta from Attabiy, the place in Baghdad where it was woven; its irregular patterns gave striped cats their name.[5]

The famed overland Silk Road was not one big road, but several routes which branched off in many different directions.[6] Caravans rarely travelled its entire length from China to Venice; it seems more likely that bands of merchants traded certain goods along sections of the route, then bartered the goods they picked up there in another town further on, and so on until they made their way back to where they had started. The spice trade, too, was intricately linked with the trade in textiles.[7] Overland and, later, sea routes carried goods from the East into Rome; during the Middle Ages, Venice and other sea-faring city states exercised a monopoly over the last stages of their distribution. But after Vasco da Gama's arrival in India in 1498, control over trade and the resulting wealth and power eventually shifted to Portugal. Europe's merchants sent manufactured goods—woolens, clocks and watches, wines, mirrors and crystal glassware, musical instruments, cheese, iron, and lead—in return for goods from Asia, such as spices, pearls and jewels, silk, gold, ivory, carpets, perfumes, and cottons.[8]

China was and still is the land of silk. Chinese archaeological excavations have unearthed evidence of ancient sericulture including spindle whorls from 5000 BC, a cup with silkworm imagery, fragments of woven silks, and loom parts from at least 3500 BC. In burials dating from 1600–1027 BC, very faint impressions of chain-stitched silk embroidery have been found on bronze drinking vessels placed nearby. It is not known exactly when silk was first traded, but from at least 2100 BC the fiber is known to have been exported from China. In the sixth century BC silk thread was brought into Persia, and by the fourth it had arrived in India;[9] by the second century BC, woven and embroidered silks and silk thread had reached the Mediterranean region. Archaeological finds along parts of the numerous silk routes have revealed second-century BC embroidered Chinese silks as far northeast as Mongolia and as far west as Syria.[10] By the seventh century AD silk brocades, tapestries, and embroideries were routinely sent on the Silk Road via Tibet into Sogdiana, the ancient region of Central Asia along the Oxus River. Tibet's eastern border with China also facilitated contact with Chinese silk-producing centers, from which immense amounts of silk were acquired for Tibetan palaces and monasteries. An inscription on a pillar near the Potala Palace in Lhasa records that in the eighth century AD, China's annual tribute to Tibet amounted to 50,000 silken textiles.[11]

Knowledge of Chinese silk-production techniques spread only slowly. The ancient kingdoms of Assyria, Babylonia, and Persia craved silk for its delicate coolness, smoothness, and luster. Silkworms first reached Persia between the third and sixth centuries AD.[12] In the following centuries, Central Asia and Persia supplied silk to Byzantium. The Emperor Justinian established a textile monopoly which lasted until AD 540, when war with Persia closed a vital supply link resulting in the migration of many Syrian and Lebanese silk weavers to Persia. When Persia conquered Byzantium it gained control of the silk supply,[13] and with the Arab conquest of Persia, the resulting silk production began to threaten China's silk industries, because the Islamic world controlled vast stretches of the overland trade routes. Muslim rulers opened their own workshops and made textile gifts an important part of their political and social lives. Syria, with its strategic placement on the Silk Road, developed an important silk industry. By the eighth century it was known as a center for luxury silk, and was producing silks for the Islamic world. Syrian trade goods were exchanged with items from the Middle East, the Arabian peninsula, Persia, Egypt, India, Central Asia, and China.[14] By the thirteenth century, the Islamic countries had monopolized the silk trade under Ottoman rule. The first capital of the Ottoman empire was Bursa in Turkey. By 1452, the Chinese emperor had permitted the export of Chinese silks to the Ottoman empire, which probably had a great impact on the weavers of Bursa.[15] The city rapidly became a huge trade center for textiles from other Islamic areas, and the focus of silk production, making luxury fabrics like silk-velvets and satins.[16]

The Safavids came to power in 1501, seizing control of Persia (present-day Iran). India's Mughal emperor Humayun spent time at the Safavid court at Tabriz and brought many influential Persian art motifs and craftsmen with him on his return to India. In Persia, the Safavid Shah controlled the silk industry, and his court consumed vast amounts of textiles; Shah Tahmasp, for example, changed his clothes fifty times a day, and, when he died in 1576, he possessed 30,000 rich garments. But even that amount doesn't represent every garment he ever owned; the royal wardrobe was burned every seven years to recover the precious metals used.[17] By the seventeenth century, silk was Persia's chief trade product.[18] Persian controls on goods passing overland eventually led to trade caravans circumventing their cities so that taxes could be avoided. Guilds of textile workers, as well as royal workshops, made expensive textiles for the courts. Flowers, human figures, animals, and scenes from stories were all illustrated in Safavid textiles. Many had metallic grounds and were scored with a hot iron to add a further dimension to their shimmering surfaces. Opulent textiles were in great demand at the Ottoman courts, being dispersed among members of the court, the Janissary guards, members of the royal household, and servants. Lavish wall hangings, floor covers, and pillows were also required.

In Southeast Asia silk textiles were made in, and distributed through, China and India.[19] Indonesians had been weaving warp ikats with cotton from the eighth to the second centuries BC,[20] and the Chinese willingly traded their silks for Indonesian cotton. Textiles were brought from India through the Hindu-Buddhist kingdom Sri Vijaya, near Palembang, Sumatra.

Weaving with weft ikat may have begun when Muslim traders carried *patola* (double ikats woven in silk) and other textiles from India in the fourteenth and fifteenth centuries.[21] Chinese trading communities were established in Sumatra, Sulawesi, and Kalimantan. The use of silk and metallic threads spread throughout many Indonesian cultures, and was the prerogative of the élite. By the eighteenth century, sea trade had circumvented the Islamic cities and shifted economic power to Europe; European looms began to compete artistically and economically with Asian textiles.

Silken textiles and dress were important aspects of material culture that defined a person within his or her group, country or region, and mirrored world views. Since dress announced a person's status, people clothed themselves to the limits of what they could afford or were permitted to wear by their social rank. Certain silk weaves and garments were well known by their place of origin and type of manufacture, and the highest-ranking members of societies claimed particular weaves, patterns, and luxury fabrics for themselves. Sometimes, certain cloths were produced only in the courts, while dress and the exchange of precious textiles at rites of passage was regulated by social strata and custom.

By the nineteenth century, mechanized cloth production and chemical dyes caused dress styles and domestic products to change dramatically, as cheaper mass-manufactured European goods flooded world markets. Some weaving industries have been revived with government encouragement and are making old textile weaves and patterns. But the lowly silkworm's lustrous filament will never again shine as brightly as it did in its glorious past.

Dyes and Treatments

It seems that simultaneously, in different parts of the world, people utilized various materials and substances at hand to make ordinarily non-reflective cloth glitter. It is not known why fabric was first treated with some of the innovative and creative methods described in this chapter, but the end results of these practices are still much sought after.

In many places around the world, it was discovered that cloth became shiny when rubbed repeatedly with a starch, glue, or albumin substance. Asian polishing practices can be traced back to India, to the Arabs and Persians, and more recently, to Central Asia. Throughout these areas, cloth-polishing workshops (*kudunggari*), workers, and tools (*kudung*) are known by the same Persian terms.[1] Sanskrit literature from AD 319–465 describes calendered textiles (which are polished to a sheen by burnishing with a hard surface while rubbing a starchy substance into the cloth) and dress worn by high-ranking people in India.[2] Until recent times, in the famous weaving center of Varanasi in India, woven cottons and gilded brocades were taken to glazing workshops before being sold.

Glazed chintz, with its floral and animal motifs, is well known today for its shiny surface which is achieved through the application of resins with heated rollers. Chintz's origins lie in Indian mordant-printed and painted textiles polished with rice starch which came from India's Coromandel Coast; because the cloth was rubbed with a chank shell (of the Turbinidae family, a shell found in the waters south of India, especially the Bay of Bengal), the process was called "chanking." During the late eighteenth century, chintz gowns were the height of European fashion, because of the opulent effect that could be achieved with the gleam of glazed chintz accompanied by the rustle of a full-silk under-dress.[3]

In Bukhara and Samarkand, workshops specialized in polishing already shiny silk-satin ikat cloth with egg-white or gum arabic. Less lustrous cloth woven with silk warps and cotton wefts was glazed with egg-white foam.[4] Another Central Asian technique involved pounding the cloth with a convex wooden hammer on a convex wooden base: the irregular pressure produced a moiré effect.[5]

In Indonesia, the Buginese, who were great sailors and traders, produced calendered cloth, called *garusu* or *geris*. They were well known for their highly polished plaid silk sarongs. Their method of polishing, which spread throughout the islands, utilized a tension pole with an attached cowrie shell which rubbed sago palm or rice flour into the cloth.[6] On Sumbawa, also occupied by many Buginese, two courts produced ceremonial red polished cloths, which were worn by the élite and bridegrooms.

Weavers in northeast Thailand used two different plant products to give woven silk a shiny finish. Handloomed silk was immersed in a solution made from either the ashes of a spinach-like plant locally called *phak hom*, or from dried, burned branches of sesame (*Sesamum indicum*).[7] In the Southern Philippines, Bagobo and Bilaan women burnished fabric made from *Musa textilis*, abaca fibers, with the cowrie shell method.[8] The wearing of shining cloth and a good appearance were linked to a virtuous character. Shining clothes honored the ancestors and demonstrated a high moral spirit.[9]

A most unusual glossing material was used with Hawaiian bark cloth made for special loincloths. *Tapa* (cloth made from the bark of a paper-mulberry tree) was dyed red with the root of *Morinda citrifolia*, burnished with hens' and spiders' eggs, and then incised.[10]

Textile producers found that incising or embossing the cloth's surface enhanced the richness of the cloth by producing highlights and shadows. After the great seventeenth-century fires that destroyed Edo and Kyoto, Japanese artisans were under great pressure to replace numerous garments; various shortcuts for imitating more time-consuming processes were devised. One technique, *uchidashi kanoko*, imitated the crinkled textures of tie-dyeing by pounding tufts into the reverse side of dot-stencilled silk.[11] Ironing was used in China, Persia, and, later, in India's Muslim courts to ornament dress. A hot iron pressed lines and grids into metallic woven backgrounds of silk brocade robes and cottons.[12] *Gaufre*, heat stamping or crimping with a hot iron, was another technique used with metallic grounds and velvets.

Patterns, even of gold leaf, could be stamped into the surface with a hot iron. The need to develop less expensive processes that imitated more time-consuming ones led in the sixteenth century to the creation of many textural surface treatments, such as embossing with *gaufre*; crushing; *devoré* (a chemical burn-out process which destroys the pile); and selective shearing or clipping into the pile.

The procurement of dye materials and the perfection of dyeing processes continued until 1856, when an Englishman named William Henry Perkin invented the first synthetic dye. Dye sources and recipes were developed slowly and kept secret. As knowledge from experimentation and accident expanded, more sophisticated formulae evolved. Of all dyes, indigo is the most ancient in continuous use; many creative techniques have been explored with it.

The word for indigo comes from the Sanskrit *nila* for dark blue. The Arabs called the dye and plant *nil* or *an-nil*. The Spanish learned *añil* from the Arabs, and the Portuguese called it *anilera*. The word aniline is derived from these words for indigo, because it was the first natural dye to be chemically created.[13]

It is not known when indigo was first used in China's mountainous southwest, but it is favoured by many of the minority nationalities in that region for their distinctive dress. Dyed garments used one of three variations with indigo: those dyed deep blue-black; those with both indigo and a red-violet sheen; and those that are iridescent-polished and/or pounded with indigo.[14] Miao and Dong women were skilled in achieving special shiny effects on cloth; some of their formulae include up to one hundred steps. Liquid from beans, a solution of boiled ox skin and water, pig's blood pounded with a wooden mallet, a purple-colored antiseptic called gentian violet into which cloth was dipped: these were some of the many materials used. Egg-whites were also steamed onto the fabric and then burnished to created a stiff and lustrous surface.[15]

Yoruba women and Hausa men of Nigeria are famous for their indigo-dyed cloths, such as resist-dyed *adire* (indigo-dyed) examples and those made of narrow handloomed strips, which are dyed and pounded to a lustrous finish. Because indigo is expensive and requires many dippings to make a dark color, it is a prestigious dye. Many high-status garments dyed and pounded with indigo use voluminous amounts of fabric or labor-intensive processes as well to enhance yet further the status of the cloth. The Hausa weaving center, Makoro village, is located near the indigo-dyeing pits of Kano and Kura. Long narrow strips of handloomed cloth are taken there for indigo dyeing and pounding until they gleam.[16] These cloths are used by the Tuareg and the Wodaabe of Niger, too; often the pounded indigo rubs off on the skin.

In the Arab world, indigo has been in continuous use for over four millennia. With its strategic geographical placement in the major trade network connecting the Indian Ocean and East Africa, South Arabia was known for textiles.[17] Many Arabs still use indigo for daily dress. Indigo pounding was a separate profession from indigo dyeing, and cloths were calendered with stones to produce a metallic sheen. Polishing windproofed the cloth and minimized indigo rub-off.[18] In *tasmigh* (a gleaming, iridescent indigo cloth), gum arabic resin from *Acacia ehrenbergiana* was also polished into the indigo to produce mirror-like effects.[19]

Certain tree barks, leaves, roots, and saps have been exploited for their potential to shine and embellish textiles. In Oceania, *tapa* cloth was stamped and painted with glossy tree and plant extracts, and in Sulawesi a sticky black ink from the Nompi tree was used by the Toraja people.[20] Some plant products leave stiff, shiny encrustations; others make surfaces waterproof.

Lacquer was one of the most significant tree products which made important contributions to the textile arts. Lacquer comes from the sap and seeds of trees native to China; the most widely used is *Rhus verniciflua*, but many other species exist that produce the necessary ingredient. Lacquer is an ancient waterproofing substance that was applied to baskets and cloth. Lacquer objects have been found in tombs dating from as far back as the fourteenth century BC.[21]

Pieces of armour made of lacquer-coated leather have been found and dated to the eighth or early ninth centuries AD. Lacquer headgear, too, was common in Asia: in Tibet, lamas wore several kinds of lacquered hats,[22] and in China the hats of scholars and military officials were made of lacquered gauze; Japanese court dress utilized lacquer headgear and shoes, too.[23]

One example of lacquered waterproofed cloth came from northern Thailand. A small cloth sometimes embellished with gold thread and mirror, the *pha chet noi* was used by betel-chewers to wipe their mouths.[24]

Adinkra cloth from the Asante people in Ghana uses sap, which is used to stamp impressions of symbolic patterns. The making of *adinkra* attire was one of the funerary arts that included songs, dances, pottery, and burial offerings. This special attire paid respect, and indicated the wearer's relationship to the deceased. Now a popular form of Akan and Asante dress, *adinkra* is no longer strictly reserved for funerals.[25] At one time, over two hundred symbols were used in *adinkra*, many of which have associations with proverbs and moralistic teachings. In early *adinkra*, narrow cloths were stitched together prior to stamping and the seams were embellished with multicolored seam treatments and embroidered stripes. The stamps are carved from calabash gourds and the shiny brown-black sap dye used for the stamping was made by specialists and called *aduro*, "stamping medicine"; it came from the sap of the Badie tree, *Bridelia micranta*.[26] A shiny stiffness has always been an important feature of *adinkra*; in order to project a fresh, well-to-do appearance for the wearer, it is important that the cloth looks crisp. *Adinkra* is never washed, to prevent the sap from coming off.

The use of such a great variety of natural substances, ranging from boiled tree sap and burnished spider eggs to pounded-in purple gentian and polished rice flour, demonstrates human inventiveness and persistence in creating shining cloth.

19, 20 Jacket, and detail, Miao people, southwestern China. The Miao wear shiny, indigo-dyed cotton for festive dress, but in Huanping county silk garments are colored with pounded gentian violet, an antiseptic used for the treatment of skin diseases, which produces iridescent bronze hues on damask-patterned silk.

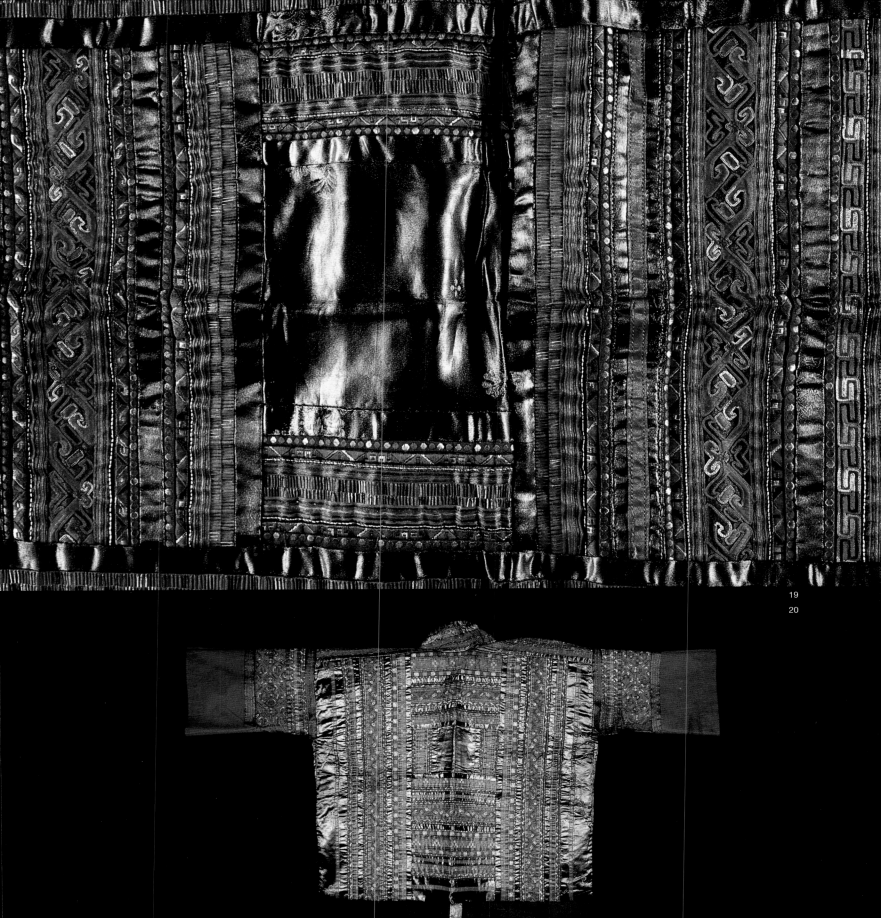

21

22

23

Silk, texture, and light

Highlights and shadows are achieved through processes as diverse as patterning fabric with stitch-resist dyeing, embroidering directional stitches with untwisted floss, and stacking multiple pieces of appliqué silk.

21 *Gahng-ah-mao* apron, detail, Miao people, Zhouxi area, southwestern China. Miao women make *gahng-ah-mao* silk by placing thousands of silkworms in special containers to form communal cocoons. The resulting felted silk is dyed and appliquéd onto festive dress.

22 *Roundie*, detail, Bukhara

23 Jacket, detail, Miao people, southwestern China. In the padded appliqué technique, small pieces of silk are stiffened in soap-bean pod juice, folded into triangles, and assembled in graduated layers with invisible stitching to produce contrasting edges of light and shadow.

24 *Selendang*, detail, Palembang, Sumatra. Many shoulder cloths, *selendang*, made in Sumatra were inspired by tie-dyed textiles from India. Lustrous silk fibers retain memories of scrunching and pleating, a result of the bound and stitch-resist process.

25 *Tritik* fabric, Cambodia. As early as the ninth century, *tritik* and *plangi* (stitch and resist processes) reached the Khmer region from ancient Hindu-Buddhist kingdoms in Indonesia via trade with India.

24

25

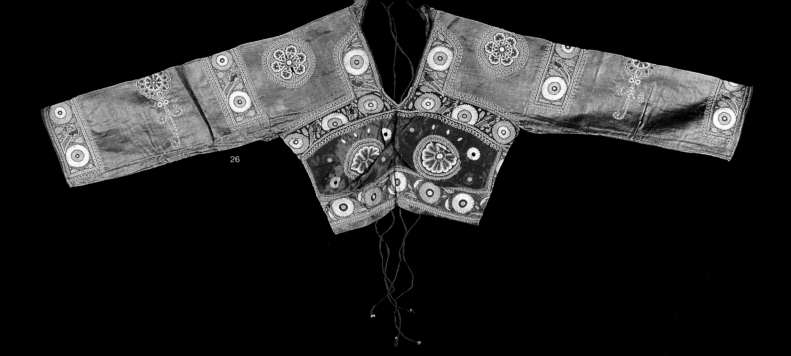

26

27

28

29

Silk embroidery and directional light

Embroiderers create rich kinetic effects by altering the texture of stitches and the directions in which the needlework moves about the cloth's surface. When worn, embroidered clothing with masses of compact, parallel stitches reflects interesting surface variations and color modulations.

26 *Kapada*, Mochi *bharat* embroidery, Kutch, western Gujarat, India. The ruling élite and wealthy of Kutch commissioned professional male embroiderers from the Mochi caste to work silk garments, like this backless bodice, with tambour needles.

27 *Libra dubu* or *kasugu*, Kotoko and Kanouri people, Chad, Africa. Prestige dresses with labor-intensive embroidery were called *libra dubu* ("one thousand needles"), or *kasugu* ("big deal"). Silky, untwisted cotton floss achieved similar light-reflecting effects to silk.

28 *Phulkari* headcloth, detail, Punjab, India. *Phulkari* (flowering work) is a technique of embroidering untwisted silk, or more recently rayon thread, on earthy, handloomed cotton to create ceremonial wedding headcoverings.

29 *Ghaghra*, detail, Saurashtra, Gujarat, India. Reflective flossy silk, called *hir*, was used on the *ghaghra* (full, gathered skirt) to create directional changes of light. Mochi-style motifs were commonly adapted with distinctive regional flair by small courts and wealthy merchants.

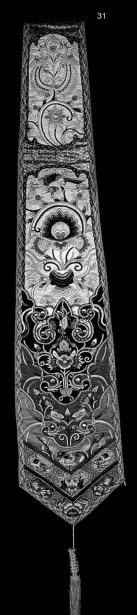

Painting with needle and thread

With tambour hook or needle and thread, stitching is equated to brush painting; images are drawn onto the cloth, one stroke at a time. Varied stitches, overstitching, and color gradations are used to create detailed representative imagery.

30 Sleeve bands, China. From at least the seventeenth century, fashionable Chinese women wore embroidered robes. Pairs of needleworked bands for the cuffs were created, often using auspicious, happy images such as flowers or butterflies.

31 Wedding hangings, Straits, Nonya, or Peranakan Chinese, Malaysia. Pairs of tongue-shaped textiles were believed to repel evil. At weddings, bridal chambers were decorated with rich textiles which symbolized the merging of two families, exhibited wealth and taste, and alluded to protective forces.

32 Mochi *bharat ghaghra*, detail, Kutch, India. Royal and wealthy women's silk *ghaghro* (skirts) could contain up to twelve meters of fabric. Professional embroiderers' designs included Persian-inspired *butti* (bouquets), and color gradations inspired by Chinese needlework.

33, 34 Sleeve band details, China. Minute silk stitches render life-like auspicious and seasonal images from nature on sleeve bands attached to the cuffs of robes. Butterflies signify wishes for longevity, while flowers evoke the seasons in which they bloom.

32

33

34

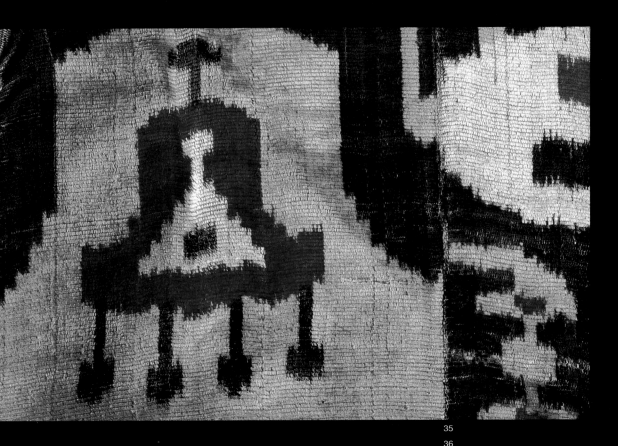

35

36

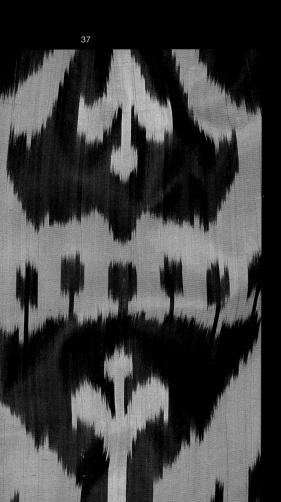

37

Ikats: tongues of the bird and clouds of silk

In Central Asia, silk ikat robes were an index of a person's wealth and favor. The most admired were those of pure silk-satin (*atlas*), although weavers developed mixed cotton and silk *adras* blends, iridescent weaves, pile-velvet weaves, and burnished surfaces for shimmering effects.

35, 36 *Baghmal* robe, and detail, Bukhara, Uzbekistan. *Baghmal* (velvet ikat) was the pinnacle of Central Asian ikat-weaving, which combined the skill of ikat-dyeing with laborious weaving to produce a multicolored pile-velvet fabric. Such *baghmal* robes were unique to Bukhara.

37 *Qanawaz atlas kamzul*, detail, Bukhara, Uzbekistan. In the late nineteenth century, Central Asian weavers achieved radiant effects with silk ikat-dyed warps and fine rosy or orange unpatterned silk wefts called *qanawaz*. A *kamzul* was a woman's robe which was gathered to accentuate the waistline.

38 *Qutni hidim*, detail, Aleppo, Syria. Staggered stripe and arrowhead motifs were called *lisan al-asfur* (tongue of the bird). Ikat- or *qutni*-patterned robes and *hidim* (cloaks worn on the head by men) were important wedding gifts often worn at festivals.

39 Women wearing *atlas ucetek*, Turkmen Festival, Turkey. The *ucetek* was a Turkmen woman's robe often made from ikat-patterned fabric. Arab and Islamic nomadic and rural peoples' traditional demands for *alaja* or *atlas* (silk-satin) fabrics ensured their on-going manufacture.

41 *Rong*, detail, China. *Rong* (pile velvets) were frequently used as chair, table, or bed hangings. Weaving was carefully planned so that images could be precisely positioned on chair seats and backs. Textiles brought an element of softness to sleek, pared-down interiors.

42 Tibetan robe, detail, Chinese silk. Silk was an important tribute item distributed from China to Tibet, from at least the seventh century AD. Imports were frequently remanufactured into high-status clothing and textiles for Tibetan taste.

43 *Rong*, detail, silk cut-pile velvet and satin, China. Velvet-weaving requires a secondary warp to produce a pile above a foundation fabric. Pile loops are sliced open for plush, cut-pile surfaces.

44 *Obi*, detail, Japan. *Obi* evolved from narrow sashes to bind kimonos into stiff but spectacular woven art forms wrapped around the waist. *Nishiki*, a handloomed silk brocade technique, developed from the Nishijin weaving district outside Kyoto.

40
41

42

Silken weaves

Silk is woven into countless shimmering surfaces. Elegant damask weaves with self-colored patterns, supplementary weft-inlaid motifs which rival embroidery, and plush velvets were artistic, technically demanding, and of great economic importance in many places around the world.

40 *Pha biang*, detail, Tai Lua people, Laos and northern Thailand. *Pha biang* (shoulder cloths) could require a thousand shed sticks to create the intricate supplementary weft patterns. Some weavers use long porcupine quills as tools to lift warp threads to be wrapped with silk wefts.

45, 47 Bizarre silks, details, Italy/France. Bizarre silks were popular from the late seventeenth to the early eighteenth centuries, although they appear much more like the Art-Deco styles of two hundred years later, with their Oriental-inspired imagery and non-directional patterns.

46 Woman's upper-body garment, detail, Myanmar. Women of many cultural sub-groups from the northwest strip of mountain territory spanning the western border of Myanmar and northeast India were skilled weavers, and their articles of dress were frequently woven with supplementary weft.

43

44

45

46

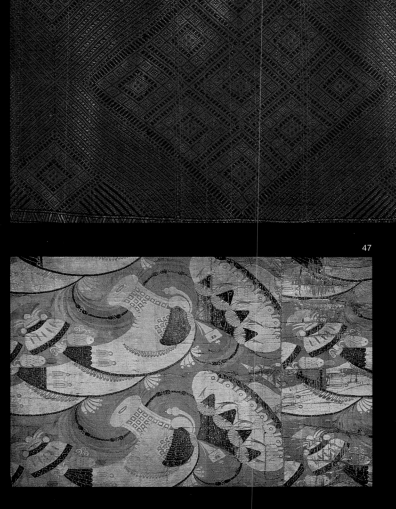

47

43

48

Cloth polished to a shine

Calendering, glazing, and *garusu*, or *geris*, are terms to describe cloths polished to a high shine by burnishing starchy substances into fabrics. Indigo dye also yields glossy surfaces, when pounded or steamed with egg-white and other substances. The shimmer adds to the prestige and ceremonial value of the textile.

48 *Salwar* (trousers), Bagobo/ Bilaan people, Mindanao, Philippine Islands. Clothing made from the abaca plant was polished with rice flour using a cowrie shell. Spiritual metamorphoses were frequently displayed by a change from poor to splendid, glittering clothes at transitional rites of passage.

49

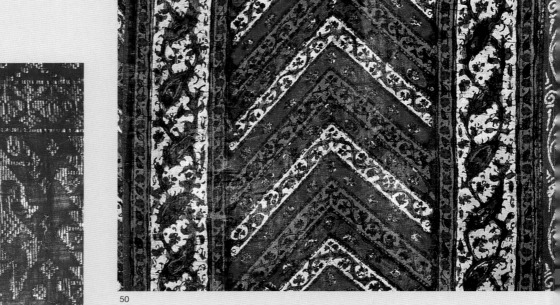

50

51

52

53

49 *Kre alang* or *selungka* (lower-body garment), detail, Semawa, Sumbawa. Calendered textiles, dyed red with *Morinda citrifolia* and patterned with *songket* (metallic-thread brocade), were a speciality of the courts of Bima and Semawa. The dye's medicinal and protective properties meant that it was often used for bridegrooms' clothing.

50 Calendered prayer cloth, detail, Iran. Many textiles were block-printed, mordant-dyed, and calendered to a high sheen in southern India. A nineteenth-century royal monopoly on printed goods in Iran meant that it was often cheaper to import cloths from India.

51 Young Miao women in *yan bao*, Gedong village, Guizhou, China. Miao and Dong women are expert at creating shining *yan bao* cloth with pounded indigo, steamed egg-white, and other materials. Each nationality wears a distinctive form of festive dress to proclaim ethnic identity.

52 *Yan bao* jacket, White-collared Miao, Sanho village, Kweichow province, China. This special-occasion *yan bao* jacket features spiral-patterned batik panels, an angular neckline in front, and pendants suspended at the back. Women wore jackets with trousers and multi-paneled overskirts.

53 *Yan bao* jacket, Dong, Guizhou, China. Dong women use fresh cow or pig hides and blood, which is pounded into the cloth, to impart a reddish violet sheen. Steamed egg-white, certain tree barks, and burnishing completed the effect.

56

57

54

55

58

59
60

61

60 *Tapa*, detail, Fiji or Samoa. *Tapa* (pounded bark cloth) was sometimes painted with glossy brown sap called *togo*, from the mangrove tree, *Rhizophora mucronata*, in contrast to the soft patterns derived from rubbing the cloth on a relief-carved design tablet to take its impression.

61 *Barkalla qamis*, detail, Bedouin, San'aa, North Yemen. In the harsh climates of Yemen, Oman, and areas of Saudi Arabia, pounded indigo garments were prized for their durability and resistance to strong desert winds. Rural women wore wide-sleeved *qamis* (robes), and *barkalla* with embroidered neck and hems for festive or bridal attire.

Part Two: Materials from the Earth

62 *Halili*, Toraja people, Oenta or Tole area, Sulawesi. Embroidered and appliquéd mica designs on *halili* (women's upper-body garments) were connected to headhunting, fertility, and Toraja mythology. *Halili* varied by region, with the result that wearers' origins were frequently distinguishable through their embellishment.

Gold

Gold has always provoked a powerful response in humans. Ancient Sumerian, Egyptian, and Andean peoples revered gold and some considered it the sweat or seed of the sun; among the Hindus it was believed to have been created by the fire-god Agni. Gold was widely thought to be the most perfect form of matter and was therefore imbued with healing properties. The Scythians believed that it fell from the heavens and worshipped it because its color resembled the sun. Other peoples feared it. To some in Indonesia, mining gold was a theft from the earth;[1] West Africans believed that gold had a spirit of its own which could drive a person insane.[2] Perhaps they were right: the history of human quests for gold is as filled with heartbreak and greed as it is with splendor and beauty.

Nothing looks or feels quite like gold. Since it does not corrode or tarnish, the precious metal, with its weight, warmth, and gleam, represents immutability, purity, and indestructibility. From earliest times, weapons, vessels, and amulets were made from copper and meteoric iron, but, by at least the middle of the second millennium BC, gold was being used to express sacred concepts and social hierarchy.

Surface applications of gold to embellish articles of dress were the earliest use of the metal, because early civilizations lacked the technology to weave complex patterns. Gold was pounded into flat sheets from which shapes were cut and then stitched onto cloth and leather. Drawn wire was attached to the surface with a second needle and thread. The couching technique (in which a needle and thread anchor the metal into place) was frequently used because the filament was fragile. Some of the most sophisticated ancient metal-working techniques ever devised were developed by the Andean civilizations of South America, such as the Moche (100 BC–AD 800) and Chimu (AD 1150–1476), many centuries prior to European contact. Alloys of copper, silver, and gold could be treated so that the surface appeared to be made of gold or silver alone. Any silver scale or oxidization was removed with salt. A similar technique for bringing the more precious metals in an alloy to the surface involved repeated hammering and heating. Copper on the surface reacted with oxygen in the air to form a black scale of copper oxide. When this was removed, more silver appeared as the copper was depleted. Electro-chemical replacement was achieved with corrosive soils which acted like acids to dissolve gold into an aqueous solution which was applied to the surface to be gilded and then heated. The heat caused the gold in solution to bond to the other metal.[3] Interestingly, Old World and New World motivations for discovering new metallurgy techniques contrasted sharply. Warfare, transportation, and agriculture stimulated the development of bronze- and iron-working in the Old World, because stronger weapons and tools were desired. In the New World, metal objects were associated with the display of political power and religious beliefs.[4]

From evidence on ancient images on seals and garments depicted in bas-reliefs and sculpture, we know that the people of Elam, a kingdom at the head of the Persian Gulf near the Rivers Tigris and Euphrates, used golden squares, circles, and rings to adorn their solar deities. These ornaments had rings soldered to the back or had small holes, through which they were stitched to the gods' clothes. The practice spread to nearby Mesopotamia, and eventually, by the twelfth century BC, had filtered into the dress of kings and royal attendants. In Mesopotamia, golden shapes more specific to the Babylonian and Assyrian cultures, such as rosettes, eight-pointed stars, and crenellated shapes, evolved. Only Assyrian gods and kings had been depicted using gold ornaments; the sacred character of their sun-gods was thus transferred to their kings. These gold-patterned arrangements and shapes appeared in later Sassanian textiles, when weaving technology was sufficiently advanced to create desired images.[5] From Iran, the use of gold to depict the sacred nature of solar gods and kings spread to Byzantium, and from there to Syria, Egypt, and the Mediterranean world in the centuries immediately before Christ. Simultaneously, the use of precious, high-status golden and purple-dyed mantles spread into Europe.[6] Another study indicates that the Sumerians, Babylonians, and Assyrians traded clothing embroidered with pure gold-wire thread, and that the gold may have come from Arabia, Egypt, India, and Central Asia.[7]

Some of the best-preserved examples of clothing ornamented with gold come from Scythian and Saka burials of the fifth to fourth centuries BC. At one time these nomadic peoples ranged across the Russian steppes to north of the Black Sea and as far west as the Danube. Their rulers lived in great pomp and splendor, as is indicated by their ornaments, dress, and regalia, which are made of gold or covered with platelets and sheets of gold leaf. The famous "Golden Man," a fourth-century BC Saka nobleman found in 1969, had more than 4,000 gold platelets stitched to his garment. Minute spangles trimmed even the seams of his trousers, and natural and mythological animals were symbolically placed about his dress and headdress.[8]

Scythian gold was mined in present-day Kazakhstan and Altai. The name Altai comes from the Turkic-Mongolian word *altan*, for gold.[9] Herodotus tells of a trade route through the Altai Mountains in Siberia to Olbia, the Greek city on the Black Sea. Gold that came to Olbia and other ancient Greek cities originated in Scythian mines in present-day Russia, Transylvania, or the Caucasus, where the legend of the Golden Fleece originated. In an ancient gold-mining process, river sand and water were allowed to flow over woolly sheepskins, which caught minute gold particles, thus creating a golden fleece.[10]

Some of the most spectacular goldwork from ancient times comes from the Thracians. They left no written language or architectural ruins, and their culture was gradually absorbed by the Greeks from the fourth to first centuries BC. But evidence of the finest of Thracian material culture dating from 1000 BC lives on in their stunning golden masterpieces.[11] By at least the first century BC, the Persians, too, were known for their textural goldworked clothing: the Persian King Darius (521–480 BC) wore a famous golden mantle.

The practice of incorporating gold and silver along with highly prized silk into prestige dress became well defined in Persian and, later, Ottoman culture. Instead of awarding medals, Persian rulers gave their subjects precious textiles or articles of dress for meritorious service. These garments were known as *khalut* and later, *tiraz*. The term *tiraz* came from the word for embroiderer, but was later used for prestige dress, since the embroidery often utilized precious silk and metals. Originally, embroidered decorations consisted of calligraphic designs of the bestowing ruler's name. The first workshop to create honorific textiles was established in Persia by Aba al-Malik, the Umayyad Caliph, around AD 685.[12]

Long before *tiraz* was used to bestow honors in Persia, the Chinese had developed highly refined textiles using gold and silver. Their sophisticated technologies and their proficiency in sericulture helped them to maintain a monopoly on the silk and gold thread trades until the sixth century AD. Gold was overshadowed by a preference for jade and ivory, until Persian influence reached the Chinese courts during the Eastern Zhou Dynasty, from 770 BC, and the Han Empire, between 206 BC and AD 220.[13] As a result, the Chinese recognized the importance of gold as a prestige material; its use to reinforce power and display affluence became widespread in later dynasties. By the West and East Han periods, emperors and aristocrats were buried in jade platelet shrouds stitched together with gold, silver, or copper wire, depending on status. Prince Liu Sheng's burial suit, unearthed in 1968, consisted of 2,498 jade pieces and 1,110 grams of pure gold.[14] By the Zhou period, hierarchical systems of dress had been developed to distinguish those in authority from ordinary people. Emperors wore dragon robes with twelve symbols at the various sacrificial rites, and badges were used to denote the rank of court officials.[15] Later court dress used silk and metallic elements; commoners were forbidden to wear gold embroidery. By the Qing Dynasty, dress was so highly regulated that everyone could understand rank and position through outward appearance.

The Japanese courts were highly influenced by Chinese gold and silk textiles. Their artisans adapted *surihaku* (a technique of glueing metal leaf to fabric); *ginran* (the glueing of silver leaf to paper and incorporating narrow strips of it into weaving); *kinran* (the same technique using gold leaf); and *nuihaku* (embroidery with metal thread) from Chinese sources. The golden age of Japanese dress lasted from the mid-sixteenth century until the mid-nineteenth. Artistic outer garments called *kosode*, *shozoku* (Noh theater costumes), and *kesa* (priests' robes) were particularly sumptuously decorated with gold and silver metals.

Japanese society was divided into classes consisting of the samurai or military ruling class, the *chonin* (townspeople and artisans), and the farmers; their dress conveyed their economic differences. The Shogun class system was based on the ancient rice economy, where both the samurai and the farmers paid rice taxes. Merchants and artisans were mostly untaxed and grew rich from either brokering rice or increasing the price of their expensive robes and goods. Competition between the increasingly wealthy *chonin* for innovative and exquisite dress spurred the textile arts on to new heights, and they came to be regarded as an important art form, with textile makers being celebrated as great artists.[16]

In India, too, gold cloth has an ancient history. Since Vedic times around 1500 BC, stories of the gods told of their golden dress.[17] Gold, which was associated with the sun, was valued for its purifying and life-giving powers. The god of fire, Agni or Hiranyakt, was believed to have created gold; indeed, one of its Indian names, *hiranya*, has its roots in his name. Gold is also associated with Lakshmi, the goddess of wealth, and several other Hindu deities. In India, unstitched garments, many of which were combined with gold, expressed purity and were used in worship rituals. Through design inspiration from Persia, Indian textile artisans still fashion countless forms of sheet gold and drawn gold wire into shapes and textures that are applied to the surface of cloth. The elements seem to float on top of the fabric, as they are cut to the required size of a design motif and held in place with anchoring threads that pass through or over them at strategic places. The term *zardozi*, from the Persian *zar* for gold, defines this type of gleaming dimensional textural work. The elements are distinguished by their shapes and weights—*salma* is a square-sided coil of metal, *dabka* is finely coiled wire, and *gizai* is a stiff twist used for outlining shapes. *Sitara* (sequins), *badla* (flattened strips of metal), and *kalabatun* (gold-wrapped thread) add further variety to the textures of gleaming reflected light.

The earliest date is hard to determine but from at least the seventh to the fifteenth centuries, trade in sumptuous and exotic silks and gold-thread weavings from China and India was vigorous.[18] Ancient seaports at Broach and Cambay in Gujarat were active, with traders distributing woven ikat silks, golden brocades (*kinkhabs*), and vegetable-painted and wax-resisted or batik cloths from India to the Arabian peninsula and Southeast Asia.

Central Asians and Persians slowly established themselves in India over several hundred years and came to power in the late 1400s. As we have already seen, the second Mughal emperor, Humayun, was exiled to Persia between 1539 and 1554, but on his return to India he brought Persian artists who influenced all the Indian courtly arts after that time. After Mughal control was decentralized, artisans found new sources of patronage in the princely Rajput and Muslim states. Wealthy traders, too, began to place orders for exquisite gold and gilded textiles, which had once been mainly the preserve of the courts. After Indian independence in 1948, many artisans lost their patrons as royal durbars were disbanded and princely families gave up their states and many aspects of their opulent lifestyles.

The 3,000-mile-wide arc of Indonesian islands had been reached by the Chinese by the first millennium BC, and by at least the first century AD Indian traders brought gold and silver brocades and aspects of their culture to the Hindu-Buddhist kingdoms in Java, Sumatra, and Bali.[19] By the thirteenth century, Islam had spread to Indonesia, and with it came the opulent textiles and status dress of Islamic India, Iran, and North Africa.[20] One of the main ports along the ancient Southeast Asian water trade route, a major channel of trade and cultural exchange regularly plied by Arab, Chinese, Malay, and Indian merchants, was Palembang on the northern coast of Sumatra. Sea and forest products and minerals were transported to China, India, and the Middle East, along with spices, kingfisher feathers, and cotton, while sophisticated woven and dyed cottons came from India.[21] The textile arts synthesized imported design motifs, luxury materials such as gold, and expressions of deeply philosophical spiritual concepts. Through the port of Aceh at the northern tip of Sumatra, both trade and religious activity flourished, as Aceh was a stop for Islamic pilgrims bound for Mecca.[22] Sufism, with its tolerance of older social and religious customs, brought imported golden elements with mystical concepts of heaven and earth; the beauty, luxuriousness, and abundance of wealth incorporated in the textiles represented divinity and Paradise. The accumulation and display of rich textiles was therefore an expression of ecstasy, like that of a person united with God in a profound spiritual experience.[23]

By the sixteenth century, European traders were attempting to dominate the extremely lucrative spice trade. Both the Portuguese and the Dutch were active in Southeast Asia, but it was the Dutch who really came to understand the pivotal role Indian textiles played in the spice trade with Indonesia. Textiles from Gujarat and the Coromandel Coast were traded in Palembang for pepper and gold. Many of these were heavily imprinted with gold leaf or painted with gold after they reached their destinations. The Dutch took Indian textiles to Japan, too, and both Portuguese and Dutch traders brought textiles with patterns specifically created for Southeast Asian taste to the ancient capital of Siam at Ayutthya, and to the Tonkin port in Vietnam.[24] In Ayutthya, Indian textiles were the most important trade commodity, and throughout Southeast Asia people acquired imported Indian and Chinese textiles as signs of wealth and status.[25]

Indian traders reached other geographical areas, too. Quseir Al-Qadim along the Red Sea and Fustat near present-day Cairo, which linked the Nile to the Red Sea, were once important trade centers. Fragments of mordant-printed and resist-dyed textiles from India's Coromandel Coast have been found there, dating from the fifteenth century.[26]

Maritime trade along the eastern seaboard of Africa existed since at least the second century BC. Camel caravans traversed Africa with gold from Ghana and Mali destined for Egypt.[27] Medieval Arab traders and travelers left reports of the elaborate gold regalia used in Ghana and Mali, and later reports from Portuguese, Dutch, and other European merchants described the abundance of gold worn by West Africans. The Akan of Ghana were famous for trading in gold, and by 1471 Europeans had begun to trade there, on the Gold Coast, a name which endured until Ghana's independence in 1957.[28] The Akan and Asante groups of Ghana are closely related culturally, and the European traveler Thomas Bowdich described the golden ornaments, regalia, and dress of their Asantehene (king) and his entourage in 1817. About the feet of Asantehene Osei Bonsu were "ancle [*sic*] strings of gold ornaments of the most delicate workmanship, small drums, sankos [harp-lutes], stools, swords, guns, and birds, clustered together; his sandals, of a soft white leather, were embossed across the instep band with small gold and silver cases of saphies; he was seated in a low chair, richly ornamented with gold; he wore a pair of gold castanets on his finger and thumb, which he clapped to enforce silence." Other Asante chiefs wore "rude lumps of rock gold, hung from their left wrists, which were so heavily laden as to be supported on the head of one of their handsomest boys…Wolves and rams heads as large as life, cast in gold, were suspended from their gold-handled swords, which were held around them in great numbers."[29] Textiles and golden objects were considered part of the wealth that was publicly displayed. Many of the gold items were cast as purely representational images connected to proverbs and messages, but some gold fetishes and ornaments contained powerful talismanic spells and protective qualities too.

Precious metals also figured prominently in the religious beliefs of the ancient Andean cultures, where gold's associations and properties led to its becoming a representation of divine power. The oldest examples of ancient Peruvian metalwork date from 1500 BC, and by 1000 BC, the Chavin religious cult spread through the Central Andes, carrying with it a belief in metals' divine origins.[30] To the Andeans, like so many other peoples, gold was sacred and associated with the sun; it was used for votive offerings, paid in tribute, and buried with high-ranking people. Gold flakes and nuggets were found on the eastern slopes of the Andes, and large amounts came from the River Tumbes in the north. Copper was also mined, but silver was rare as it is usually not found in pure form. The Andeans considered the mines sacred shrines and prayed to their gods to release the metals.

The ancient Andean civilizations produced stunning textiles with metal platelets, feathered garments with metal attachments, and precious metal objects, which evolved from a complex political and social framework. Textiles were produced for everyday use and for the payment of taxes; more extravagant, complex examples were created for the élite. Extended trade-and-exchange networks existed, whereby people could obtain goods from afar, such as crops only grown in certain agricultural zones, or colorful feathers from the Amazon. The Inca élite, who claimed that they were descended from the sun-god Inti,[31] wore the best quality textiles made by their subjects who were taxed with spinning and weaving. To reinforce visually his relationship to the sun-god, the Inca emperor wore gold-embellished clothing and ornaments.

From ancient times when it was revered for its associations with the life-giving, fertility-providing sun, people have attached symbolic meaning to gold. Humans have incorporated this malleable metal, the ultimate symbol of power and wealth, in many kinds of shining cloth with brilliant artistry, so that it is often difficult to determine where heavily embellished fabric ends and jewelry begins.

Silver, Other Metals, and Sequins

If gold was the glow of the sun, then silver was the light of the moon. Gold was principally a symbol of wealth, but silver's associations had more to do with protection. The white gleam of silver was visible by night or day, and thereby provided round-the-clock defense; white, among many peoples, was also linked to attracting blessings from ancestors.[1] Silver sequins, amulets, and platelets in myriad forms promoted fertility and offered protection from the evil eye. Of course, silver was valuable as currency, too. Gold and silver were hoarded as wealth; silver coins, often worn to adorn clothing, also functioned as easily detachable currency. When used for ornament and jewelry, silver's associations with money ensured prosperity and the fulfillment of wishes.

There has always been a tension about metals: people were caught between the desire to possess metallic objects and a fear of their powers derived from supernatural legends about the origins of metals. Silver and iron were thought by some to possess power over good or evil; some believed that metals had souls. Others thought that mining precious materials from the earth constituted stealing. Among Hindus, gold and silver were considered sacred, and human life was believed to have been created from a golden and silver womb: when the womb opened, the golden half formed the heavens and the silver half created earth.[2] Early Turkic people believed that heaven and earth were once a totality. They separated, but the elements remained in contact as thunder, lightning, and fog. Metals were regarded as embryos of the union of heaven and earth, a union which metalsmiths could advance to completeness through their work.[3] Similarly, Arctic women were believed to mediate between hunters and the souls of hunted animals by creating garments from hides.[4] In this way, metalsmiths acted as "midwives" by transforming raw metals into useful forms.

Like so many of the myths that surround it, silver usually requires transformation into useable form. Because it does not occur in large lumps or flakes like gold, natural silver is one of the most difficult metals to obtain; it must be extracted from other materials and consequently was not often seen in ancient metalwork until metallurgy processes had developed. Silver and gold are often found together and the two are sometimes alloyed to produce electrum. An early source of silver was lead sulphide or galena, which was smelted to yield silver. Silver extracted in this manner always contained a proportion of lead.[5] In Egypt, because of its rarity, silver was more valuable than gold until Ptolemaic times.[6] The Egyptians imported most of their silver, probably from Western Asia and, later, from Greek mines. In Asia Minor there were over two dozen silver and galena deposits: Armenia, Afghanistan, and Kurdistan possessed some of the known world's richest deposits. These areas developed silver-working technologies from the fourth millennium BC onwards. Asia and the Middle East, Iran, Armenia, and India contained galena deposits, as did Yugoslavia, Bulgaria, and Hungary in Eastern Europe.[7]

Other metals, including platinum, copper, tin, and bronze, have been appreciated for their utility and beauty since early times. Platinum was used in Colombia and Ecuador, where it was recovered as grains and occasional nuggets found in gold-bearing river deposits.[8] In the Middle East, lead smelted from galena was used for ornaments. Because of its low melting point, the soft metal was easily formed and cast. Lead jewelry was found prior to the third millennium BC in Egypt and Mesopotamia, but was more common in Rome.[9] Copper was mined near Agades in Africa from 2000 BC; both copper and meteoric iron were used for decorative purposes in that continent.[10]

Lead dangles and beads are incorporated into many textiles and ornaments made by the Banjara groups of India. The Banjara are nomadic peoples scattered throughout Gujarat, Rajasthan, Uttar Pradesh, Madhya Pradesh, Maharashtra, and Karnatika states. Lead is sacred to the Banjara,[11] and the use of lead embellishments in dowry textiles may be related to ritual songs (*dhavalo*) sung to instruct a bride on proper behavior. Before a Banjara bride leaves for her new home, she sings a *dhavalo*, a hymn vowing to bring honor to her people. She sings that she will be "soft as lead" and obey all the elders, and that she will "withstand the hard life as silver withstands heat."[12] Perhaps the malleability of lead serves as a greater metaphor for Banjara life, for lead beads in adornment, dress, and functional textiles are used by men as well as women to symbolize "Banjaraness."

Tin, too, was used in personal adornment, but primarily as an alloy. The combination of tin and copper to produce the alloy which gave its name to the Bronze Age was an important moment in the development of metalworking. It seems that Cyprus, Turkey, Palestine, and Iran provided much of the Bronze Age's copper.[13] Cornwall, England, has generally been regarded as one of the oldest tin-mining centers,[14] but Cyprus is more ancient: Cypriots were mining, melting, and distributing tin on well-established trade routes from the sixteenth to the eleventh centuries BC.[15] Later, Southeast Asia became well-known for tin; great quantities were found there in rivers and streams.

Iron was another substance favoured by ancient peoples. Meteoric iron was considered the most powerfully protective metal, because of supposed mystical properties derived from its fiery arrival on the Earth's surface. Since its appearance and magnetic properties couldn't be accounted for, it was considered a magical material that repelled malevolent spirits. Amulets made of iron and worn on the body were especially powerful for this purpose.[16] In central Tibet, bronze, copper, and iron shapes found in the soil (called *thokchag*, from *thokde*, "stone fallen from the sky") were believed to have supernatural origins and to possess supernatural powers.[17] Some *thokchag* date from the fourth to the third centuries BC, and, although they were believed to have come from the sky by the people who found them, it seems that their origins were mostly terrestrial, from Central Asia or the Middle East.

Iron was very important in the special dress of Siberian shamans. Pieces of forged iron found in ancient shaman burials and the prevalent use of the metal for protective means date from at least 1000 BC to AD 100.[18] Iron rattles, hooks, and plates created protective coverings on the shaman's reindeer-hide garments. Some iron was worked to imitate parts of the bodies of sacred animals, such as deer, bears, and birds. Other iron objects on shamans' dress included images of suns and moons, metal mirrors and earth discs, and spiritual helper figures. Although the full symbolism of iron's presence in shamans' dress has not been revealed, it is clear that the material contributed to the spiritually protective aspects of the garments. Some of the earliest forms of shaman's dress, such as tall thigh-high boots, gauntlet gloves, horned metal headdresses, and metal dangles, are reminiscent of physically protective clothing, like armor to ensure safe return from supernatural battles.[19]

Peoples all around the world have attached pieces of silver or other metals to their clothing for protective and auspicious purposes. *Hagab*, the Arabic word for veil, curtain, or wall, was also the word for amulet,[20] and suggested that amulets shielded or hid the wearer from malevolent forces. Amulets protected against evil, while talismans, from the Arabic word *talasm* for charm, were believed to bring good fortune magically. Amulets repelled, while talismans attracted, and both reflected the world-views of their makers. Although they were worn on the body, amulets and talismans differed from purely decorative jewelry.

Many objects worn on the body and on clothing were intended to repel the malevolence of the evil eye. Some Babylonian and Assyrian clay tablets inscribed with cuneiform characters from the third millennium BC describe a myth whereby death was caused by the evil eye.[21] Those who could cause injury by their glance were called "fascinators"; such looks stemmed from jealousy, anger, and greed. Many cultures developed beliefs that fascinators could harm those most sensitive to attention, such as babies and brides. Therefore protective means were used either to deflect the evil eye or to prevent a vulnerable subject from receiving malevolent glances.

Since the first glance was the most powerful, objects that caught the initial gaze were believed to absorb the worst of the negative energy from the wearer. And since silver was gleaming and white both by day and night, it was the perfect choice for engrossing the evil eye. The dazzling silvery reflections of fish in water gave rise to the use of fish-shape motifs, which were also believed effectively to combat the evil eye.[22] Fish shapes are widely seen in Tunisian bridal dress for this reason and are also used as fertility symbols. The moon's silvery glow is associated with ancient fertility goddesses, and silvery reflections evoke protection from these deities.

To nomadic peoples, fertility was essential for day-to-day survival, for progeny assisted with agriculture and cattle-raising as well as preserving the continuity of the group in the longer term. Images such as curving antlers and horns, the tree-of-life, flowers and plants, sun and moon disks, and protective hands suggested the regenerative powers of nature and protective aspects of the heavens, as the sun and moon were considered deities. Some ornaments expressed contrasting polarities such as male–female, sun–moon, and water–dryness.[23] Many nomadic and semi-settled groups wore amulets to express their wishes for offspring; embroidered clothing served a similar function as well as its protective role. Personal adornment was secondary to the amuletic quality of ornaments: nomadic women after child-bearing age usually wore less embroidery and jewelry. At one time, Turkmen women in parts of Central Asia wore ancient images of Anakhita, the goddess of water and fecundity, on their headdresses to promote reproductive fertility.[24] The nomads' selective placement of amulets and embroidery over the breasts, the chest, the nape of the neck, the reproductive organs, and around the openings of garments echoed ancient protective and regenerative powers. Silver platelets and amulets were also important elements of customary regional styles of dress whose use established identity and provided the wearer with links to tradition.

Unlikely as it might seem, fish scales and coins have something in common: both were early forms of sequins. Iridescent, and later gilded, fish scales were used in European needlework and fashion. Fish scales were commonly listed as supplies for "fancy work," along with ribbons, metal cords, and beetle wings.[25] The evolution of the sequin was more complex. The word had its origin in *zecchino*, a term for the Venetian ducat, a gold coin minted in around 1280 which became important in world trade. Imitations flourished throughout the Eastern Mediterranean and into the Levant and South Asia. The word chequeen for the coins first appeared in the English language in the late 1500s, and a later form, sequin, was credited to the French. Chequeens were prominent in European commerce with India, and were gradually transformed from currency to ornamentation, when imitations with illegible or nonsensical inscriptions were struck from thin sheet gold or gilded copper.[26]

Sequins are made from drawn wires of gold, gilded silver, copper, and brass which are twisted around small-diameter metal rods. The spiralled coil is sliced off the rod, and the resulting rings are hammered flat. True handmade sequins can be recognized by a slightly visible line which represents the ends of the metal ring. Some sequins' edges are slightly bent upwards in order to reflect more light; these are known as "cupped sequins." Contemporary sequins are usually made of painted, stamped plastics; they come in many varieties of sizes and finishes such as fluorescent, variegated, and brilliant laser foil.

When multiple shiny spangles are stitched side by side, there is a strong visual and perhaps metaphorical relationship between sequins and mirrors.

In Haitian Vodou, *drapo* (banners) are covered with numerous sequins which dazzle and reflect broken light, like sunlight gleaming on water.

Whether suggesting glinting water, fishes' silvery scales, or the glow of the moon, the cool white light of silver and sequins has protected humans for millennia. In the form of coin and coin-like shapes, or representational and symbolic talismans and amulets, silver was not as monetarily valuable as gold, but was rich in meaning. To some, the gleaming white light of silver is simply dazzling, but to others, its reflective protection is a matter of life and death.

Minerals

Sparkling outcrops of mineral earth are found in many places. After the rains, or when earth is moved or mined, shiny particles, flakes, and nuggets of mica, pyrite, and hematite surface. To some, these are sacred. To others, they are delightful curiosities to be exploited for their expressive light-reflecting qualities. Perhaps these glittering gifts from the earth convey awe or respect for the land's fertility and regenerative powers. With sunlight gleaming from their surfaces, these raw materials transform the sun's creative energy, vitality, and life-force. We can marvel at the innovation and delight of people who, long before our time, made objects embellished with glittering minerals. When the songwriter Paul Simon wrote about the woman who had "diamonds on the soles of her shoes," was he using a poetic metaphor or writing about a real person—perhaps the Scythian princess with pyrite "diamonds" on the soles of her boots, who lived 2,500 years ago?

It is impossible to speculate on humankind's first use of shiny minerals. Evidence and references exist, but they give no clues to the true antiquity of people's curiosity about reflective minerals. Dyes used during China's Han dynasty for block-printed textiles have been analyzed: mercuric sulphide, vulcanized lead, mica, hematite or iron red, and powdered gold were some of the minerals found in the coloring matter. Lead was mixed with ground mica to create a silver colour, and records mention a famous color called "cloud silk," which also used mica.[1]

Mica is a material found commonly around the world. A silicate of aluminum and potassium, it is combined with compounds of iron, magnesium, potassium, or sodium. Often found in rocks such as granite or gneiss, it is sometimes called muscovite or isenglass. In North Africa, mica was found in the silt of the Nile. Mirrors made of mica were found in Nubian tombs, and excavations at Kerma in Sudan uncovered caps decorated with mica fragments dating from the Middle Kingdom period of Egypt (2160–1788 BC)[2] while mica beads were discovered at other sites dating from both Middle and New Kingdom eras.[3]

Because of its natural characteristics, mica has been used in a number of diverse ways. A poor conductor of heat, it has been used for insulation.

Because it is easily split into thin sheets and is translucent, it has been used for making windows and lampshades. Because it is lightweight and shiny, whole pieces of mica have been stitched onto cloth like mirror rounds; ground mica, perhaps our first glitter dust, was glued onto cloth in shimmering trails and outlines. We know from seventeenth- and eighteenth-century *sarasa*, Indian printed textiles made for the Japanese, that some cloths were ornamented with mica and gold outlines. Indian chintz and Indonesian batiks were frequently accented with gold leaf, ground mica, or both.[4]

In India, where it is called *abrak*, mica was widely distributed, but is most commonly seen in textiles from the northwest.[5] In Rajasthan, powdered *abrak* was sometimes temporarily adhered to men's turban cloths and women's headcovers with laundry starch and water. In Kutch, in western Gujarat, mica, gold, or silver powder was sprinkled onto cloth covered with patterns drawn in a viscous material called *roghan*. Contemporary cloths called *khadi* prints, named after the white paste which is squeezed through pierced metal boxes onto the cloth, are sprinkled with mica flakes or glitter. *Khadi*-print cloths are worn as saris, headcoverings, and *dupatta* (shoulder cloths).[6]

The Toraja people from Sulawesi in Indonesia applied mica to garments, but for them the mineral was probably more symbolic than decorative. Women's cloth upper-body garments, *halili*, and men's headcloths, *siga*, frequently incorporated stitched-on mica pieces or ground fragments glued with sticky tree sap. Mica glints and reflects sunlight, and was found in combination with images connected to the upper echelon of the Toraja cosmos and land of the Toraja sun-god. Because of its glittering reflective qualities, mica was probably associated with the sun and upper world too.[7]

Although not itself a shining material, asbestos warrants mention here for its connection with fire. Asbestos, or stone wool, is a mineral that was once considered magic. When heated, it glows red but it is not consumed by fire; its name means inextinguishable. The Chinese, Arabs, and Greeks knew how to weave with asbestos. In ancient times, woolly asbestos fibers were twisted into wicks for lamps. Fibers were spun and woven into napkins and handkerchiefs, which were tossed into a fire for cleaning.[8] Pliny calls asbestos *amiantus*, undefiled, and tells of people trying to pass off pieces of asbestos as the true cross of Jesus because it would not burn.[9] Asbestos was also used for royal funeral shrouds, so that when royal personages were cremated their ashes were kept from the coals. Arab soldiers were said to have worn asbestos suits when burning villages,[10] and even today, asbestos creates the illusion of glowing coals in artificial gas fireplaces.

Pyrite, or Fool's Gold, is an iron disulfide that is very shiny, heavy, and brittle. If hammered or smashed, the crystals give off the smell of sulphur. Pyrite's original name in the western world was *haephestites*, after Haephaestos, the Greek god of fire equivalent to the Roman god Vulcan.[11] Pyrite's fiery name was perhaps related to the belief that if held, it would burn the hands. There is some truth in this: as it breaks down, pyrite produces sulphuric acid which in a moist hand would set off a mild chemical reaction that would generate some heat. Pyrite is commonly found in India, Turkey, and Russia; some Iranian pyrite beads have been found dating from the early Iron Age.[12] Marcasite, a glittering mineral used in jewelry, is related to pyrite but is more gray-gold in appearance.

One of the most interesting ancient examples of the use of pyrite for garment decoration is a pair of exquisite boots. In the Scythian territory of the mineral-rich Altai Mountains in Siberia, gold, tin, copper, and silver were mined; cinnabar and pyrite were also found there. Tin was highly valued and often used like gold leaf to cover various articles.[13] It was a metal commonly found in underground burial chambers with other treasured materials belonging to deceased members of the Scythian élite. A pair of ornately embellished, soft red leather and felt booties was placed in a princess's grave in the famous Barrow Number Two, dating from about 500 BC. The ornate display boots were embellished with couched, tin-wrapped sinew threads. On each sole were forty-one diamond shapes of pyrite crystals, which had been drilled and stitched into two larger rhomboid configurations.[14] The boots were not intended for outdoor use, but for sitting inside, where their soles could be seen and admired.

Another naturally shiny mineral is obsidian, a volcanic glass. The Maya made blades of obsidian, and it was highly valued, too, among northern Californian Native Americans. Perhaps the material was associated with water because of its dark gray to almost translucent glass colors. The most prestigious and sacred obsidian was carved into elongated oval blades with pointed ends. The blades were displayed in the White Deer Dance of the Hupa people, when men called Packers carried the blades in procession.[15] Smaller obsidian shapes were made into arrowheads or tethered dangles, called *tintiin*,[16] which were attached to women's ceremonial clothing. Heavy and fragile, obsidian was not practical as currency. Rather, its presence suggested wealth, because it was ceremonially displayed with other precious objects.

One of the most curious mineral substances is hematite, because it is both highly reflective and opaque. It possesses a cold, dark-metallic gray outside, but if cracked open, a dull red is revealed. If rubbed against a rough surface, the mineral leaves a reddish mark; its name is derived from the Greek word for blood, *haima*.

Hematite was well-known in China as a dye and in Egypt for jewelry. In the Mediterranean world, it perpetuated a myth for many years. Near Baalbek, it was believed, Tammuz, the Phoenician equivalent of Adonis, was killed. At the same time every year a nearby river ran red with his blood. This was in fact due to the large amount of hematite in the area, which flowed into the rivers during periods of heavy rainfall; since it is an oxide of iron closely related to red ochre, the mineral turned the river red.[17]

· Hematite and a related mineral, goethite, were important trade items among Alaskan peoples long before European contact.[18] Aleuts in search of obsidian or mineral pigments for coloring, such as hematite, often entered the territory of their neighbors; numerous conflicts were caused by the quest for special pigments and minerals.[19] Hematite was given as a gift to strangers, and the iron-colored, shiny earth was also smeared across the nose and cheeks.[20] The mineral also held great symbolic importance: red had magical meaning for the Inuits (Eskimos) and Aleuts. Every Inuit and Aleut group made a red-colored hematite paste and applied it to ceremonial objects and hunting implements; it was among the mineral materials frequently used to attract sea mammals.[21] In the Aleutian Islands, a common charm tied to kayaks was a small piece of ivory in the shape of a sea otter. The charm was drilled and filled with hematite, which was said to attract otters and whales.[22] Perhaps the dark shiny exterior and deep red inside of the mineral symbolized a wet sea mammal and its life-sustaining flesh, or perhaps the highly prized red color was considered a type of offering to the animals.

Some objects of Aleut culture, such as caps and bags, used ground hematite as a glittery, perhaps decorative, material in conjunction with objects painted in red and black pigment. Many of these pieces were made for sale to Europeans. Since hematite was so highly prized, perhaps these ornamented objects were imbued with magical associations. No one knows exactly where hematite originated: like its ceremonial meanings, the shining mineral's sources remain shrouded in mystery.

The earth yields many glittering treasures, and glinting minerals have universally been found irresistible. Numerous imaginative methods have been discovered to incorporate sparkling, naturally occurring minerals in dress and adornment. The twinkling surfaces of natural substances remain enchanting, whether they reflect the sun's energy, embody a rare form of wealth, or just delight us.

Mirrors

The desire to replicate one's image is universal. In mythology and folklore, mirrors hold fascinating levels of meaning and significance around the world. They reflect sunlight and moonlight, and their shining surfaces provide a medium for introspection. Some believe mirrors deflect evil, while others think of them as portals through which malevolent forces can enter the home. In Turkey, mirrors were treated with reverence and were covered with lovingly embroidered cloths or placed face down when not in use. Like sequins and shiny materials, they protect humans with their dazzling capabilities to attract or hold the attention of the evil eye. Mirrors deflect light, and thereby blind and confuse evil forces. These protective beliefs are deeply rooted in the universality of ancient solar worship.

In numerous cultures, mirrors are used as tools for divination and sorcery. They separate the spirit world from the realm of reality. Among Haitians, mirrors symbolize the passage between life and death. They signify water, the domain of the Haitian *Lwa* or deities. After humans die, their souls reside with the *Lwa* in their watery underworld for a year and a day. In this other world, the soul sees "the other side."[1]

In mirrors, objects reassemble themselves in reverse, something probably both perplexing and compelling to early people. Perhaps this might help to explain how mirrors are connected with magic. Since mirrors return light and multiply it (if several are used to reflect one light source), hope and vitality are expressed through their use. They capture vital sunlight and are used to light the way literally and metaphorically. Mirrors made of shiny minerals, like crystal, pyrite, and obsidian, as well as manufactured polished metal and metal-backed glass examples, have been created all around the world. Records tell of small mirrors made of polished pyrite which were used by Peruvians and Mexicans,[2] and Tahitians made mirrors of highly polished basalt, the volcanic rock, which were hung around the neck.[3]

Polished metal mirrors, which probably originated in Siberia,[4] were placed in ancient Chinese and Scythian burials. They were frequently incised with solar images, which suggests not only a connection between mirrors and the sun, but also the importance of the sun's daily return as a parallel to beliefs in the afterlife. The mirror, the sun's surrogate, guided the soul's safe passage to the afterworld. Bronze, silver, and electrum mirrors with knob handles have often been found in nomadic burials from the eighth to the fourth centuries BC. Later mirrors, with flat handles, came from the Greeks.[5]

Shamans of Siberia employ mirrors to enter the spirit world and capture lost souls, using them again to shield themselves from evil and to ensure a safe return to earth.[6] As protective shields, the mirrors deflect blows from evil forces, and are often layered, armor-like, to cover the shaman's vital organs. Mirrors also assist shamans to see into other realms of existence.

While we know of examples dating back at least 4,000 years, reflections from water were undoubtedly humankind's first mirrors. People saw their reflections and probably tried to recover these fleeting impressions of their appearance. Perhaps their images were perceived as visible manifestations of their souls. Maybe they thought they were drinking in their own essence or life-force when consuming the water that had reflected them. In desert communities where mirror embroidery is prevalent, access to water is a primary concern. As reality dissolves into illusion, a mirage teases the viewer into believing that water is near. Mirrors flash light like the glinting rays of the sun reflected on a lake: with their ability to sparkle, mirrors allude to all the literal and metaphorical meanings of water and the sun.

Studies by scientists have demonstrated that infants and children are drawn to mirror surfaces, which they are naturally compelled to lick and mouth. Furthermore, they have found that children and adults first identify shining, glossy surfaces with the presence of water, which may be the result of five million years of natural selection. Humans survived because they were able to interpret just such optical information. The remnants of these survival mechanisms may help to explain our delight in glinting, shimmering surfaces.[7]

While most of today's mirrors are made from coated glass, the earliest antique examples were made of metal. The round bronze mirrors found in many tombs were most probably manufactured in Susa, the ancient capital of Elam in present-day Iran. Metal mirrors found in Egypt, Greece, and Etruria probably came from Susa.[8] Some Egyptian mirrors have been dated to as far back as 1500 BC.[9]

As early as 3500 BC, Egyptians possessed the technical knowledge necessary to make glass. Quartz could be melted, and stone with silicic acid deposits would make glaze if salt or soda were added. The first glass was probably discovered accidentally by a potter who dug clay from the mud of inland lakes containing salt, potash, quartz sand, or lime; when heated, these ingredients make glass. In North Africa, thousands of such lakes exist.[10] No one knows when glass mirrors were first made. They may have originated in Egypt or the Middle East and been distributed throughout the Mediterranean basin by the Moors.[11] Aleppo, in Syria, was a famous center for the manufacture of glass mirrors. Eventually, metals such as gold, silver, mercury, and lead were used to coat the glass and capture reflections.

It is not known when *shi-sha*, small mirror pieces, were first used in embroidery. But their protective aspects, combined with the ancient talismanic and protective associations of embroidery, forge a powerful alliance. There are also strong links to solar worship and fertility, since mirrors dazzle and reflect the sunlight. Notice that mirror embroidery is often placed at the breasts and over reproductive organs in dresses or aprons; placement around neck openings, the nape of the neck, the cuffs, and other garment openings created barriers to prevent malevolent forces from entering the body.

Present-day practices of creating mirrors for use in embroidery have changed little since ancient times. Glass mirror pieces can be purchased in bazaars throughout northwest India. Most of them are manufactured at an ancient factory in Kapadvanj, a town in central Gujarat, India, where generations of the Sishger family have used traditional methods to make mirrored spheres. River sand rich in soda ash, called *ush*, was gathered after the rains. When heated to melting point, the *ush* created glass. Although recycled glass is used instead of river sand these days, the mirror-making process remains the same. Large, hollow spheres of red-hot glass are coated with a molten mixture of five percent zinc and tin and ninety-five percent lead. As the spheres are rotated, a continuous spiral of molten metal silvers the inside of the glass. When they are cool enough to handle, the silvered balls are broken into large chunks. Pieces are packed into boxes and sent to the town of Limbdi, about fifty kilometers away. There, women cut the chunks into various sizes of circular pieces with special scissors. Limbdi merchants sort and package the mirror disks, and ship them throughout the subcontinent to be sold in numerous bazaars.[12]

In India and Pakistan, mirrors have been incorporated into richly embroidered clothing and used to ornament varieties of household and dowry textiles. They have been embedded in the walls and furniture of indigenous desert-dwellers and to create fantasy mirror-rooms in Persian and Mughal Indian palaces from the seventeenth to the nineteenth centuries. Whether used for clothing or for interiors, the bubbled, slightly convex surfaces created by these hand-blown spherical mirrors enhance the play of sun and candlelight, and their irregular surfaces delight the senses with magical, twinkling light.

Mirror embroidery was widespread in the area which ranges from Iran, into Baluchistan and Afghanistan, through Pakistan, across northwest India, and south into the Deccan plateau. Throughout this desert "mirror belt" were seen numerous forms of *abhala bharat* (embroidery with mirrors). Much of the region has been under Muslim rule since the seventh century, and throughout Islam, mirrors were used to absorb or deflect the influence of the evil eye. But, as we have seen, the oldest uses of mirrors in embroidery— as symbols of solar deities and water—were deeply embedded in the psyche of desert-dwellers.

Throughout areas of *abhala bharat* production, there existed many regional stylistic differences and subtleties. Facts about the wearer's cultural background, community, village, marital status, and even occupation could be determined from their clothing. For example, many diverse dress styles were seen among the inhabitants of Gujarat and Rajasthan states in India and Sind in western Pakistan.[13] As peoples migrated from Central Asia, Iran, and Baluchistan, or mingled with the original settlers of India and the Indus Valley, each community developed its own styles of embroidery and clothing. The practice of creating richly embroidered textiles for young women's dowries continues among a few communities, a loving activity which preserves the area's artistic *abhala bharat* and other needlework traditions.[14] Imagery, size of mirror pieces, embroidery stitches, types of floss, and color schemes are all regionally variable features of these textiles. Objects made for home decor, clothes for festive occasions, and decorations for animals, such as forehead ornaments and leg straps, bear the stamp and taste of the maker's community.

In some areas of Rajasthan, women embroidered distinctive patterned skirts with large mirror pieces, which conveyed their tribal identities. Throughout central India, the Lambani (members of a larger group collectively known as the Banjara) were also known for their use of large circular mirror pieces.[15] The convex shapes, pits, bubbles, and other irregularities common to hand-blown mirrors are easily seen in these huge pieces. Bold mirrors were incorporated into colorful, grid-like configurations using appliqué and embroidery. Other peoples, like the Mutwa, were known for their work with tiny mirrors and stitches. With numerous regional styles, constant adaptations and inspirations from other embroiderers, and shifting tastes, it can be quite difficult to distinguish the embroidery of one area from another.[16]

The idea of using mirrors in Indonesian embroidery probably came through the textiles trade with India. A collection of nineteenth-century Indian *abhala bharat* pieces was found in the Lampung region of Sumatra, and is now housed in the Rijksmuseum voor Volkenkunde in Leiden.[17] Although it is difficult to state when or how the use of mirrors in textiles first appeared in Indonesia, it is known that contact with India was established as early as two thousand years ago. The Sumatran ports were visited by Indian, Chinese, Javanese, Arab, Portuguese, and Dutch traders who brought mirrors, locally called *cermuk*, and other novelty items like metallic threads, silks, and trade textiles.[18] Inspired by foreign goods, local Sumatran weavers used their talents to produce splendid textiles punctuated with dazzling mirror pieces.

Imported lead-backed glass mirrors probably replaced older traditions, which used mica. Some of the reflective rounds used in Sumatran embroideries were distinctively blue-green and golden-colored pieces of mirrored metal or glass. The thin rounds, most of which have splintered and shattered, were adhered to cloth with a thick brown-black substance reminiscent of the tree sap used by the Toraja of Sulawesi to stick mica to bark cloth. Such golden-colored mirrors, worked into embroidered *tapis* (tube skirts), imitated the gleam of pure gold, something which mica could never do. Embroidered hangings and clothing which use golden- and blue-colored mirrors made from recycled glass are still made today in Gujarat and, occasionally, by the Banjara people from Maharashtra.

The Kauer people from the Lampung region of Sumatra favored small gold-colored mirrors. Women invested wealth from the pepper trade in heavily embellished ceremonial clothing, sumptuous *tapis* (tube skirts) or sarongs, which incorporated tiny mirror pieces. Young, unmarried Kauer women wore jackets embellished with minute mirror-embroidered panels with their *tapis*, and were required to create both jacket and *tapis* prior to marriage.[19]

The Straits, Nonya, and Peranakan Chinese who settled in Malaysia and Indonesia also used mirrors in their textiles. These peoples' traditional ceremonial cloths for weddings and circumcisions echoed festive Chinese hangings with gold, silk embroidery, and mirrors. The Malay believed that mirrors repelled evil spirits, and their legends tell of heroes who wore mirrored clothing.[20] The mirrors on Straits and Peranakan Chinese ceremonial textiles were probably also intended to ward off evil, and to display the wealth necessary to pay for such imported goods.

Regardless of our background and economic status, we are all fascinated by glittering mirrors, for their associations with beauty and illusion, for their protective powers, or just for the pictures of ourselves which they provide. Mirrors, skilled hands, and artistic vision transform textiles into truly magical objects of delight and wonder in which ancient mystical and mythical reflections of reality can be seen—the reality that the sun will rise another day to dispel the cold and darkness of night. Sunlight reflected in mirrors' surfaces ultimately gives us hope.

Beads

Slinky and smooth, shiny and beautiful, novel, durable, and portable—the compelling qualities of beads have deeply fascinated people for millennia. Great effort and expense were involved in making or acquiring them. Some were transported great distances, and were believed to hold magical properties; others were cherished as ancestral heirlooms. Some were associated with healing; others offered protection from the evil eye. Human lives, gold, and lands were traded for beads, and in almost every corner of the world people made and treasured them. These alluring objects were not essential for life, but the ability to discriminate was fundamental to survival. By defining the rare and the unusual we establish systems of value.[1] Objects that were highly regarded within socially agreed patterns of esteem were transformed by the discovery of new materials and techniques, and were used to convey power and prestige through their display and accumulation.

Like gold, silver, or other precious materials used to embellish cloth, beads stitched onto fabric could communicate oneness with a group. People communicated their greater belonging through dress and adornment, while at the same time expressing a sense of themselves and their role within a social structure. Beads, therefore, assisted in reinforcing identity, tradition, and hierarchy.

Scholars have proposed that, on a subconscious level, people were comforted by beads with their round shapes, shiny surfaces, and resemblance to eyes and eyesight.[2] As we will see later, beads with concentric colored spots which resembled human eyes were very important among ancient civilizations in combating the evil eye. On the one hand, envious people were drawn to look at these beads, while on the other, they were forced to look away because of the beads' disturbing, staring qualities. Others believe that pleasing physical sensations derived from the comforting tactility of beads contributed to their mass appeal.[3]

Among the ancient peoples, beads were significant possessions. Many have been found in burials. Perhaps it was believed that spiritual powers from animals or hunting skills were transferred to wearers of bone or tusk beads. Beads were appreciated for their beauty, for adornment, and for conveying status; and they expressed the desire for spiritual protection. Laden with these complicated concepts, beads constituted early forms of abstract thinking.[4]

Around 28,000 years ago, early craftsmen possessed the technical ability to drill holes in shell, stone, bone, and other natural substances.[5] The earliest drills were hard vegetable stalks used with wet sand. Crushed flints, or powdered beads themselves, were used as abrasives.[6] Ivory beads from mammoth tusks and ostrich-shell beads were stitched onto clothing found in Siberian graves dating from 12,000 to 11,000 BC.[7] Both Mycenaeans and Egyptians made molded glass beads and amulets in the second millennium BC.[8] Egyptian beads dating from the Neolithic period ending around 5000 BC were used as amulets and charms,[9] and Tutankhamen's tomb contained thousands of beads made of minerals, glass, dark-red resin, and gilded wood. In the royal graveyard at the Sumerian city of Ur, archaeologists found Queen Puabi's beaded cloak from 2500 BC, with its imported carnelian, lapis lazuli, and agate beads.[10] Noble female Scythians were buried with many gold ornaments, quantities of jewelry, and bracelets made from imported pearls.[11] Beads dating from 2000 BC have been found in India,[12] but it is not known when they were first stitched onto cloth there.

Different substances for bead-making and adornment have been valued at different times. Amber was one of the oldest: beads were traded as early as 8000 BC. After 4500 BC, jade was considered precious in some parts of the world, and ancient jade-mining industries were located in present-day Mexico, China, and New Zealand. But in Asia, Egypt, and India, gold was the most highly valued commodity during the same period. Around 3000 BC, lapis lazuli and chalcedony were much prized, and after 300 BC, gemstones rose in value in Europe and Asia.[13]

The ancient Egyptians believed that beads brought good fortune. The Egyptian word *sha* meant luck, while *sha-sha* meant bead, which suggests that beads possessed an amuletic quality.[14] The protective function of beads is further revealed through an examination of the word bead, which was derived from the Anglo-Saxon words "bidden," meaning to pray, and "bede," for prayer. During the Middle Ages in Europe, rosaries for counting prayers started being made from beads.[15] Rosary beads probably originated in India, but it is most likely that Christians learned about beads for counting from the Arabs during the Crusades. Often rosaries and prayer beads had tassels, which were believed to ward off evil, since malevolent spirits did not like fringed edges.[16]

Beads have often been found great distances from where raw materials naturally occurred, and it is clear that they played a prominent role in global expansion and early economics. In Southeast Asia, among cultures where wealth was equated with spiritual blessings and ancestral powers, beads assumed supernatural powers through their associations with wealth. Among other communities, beads and shells were traded far inland, and took on mystical associations as they changed hands.[17] Beads enriched both the monetary and ritual value of clothing worn for important life-passage ceremonies and celebrations. Because of their durability and hardness, the beads were believed to imbue the wearer with similarly resilient and therefore protective qualities. Beaded textiles transferred the strength of hard materials to the wearer, especially if the entire body was covered.[18]

Many stones and minerals were considered medicinal and were beneficial if worn next to the skin or pulverized and taken internally. Amber was believed to prevent delirium or goiter, while precious stones could prevent drunkenness, protect limbs from injury, or even protect the wearer from fraud.[19] Because pearls came from the sea, they were associated with the sustaining element of water. Some believed pearls promoted youth and immortality, while others thought they cured eye diseases or were antidotes to poisons.[20] The curative powers of natural substances were transferred to beads made from them.

Objects with unusual shapes, rare materials, or alluring surfaces were frequently accorded value and even mystical powers. In Sarawak and Borneo, curiously shaped and glinting found items such as quartz crystals, iridescent feathers, and animal teeth were made into charm bundles called *siap*.[21] These were hung in long houses above communal fireplaces, and were believed to bring prosperity and good fortune to the residents. A glass bead with an opaque black spongy surface, called *lat ta'e pauo* ("deer dropping"), resembled amuletic tektite meteoric iron; it was considered especially protective and valuable in Sarawak.[22]

Paleolithic Western Asia may have been the point of origin connecting beads, eyes, and protective magic, for the earliest reference to the evil eye came from Sumerian clay tablets of the third millennium BC. In addition, goddess images with large eyes, large breasts, and large bead necklaces were found in ancient Syria. Perhaps the goddesses represented infants' early views of their mothers as they suckled and stared into their mothers' eyes,[23] or perhaps the figures were intended to protect babies, or to promote fertility. In many places, children and women of child-bearing age were considered especially vulnerable to the evil eye. Cowrie shells and other eye-shaped beads were used to stare back or to catch the first, most powerful, evil glimpse. Interestingly, it seems that beads used for protection against the evil eye had their own special value and were rarely used to express material wealth.[24]

The uniform size and portability of beads made them ideal trade items. Some were made from rare substances, while others were simply beautiful. The demand for beads opened vast trade networks, and ancient grave sites frequently revealed examples from other regions. A Mediterranean coral bead dating from 6000 BC was found in Turkey, while lapis lazuli from Afghanistan was transported to Sumer and other sites over routes that were established in the third millennium BC.[25] Beads were also made from shells and plant substances, such as vegetable ivory from the nut of the corypha palm.[26]

Cambay in Gujarat was a center of hardstone agate bead-making. Many agate beads from that area were traded to Mesopotamia, Egypt, China, and the Near East, where they were valued for their hardness and interesting patterns.[27] Red carnelian, also from Cambay, was associated with healing and protection, and was often made into beads which reached West Africa through Arab slave-traders. Later, Europeans took up the hardstone bead trade. In the nineteenth and twentieth centuries, inexpensive Bohemian glass beads were made to imitate older agate examples.

Amber, one of the oldest substances for bead-making as we have seen, came from fossilized coniferous tree resin from the Baltic region. It was believed to have medicinal properties, and, in North Africa, purportedly attracted sunlight and deflected darkness with its golden, sun-like color.[28]

Amber was valuable enough to have been given by the Chinese as tribute to Turkish tribes of Central Asia during the tenth century.[29]

Red coral was considered lucky because its color was associated with blood and life sustenance. It too was noted for its ability to dispel the influence of the evil eye. Coral grew in Mediterranean waters and seas off the coasts of Malaysia and Japan. The Portuguese carried red coral to West Africa for trade. Later, the Dutch and then the French entered the red coral trade. The Yoruba king, the Oba, of Benin monopolized coral and possessed a famous netted set of regalia including shirt, necklaces, and crown with the precious beads. The Oba's red coral dress was renewed annually with blood sacrifices to instill fertility into the coral and consequently to the people and land. When the Oba of Benin was forced to submit to the British in the 1880s, he wore the complete coral set.[30]

Another substance used for bead-making was brilliant blue lapis lazuli, which was mined in Afghanistan. Afghanistan was an important trade center for the distribution of lapis, which was highly coveted by the ancient Sumerians, Egyptians, and Mycenaeans for use in the making of beautiful blue ornaments which were often buried with their élite.[31]

Another highly valued blue bead was made from sky-blue turquoise. It was mined at Khorasan, Iran, from where it was widely traded in the ancient world. The Aztecs valued turquoise from North America, while in Islamic countries from at least the fourteenth century, the brilliant blue mineral was considered effective in warding off the evil eye.[32] In Islamic countries, both black and turquoise derive their prophylactic associations from mourning. Both colors are used for protection, and have been associated with death since at least the fourteenth century in Central Asia.[33]

The luminous luster of pearls was coveted for its resemblance to moonlight and its associations with deities connected to the moon. Pearls are naturally bead-shaped, and mother-of-pearl shell was cut into bead-like forms. Egyptian tomb paintings of the second millennium BC depicted pearls attached to clothing, and pearls have been found in many ancient burial grounds. The long-established trade in pearls originated in the pearl fisheries of the Persian Gulf and the Gulf of Manaar between Sri Lanka and India. One route brought pearls to the Euphrates, Babylon, and Assyria, while another distributed them from the Red Sea into Egypt. The Phoenicians probably carried Persian Gulf pearls as early as 2200 BC, with other goods, on their trade routes to India.[34] After 1908, the famous Japanese company Mikimoto successfully developed and patented pearl cultivation, with the result that more people could afford the look of pearls.[35]

Beads made from naturally occurring minerals provided numerous colors and patterns, as well as psychological associations and benefits. But they were expensive to create, because the materials had to be mined, shaped, and drilled. Between 5000–3400 BC, the Egyptians developed faience, a glassy ceramic substance made from heat-fused quartz sand. The manufacture of glass beads in Egypt, around 2750 BC, probably also came about from the use of glazing materials for ceramics containing soda-lime silicate. Faience beads were made from a paste, which could be applied onto a thread, rolled, baked, and then cut into sections. Larger faience beads were formed, pierced, coated with glaze, and fired.[36] Early glass beads were made by winding threads of glass around wires. Later, molten glass was pulled into strands, then scored and broken into beads. Faience and glass beads were readily adapted to provide less expensive alternatives to lapis lazuli and turquoise.[37] As we saw in the previous chapter, quartz pebbles mixed with wood ash from a hot fire might have led to the discovery of glass, but it could equally have been the by-product of copper smelting: wood ashes provided the alkali, such as potassium carbonate or sodium carbonate, and lime and silica occurred naturally in copper ore. The earliest glass colors were black, blue, and green; yellow and red appeared later.[38]

Several thousand years after the Egyptian pioneers, glass beads were being manufactured on an enormous scale in Europe; European explorers and traders carried large quantities with them for trade. By the late fifteenth and early sixteenth centuries, colonial expansion had begun; glass beads were to have a dramatic impact upon the social, economic, political, and aesthetic aspects of numerous lives.

The European centers of bead-making were Holland, Bohemia, and Italy. Mass-produced glass beads were used to replace handmade examples. Individually made beads were valued as much for the labor involved in their manufacture as for their inherent beauty and rarity; European glass beads cost very little compared to the value of goods for which they were exchanged. The trade in glass beads netted enormous profits, sometimes up to 1,000 percent over their cost.[39] European traders adapted trade routes that had been established for millennia and carefully noted the specific tastes and desires of the peoples who lived along them. Thousands of bead types resulted, and to keep up with changing tastes, the number of European factories increased dramatically over a 250-year period. During 1764, twenty-two Venetian factories produced 44,000 pounds of beads weekly.[40] From 1830 to 1840, the Idar-Oberstein factory in Germany manufactured, among many other types, faux agate beads. Even imitations of valuable conus-shell disks, teeth, claws, and amber were produced in Bohemian glass factories at Jablonz.[41]

The story of the ubiquitous bead permeates most of the planet. Their beauty, light-reflecting surfaces, and varied textures have made an indelible contribution to personal adornment. We have been spiritually and psychologically enriched by their ability to comfort and delight us through their tactility, their protective power to fascinate the evil eye, and their religious dimension to transform light and color. And like our predecessors, who counted beads as significant possessions, we are still equally attracted to them today.

63, 64 Ceremonial mattress edging, details, Straits Chinese, Malaysia. Chinese immigrant beadwork, with angular-edged beads called *manek potong*, produced particularly glittering reflections. Bridal chambers displayed auspicious textiles. Pairs of fish conveyed conjugal happiness while deer symbolized longevity.

63
64

65

66

67

68   69

Zardozi: dimensional gold work

Zardozi, from the Persian *zar* (gold), is gilded dimensional work on cloth. Golden textiles often convey spiritual concepts through their eternally glittering surfaces, which suggest spiritual ecstasy and divine energy. Their exuberant beauty and luxury evoke images of paradise.

65 Wedding hanging, detail, Minangkabau people (?), Sumatra, Indonesia. Auspicious golden textiles symbolize the sacred world-mountain, the tree-of-life, and nature's abundance; they were displayed on ceremonial beds and at entrances to Minangkabau weddings.

66 Ceremonial hanging, detail, Minangkabau people (?), Sumatra, Indonesia. Special-occasion textiles, displayed at rite-of-passage ceremonies, synthesized influences from Indian and Chinese status cloths in their use of rich velvet and gilded metallic elements.

67 *Zardozi* cloak, detail, Hyderabad, India. The Muslim court of Hyderabad supported a regional style of *zardozi* which incorporated small pieces of red and green lacquer-coated precious metal combined with other textures of gilded silver and gold.

68 *Zardozi* workers, Old Delhi, India. Artisans stretch fabric on a *karchob* (a frame), and then quickly fill in previously stitched outlines with wire, round and square coils, and sequins all pre-cut to size.

69 *Zardozi mor* placed on a *sonali pavari*, Kutch, India. The former Maharani of Kutch wore this ceremonial red cotton *pavari*, the requisite Rajput bridal headcovering made of *sonali* (pure gold leaf and glue work), and a *zardozi* headdress (*mor*)

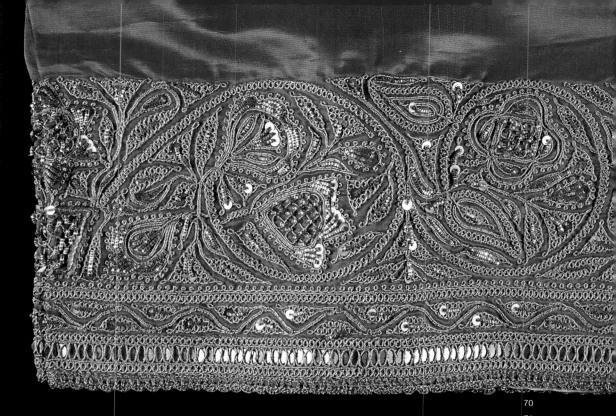

70 *Ejar*, detail, with *zardozi* bottoms, northwest India. Brides from some Muslim communities wore silk-satin tunics and *ejar* (drawstring trousers) with *zardozi*-embellished bottoms consisting of *sitara* (sequins) and *salma* (squarish tubes of metal).

71 *Zardozi* shawl, detail, northwest India. The heavily worked shawl blurs the boundaries between cloth and jewelry with couched *kalabatun* (thread wrapped with metal) lattice motifs interrupted by occasional silver-cupped sequins called *katori*.

70

71

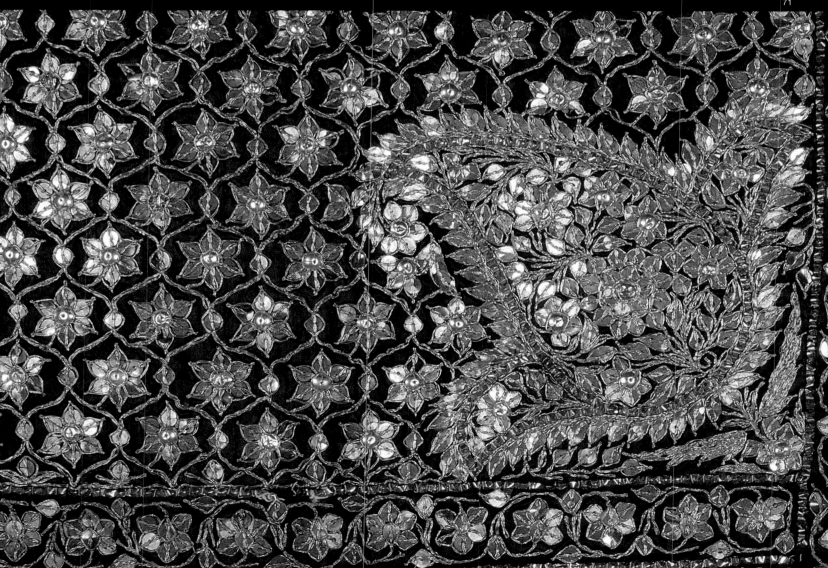

72

73

74

76

Gold leaf and gold print

Although stiff and fragile, gold-printed cloth was less costly and time-consuming to make than *songket* and *zari* (the Indonesian and Indian terms for metallic-thread weaving) or dimensional *zardozi* work. Metal foil was applied to only one side of the fabric and sometimes only to outer, visible areas.

72 Dance skirt, China. Pointed pendant aprons, like this one with gilded leather outlines, first appeared in ancient court dress and may have served protective purposes with their sword-like points. They were used in theatrical productions or worn by wedding dancers.

73 *Sewet prado* (bridegroom's sarong), detail, Palembang, Sumatra. Gold leaf (*perada*) which enhanced the prestige of cloth, was often applied to only outer areas. Gilded and highly calendered surfaces create an opulence similar to Palembang's gold and silk *songket* weaves.

74 *Odhani* (headcovering) with *sonali* (gold leaf and gluework), detail, possibly Rajasthan, India. Gold print centers evolved in India, where wealthy merchants and small kingdoms provided markets for expensive products after the Mughal courts' patronage weakened in the early nineteenth century.

75 *Pha lai yang khien thong* (long furnishing cloth), detail, Thailand. Merchants carried Indian-manufactured cloths specifically made for Thai clothing and hangings to the coast of Myanmar. From there the textiles were sent to the Thai capital at Ayutthya and then gilded.

76 Spread, Rajasthan, India. The luxurious play of light appears on floor-coverings and bedspreads printed in *sonali* (pure gold leaf) and *rupeli* (silver tinsel print) with a heated metal rod which scored impressions in the cloth.

77 *Perada* (gold leaf) on a batik *selendang*, Java, Indonesia. Batik-resist images on the *selendang* (shoulder cloth), contrast with crisp, stamped gold leaf and glue work. Symbolically male, metal goods complement soft, traditionally female textile goods.

78

79

80

Dressing the part: golden clothing and status

In ancient times, the sacred character of sun deities was transferred to the sanctity of rulers and reflected through glittering, golden garments. Gold became synonymous with power and, eventually, wealth. By the nineteenth century, leaders were no longer considered sacred, yet expensive dress continued visually to reinforce stratified societies.

78 Woman's jacket, Persia. Rural Arabs and Persians favored quality over quantity in clothing. By the nineteenth century, short jackets with flaring peplums and gold couched threads were fashionable and often worn over transparent undershirts and trousers or voluminous skirts.

79 Men's *salwar*, detail, Gujarat, India. Woven in a brocade style called *Ganga-Jamuna*, after the golden and silver-colored rivers of India, this splendid silk- and metallic-brocaded *salwar* (pair of drawstring trousers) belonged to the former ruler of Kutch.

80 Dragon robe, detail, China. *Kesi* or *ko-s'su* (interlocking tapestry weave) and gold thread enriched the prestige of a dragon robe. Chinese bridegrooms often wore them, for the attire raised the groom to greater prominence on his wedding day.

81 *Chab-blug* (holy-water flask case), Tibet. Buddhist monks carried ritualistic holy-water bottles on their belts. Clothing made of pure gold thread and detailed Chinese weaving was a privilege of high-ranking lamas, ministers, and their families.

82 Court dress, Thailand. Nineteenth-century Siam court dress consisted of a *pha nung* (lower-body garment), a sash, a *salung* (jacket), and an overcoat. *Zari pha nung* were often woven in India, and such sets of clothing were frequent gifts from the Thai king to political allies.

83 Robe of state, Thailand. Specially trained, high-ranking royal women made the finest robes, which consisted of a twelve-karat-gold netted structure supporting patterns in raised embroidery in twenty-four-karat white and yellow gold.

82

81

83

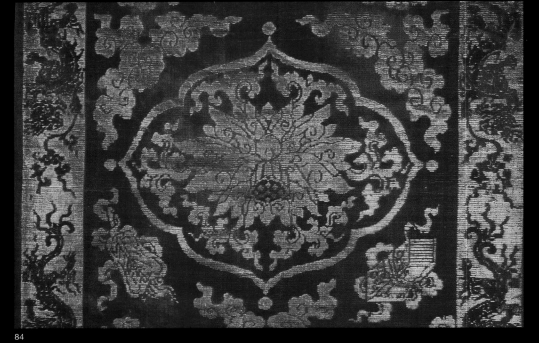

84

85

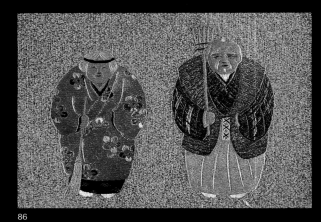

86

87

Golden Chinese and Japanese textiles

Golden textiles graced temples and homes, covered ceremonial gift presentations, and conveyed the wearer's elegance, taste, and success. Woven and embroidered images often communicated subtle meanings and associations which, when understood by the viewer or recipient, enhanced the role of the textile.

84 Silk cut-pile velvet and gold brocade, detail, China. Chinese velvet furnishing fabrics were woven in numerous variations including cut and uncut piles, multicolored brocades, damask and satin grounds, and velvets with supplementary gold threads.

85 *Iwato Yama Gion Matsuri*, Japan. Every July an ancient festival with precious textile-laden carts called *Gion Matsuri* occurs in Kyoto. Floats are presided over by Shinto images and honor Amaterasu, the sun-goddess.

86 *Fukusa*, detail, Japan. The elderly couple sweeping pine needles on the shores of the island of Takasago symbolize the spirit of two pine trees that grew into one. The *fukusa* (wedding-gift cover) conveyed wishes for a long and happy life.

87 Wall hanging, detail, China. Interiors were balanced and symmetrical, with complementary furniture covers, wall hangings, and valances. The water-dragon tapestry was woven with interlocking gilded paper wefts and fine red silk warps, creating a reddish-golden sheen.

88 *Maru obi*, detail, Japan. *Maru obi* (formal kimono wrappers) are generally four yards long, folded in half lengthwise, and wrapped several times around the waist, creating great bulk. Because of the skill required to make them and the cost of metallic threads, *obi* were the most expensive elements in a woman's wardrobe.

89 *Fukusa*, detail, Japan. The
Chinese legend of the carp that
jumped the Yellow River Falls
to be magically transformed into
a dragon, and the Japanese
homonym for koi and the word
purpose both allude to the will
to succeed. This *fukusa* was
a suitable gift cover for a high
official.

90 *Nishiki kesa*, detail, Japan.
Kesa (Buddhist priests' mantles)
were symbolically pieced together
according to the monk's rank,
often from exquisite gold-
brocaded silk fabrics woven
in Kyoto called *nishiki*.

88

89

90

81

91

92

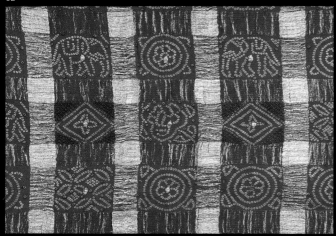

93

94

Woven gold

The Indian name for gold thread weaving is *zari*; brocade is called *kinkhab*. *Kinkhab* variations include those with predominantly gold or silver; gold or silver mixed with silk; and large amounts of silk with small gold or silver designs.

91 *Zari* sari, detail, India. Most Varanasi weavers originated in Saurashtra in Gujarat. Complex patterns are created on hand looms with a *jala* (a Jacquard device of cotton threads) which is used to lift warp patterns.

92 *Gharchola* sari, detail, Gujarat, India. The famous *gharchola* (meaning literally "cloth of the family") cotton and gold wedding sari from Gujarat consists of *zari* grids and auspicious motifs tie-dyed in ritually numbered *chowk* (squares), occurring in multiples of nine, twelve, or fifty-two.

93 *Gharchola* sari presentation, Ahmedabad, Gujarat, India. The presentation of the *gharchola* (cloth of the family) sari from the mother of the groom to the bride represents an emotional focal point of the wedding, the moment when the bride is accepted as a daughter.

94 Paithani *odhani*, detail, India. Paithani saris and *odhani* (headcovers) are known for profuse amounts of *zari*. Paithan was an ancient trade center in Maharashtra state, where weavers developed their tapestry techniques from Central Asia.

95 *Sidriyeh*, Syria. Wealthy nomadic Bedouin men often commissioned Aleppo weavers to make *sidriyeh* (vests) in silk and gold tapestry weave. High-status vests are worn over belted floor-length robes and trousers. *Abaye* (cloaks) and headcovers complete male dress.

95

many diverse ethnic groups has absorbed numerous cultural influences through its lively seaports and role in trade. Indian, Chinese, Persian, and Arabian silks, ikats, and *zari* weaves were combined with traditional textile arts, resulting in cloths conveying abundance and beauty.

96 *Tangkuluak*, Palembang, Sumatra. This type of rich headcloth, of *limar* (weft ikat) and *songket*, was worn by men for religious holidays and weddings. Its use reflects Islamic influence.

97 *Tapis*, detail, Sumatra. Regional variations in *tapis* (tube skirts) included the use of sequins or *cermuk* (mirrors), and metal threads. Older *tapis* used alternating bands of weft ikat and silk embroidery.

98 Minangkabau wedding couple, Bukittinggi, Sumatra. Splendid dress in expensive *songket* or modern Lurex is worn at important rite-of-passage ceremonies. Radiant in Muslim-style clothing, the couple inhabit an earthly paradise amidst golden luxury and plenty.

99 *Tapis tua (ta* with couched m detail, Abung p Abung women embellished tex expensive impo to express thei acquired throug coffee trade.

100 *Tapis*, deta Wedding *tapis* lavish with cou *Tapis* complete gold and sarong from Surat, the thread center i worn by the we

101 *Tangkulua* Minangkabau, Minangkabau a handloomed *so* which incorpor to *adat* (social of behavior). V *songket tangkuh* tied in various region at ceren

96
97

98

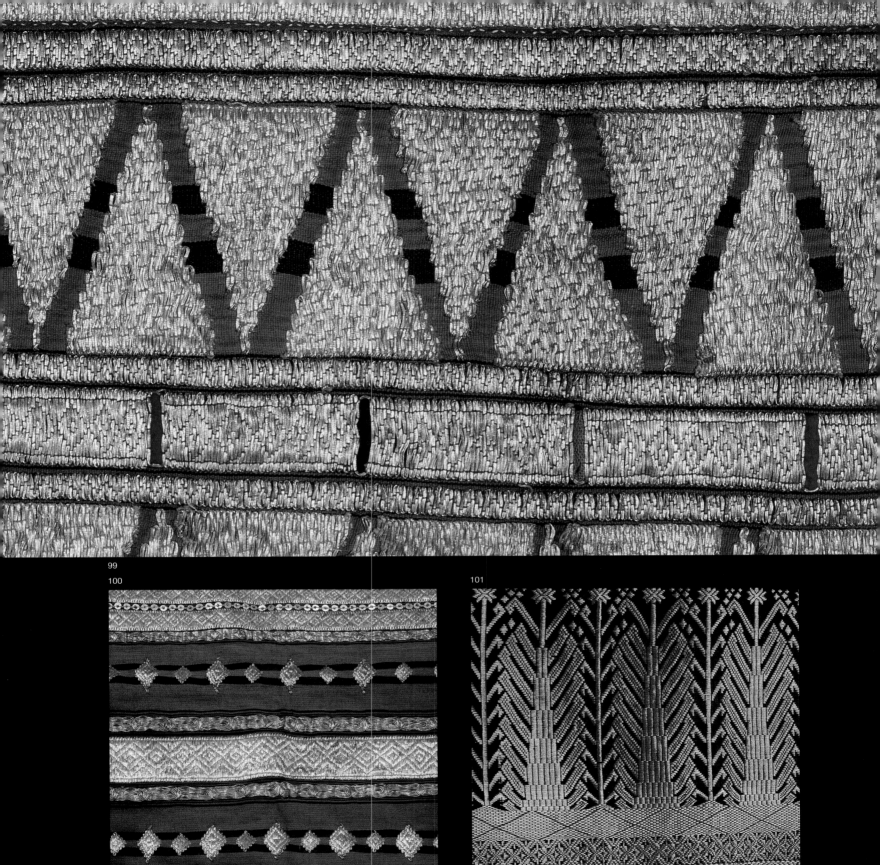

99

100

101

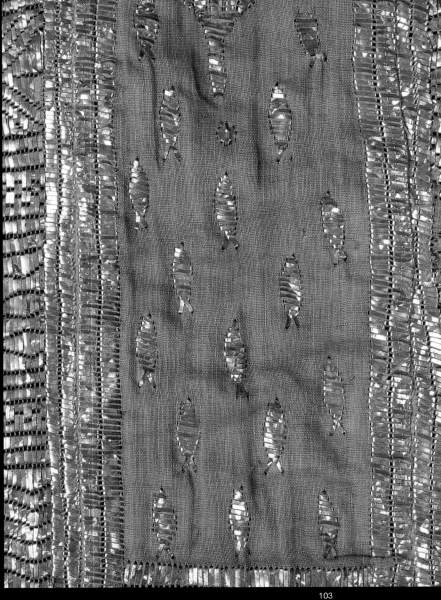

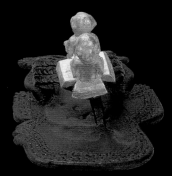

102

Gold cloths of Africa

Gold functioned on many levels: to signify leadership; to express prestige when worn at festive times; and to offer protection from the evil eye. In West Africa, high-status materials were often combined with parables and moralistic messages, while in North Africa gold expressed status and performed talismanic functions.

102 Sandals, Asante people, Africa. Both the Akan and Asante peoples of West Africa wore gold to signify authority. Sandals with gold-covered wood-carvings that conveyed proverbs were worn by kings and their families.

103, 104 *Dohlja* (golden tunic), and detail, Monastir, Tunisia. On the third day of the wedding celebration, brides wore *dohlja* when presented to the women of both families. The dazzling light-reflecting surfaces protected the bride, and the fish motifs promoted fertility and happiness.

105 *Hizam*, detail, Fez, Morocco. Fine wedding textiles, such as *hizam* (wedding belts), were woven on drawlooms in Fez. The *menbar* (stair-step) image suggested the platform where the bride and groom received wedding gifts, while *hdoub* (long tassles) ornamented the ends.

106 *Qosha del rib*, detail, Fez, Morocco. *Qosha del rib*, a heavily embossed rose-patterned fabric for robes, came from Lyons after 1921, forming just one of many layers of traditional Fez wedding attire. Motionless to avoid the evil eye, brides sat under piles of rich robes for family and friends to view their splendor.

107, 108 *Gmejja*, and detail, Raf Raf, Tunisia. Brides wore *gmejja* (sparkling tunics with lucky images) on the third day of marriage ceremonies. Seven layers of clothing, of which the *gmejja* was one, were ritually removed in the presence of family members.

103

104

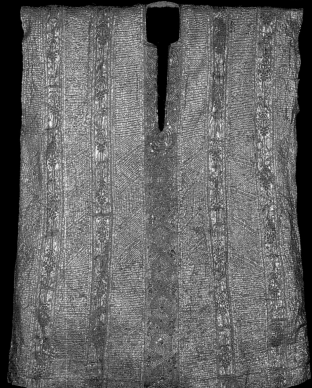

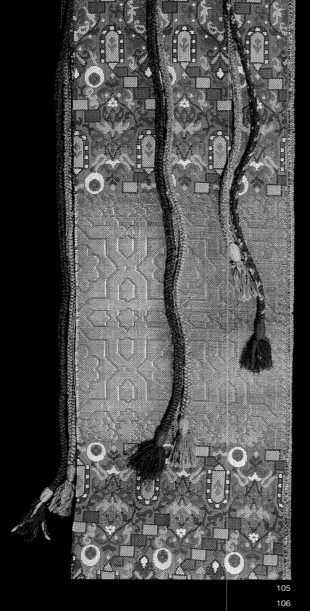

107

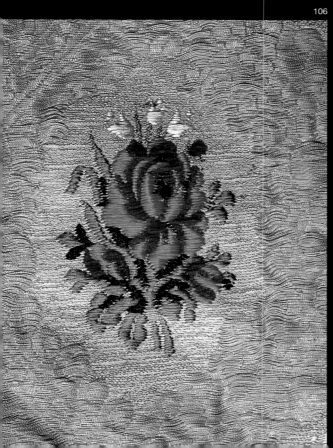

105

106

108

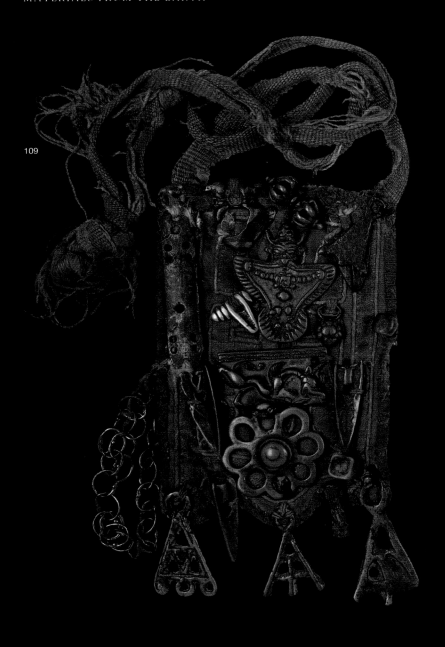

109

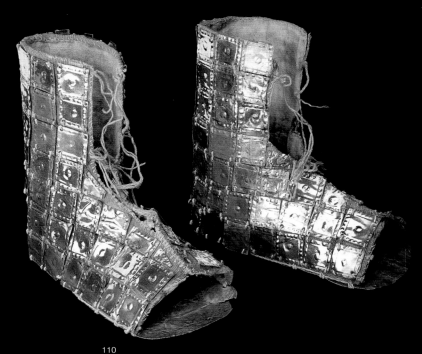

110

The value of metals

Ancient protective iron came from meteors, which was believed magical due to its origins and magnetic properties. Metals became associated with the gods and were sacred. Gold was equated with the sun and silver with the moon. Later, metal coins attached to clothing offered protection and provided cash for emergencies. Imitation coins tinkled and flashed light, and thus directed the evil eye's dangerous glance away from the wearer.

109 Shaman's cloth with *thokchag*, central Tibet. *Thokchag* (Tibetan for "things fallen from the sky") were ancient bronze and iron shards found in the soil. They were considered protective because of their associations with meteoric iron.

110 *Ataderos*, Chimu kingdom, ancient Peru. *Ataderos* (ceremonial boots) from approximately 1200 AD were covered with silver, moon-associated, *repoussé* medallions stitched onto handloomed cloth. These were probably burial offerings for an official, since only the élite in Chimu society owned metal.

111, 112, 113 *Qaftans*, Dakhala, Kharga, and Bahriyah oases, Egypt. Bedouin-style dark-colored *qaftans* were commonly worn by oasis women. Sawtooth-edged embroidery, brightly colored buttons, and shiny coin-shaped disks were believed to prevent harm, such as bad luck or infertility. Protective elements were strategically placed to protect the chest, breasts, reproductive organs, and neck.

114, 115 Water-seller and *chkara*, Marrakesh. Water-sellers with their tall fringed hats, drinking utensils, and *chkara* (coin-studded leather shoulder bags) were familiar sights in Marrakesh at one time. The reflective brass *mihrab* (prayer niche) shape and coins warded off evil, at the same time indicating the price and the type of coins the vendor accepted.

112
113

111

114

115

116

117

118

Metal in and on the cloth

Found objects, stamped and *repoussé* platelets, coins, and coin-like imitations are commonly stitched to cloth, while flattened metal strips are laid onto its surface or worked into loose weaves.

116, 117 *Mavutcekmen*, and detail, Turkmen, Afghanistan. Turkmen ceremonial dress required fixed combinations which denoted the social function and age group of the wearer. The groom's family gave a set of nine gifts to the bride, including a green coat, a *mavutcekmen*. Silver ornaments and embroidery reflected the cyclical processes of nature and wishes for offspring.

118 Turkmen women in *chalat*. Many Turkmen wore *chalat*, robes with stitched-on silver ornaments and amulets, often made from handloomed red and white striped silk and cotton fabrics. Specific types of ornaments and headdresses distinguished sub-groups, and silver expressed status, as well as offering protection.

119 *Asyut* cloth, Asyut, Egypt. Slinky *asyut* cloth headcoverings, shawls, and dress fabrics used netted or tulle fabric with flat metal strips. *Asyut* was very popular in the 1920s, when the discovery of King Tutankhamen's tomb ignited a fad for Egyptian goods.

120 *Odhani*, detail, Kutch, India. The *badla* from which this *odhani* (headcover) was made is fashioned from strips of metal flattened between two rollers. *Badla* could be couched or stitched into the cloth with a guide needle and thread. The *badla*'s weight contrasted pleasingly to springy tie-dyed silk georgette, a thin silk or crêpe dress material.

121 *Kagara*, Dogon, Mali. Bonnet-type hats were used to exhibit age and status. *Kagara* ("large opening") are Dogon bonnets made of two equal-sized rectangles of handloomed cloth stitched together on three sides. Metal strips came from recycled imported tins.

119
120

121

122

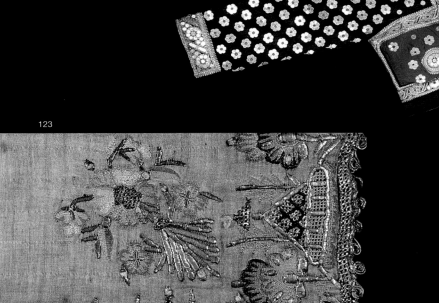

123

124

Versatile silver

Silver, used in as many diverse ways as gold, was laid onto the surface or penetrated it, through tinsel print, *gota*, *zardozi*, and embroidery. *Gota* ribbon was woven from thin *badla* strips and silk or cotton warps, and could be crimped, folded, and stitched into zigzags, formed into rosettes, or used with other materials. Silver electroplated copper wire was flattened and spun onto cotton or silk to make *kalabatun* thread.

122 *Angarakha*, back view, Kutch, India. Silver *gota* ribbons exaggerate the many seams characterizing the *angarakha*, a close-fitting garment for a man which is tied at the front and has a U-shaped front neckline.

123 *Makrama* (napkin/towel), detail, Turkey. Lavish, fine towels and napkins were embroidered by women to express the elegance, taste, and status of the household. Reversible designs used compound running stitches executed by counting threads. Metallic thread work, *pestemal*, became popular in the eighteenth century.

124 *Kapada*, Kutch, Gujarat, India. The heavy silver *zardozi* work in the *kapada* (a woman's bodice) conveyed formality. This example was worn by a member of the Kutch royal family the day before Diwali to worship the Hindu goddess Kali.

125 *Pichhvai*, northwest India. *Rupeli* or *waraq* (painted or silver leaf and glue work) was used to ornament altar cloths, called *pichhvai*, which contained images appropriate to specific times of the year. In *arti*, a part of worship using lamplight, the sacred cows of Vishnu and Krishna shimmered in the devotional glow.

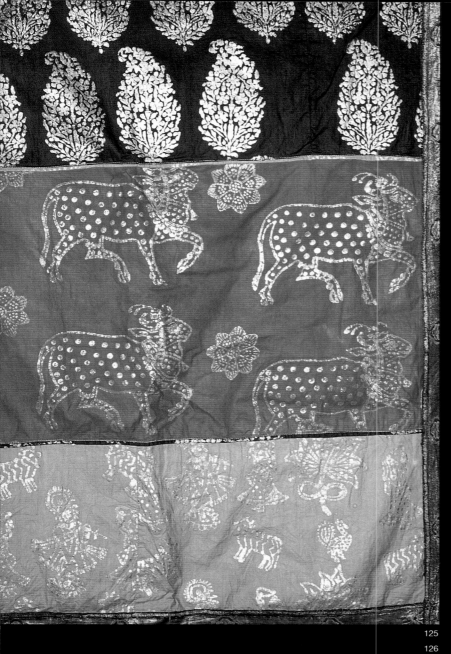

125
126

127
128

126 *Hakama*, detail, Japan. *Hakama* were loose, trouser-like divided skirts worn by women of the upper classes, Shinto clergy, and actors in Japanese theater. Stiff silk *seigo* was a favored fabric, and metal-leaf imagery expressed the hope of the coming spring.

127 *Khaddar kurta* with *rupeli*, detail, Pakistan. *Khaddar* (soft, handspun, handloomed cotton) and red madder dye contrast with the fertility-promoting designs in gleaming dots of *rupeli* (silver or metal amalgam work) on this festive *kurta* (women's upper-body garment).

128 Miao jacket, detail, Taijiang county, Guizhou province, China. Rich indigo surfaces and dimensional braid embroidery are punctuated by shimmering triangles of silver-leafed leather folded into tiny points. Women spent up to four years making their distinctive dress.

Weaving with metallic thread and silk reached high artistic levels in India, China, and Southeast Asia. With colorful or restrained color palettes, *kalabatun*, *zari*, or *songket* (supplementary weft techniques with metallic thread inserted into the wefts) gracefully glinted from the cloths' structure. Indian and Chinese textiles were widely adapted, traded, and recycled.

129

130

131

129 *Selendang*, detail, Pasemah, Sumatra. Pasemah textiles, like this *selendang* (shoulder cloth), are distinguished by somber brown ikat patterns alternating with isolated bands and borders of silver *songket*.

130 Chinese-woven *kesi* canopy, detail, Tibet. Shimmering Chinese silk and metallic brocades were used for Tibetan monks' robes, dance costumes, holy texts, drapes, and canopies. Multiple pendant hangings were believed to ward off evil with their tongue-like projections.

131 *Pha chong kaben*, detail, Thailand. *Pha chong kaben* (long sarongs brocaded heavily in metallic thread) were worn by Thai classical court dancers, courtiers, and their servants. Inexpensive examples from India were commonly worn in the Chiang Mai and Nan courts after the eighteenth century.

2

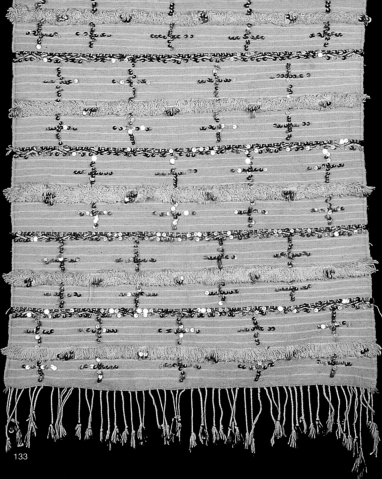

133

134

135

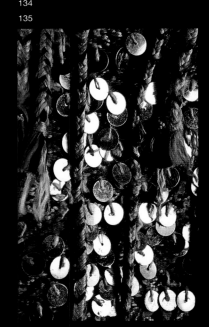

Sequins in Morocco

Many Berbers wove but did not sew. Consequently, most of their elements of dress were unstitched and draped in styles echoing ancient Greece and Rome. *Muzun* (sequins), believed to ward off the evil eye, were attached to small looped strings which dangled and glinted in the sun when inserted into weaves.

132, 135 *Ssmatt*, and detail, Morocco. Men carried wool saddle-bags, called *ssmatt*, over their horses' backs or on their shoulders. Women wove the bags with looped *muzun* and *abugs* (silky tags) on upright looms. Men stitched the pieces together.

133 *Hendira*, High Atlas Berber, Morocco. Thick woolen cloaks, called *hendira* or *tamizart*, were worn over the head or wrapped around the shoulders. Some *hendira* were decorated with sequins and had small geometric patterns woven on the inside to indicate their owners' origin.

134 Berber woman wearing a *hendira* and *muzun* coiffure cords, Zagora, Morocco. Berbers of the High Atlas were either settled or nomadic pastoral herders. *Hendira* wrappers could be worn over one shoulder or both, and were thus well-suited to the desert extremes of the High Atlas region.

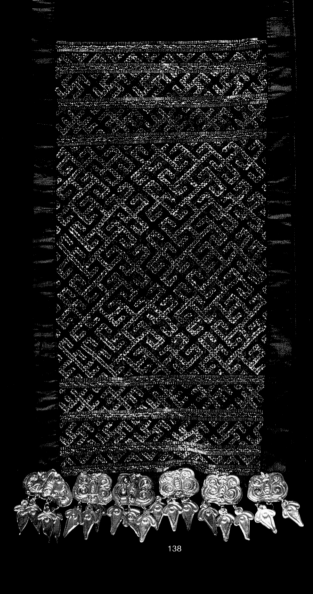

136
137

138

The power of sound

From hemline to headcovering, tethered tinklers have been attached to garment edges in almost every culture. Brass bells, *repoussé* silver platelets, old coins, or even pieces of flattened tin are all used to produce delightful noises in response to movement. These ornaments serve other purposes, too. Because the initial glance from the evil eye is believed to be the strongest, jingling bells and other noises are effective in repelling malevolent forces. Sometimes these noises are heard before the wearer is seen, with the result that the noise-producing object attracts the first gaze of the evil eye rather than the wearer. Some jingling elements are clustered into tassles, while others strike each other to make their sounds. The decorative and kinetic dimensions of diverse substances, such as beetle elytra, seeds, teeth, shells, and metal, are endless.

136 *Kandiya* (armlet), detail,
Banjara people, India.

137 *Selendang* (shoulder cloth),
detail, Bengkulu people, Sumatra.

138 Apron, detail, Miao people,
Jianhe county, Guizhou province,
China.

139 *Sapé* (upper-body garment),
detail, Maloh people,
Sarawak/Borneo.

140 *Mathravati* (headcloth
borders), details, Mathurai
people, India.

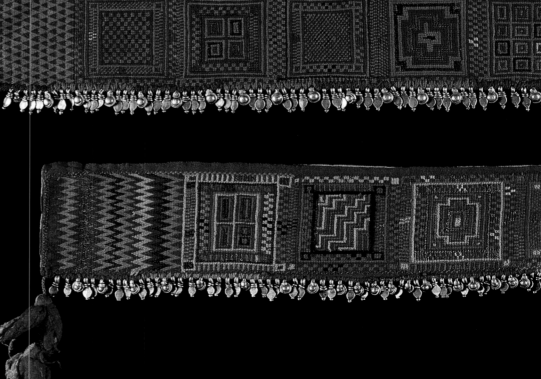

141

142

143

Anatolian sequins

Around the world, the dazzling capabilities of sequins attract and confuse the evil eye. Small silver coins and coin-like disks of white metal serve the same function as sequins. Zinc- or nickel-plated paillettes are attached to clothing and kerchiefs for everyday use and for special occasions to offer protection at all times.

141 Sleeves worn with Biga/Pomak jacket, detail, Canakkale area, Turkey. Separate sleeves with sequinned and beaded cuffs and elastic bands above the elbows are worn with cropped-sleeve jackets.

142, 144, 145 Young women's jackets, Biga/Pomak people, Canakkale area, Turkey. The jacket is one of about twenty pieces of clothing completing the dress ensemble, which includes heavy knitted socks, a skirt, an apron, a girdle, a vest, a shirt, a headcloth, and a fez. Bridal couples and young girls are vulnerable to the evil eye, so sequin-trimmed clothing safeguards their fertility and creates a festive appearance.

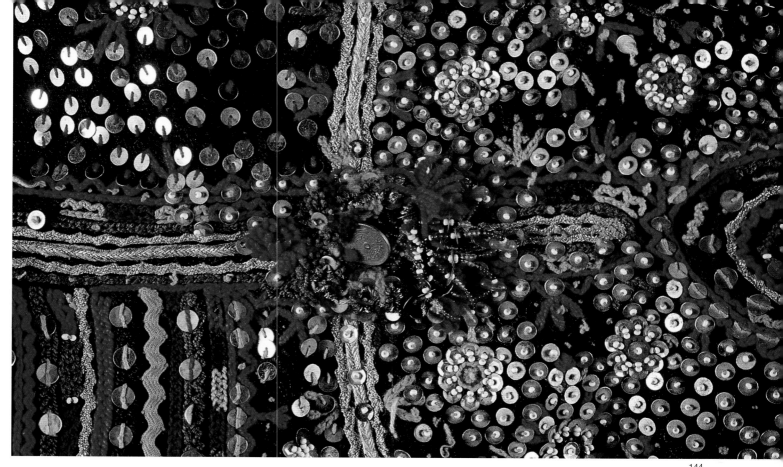

143 *Oya* (edged scarves), detail, central Turkey. Beaded and spangle-edged scarves are very prevalent among rural Turkmen men and women. Scarves play a prominent role in weddings, as the act of marriage is called "tying the head." The bride dons the headgear of a married woman, and sequinned kerchiefs are tied around the groom's waist and head at the ceremony to symbolize the transition from single to married life. In daily life, the number and color of scarves worn can also convey age and marital status.

146 Young Turkmen women at a festival wear multiple scarves and fezs, with shiny coin-like dangling elements. Frequently women bind their heads with several layers of sequin-edged scarves to touch the cheeks. The nickname for these scarves is *yanakhoven* ("cheek-flappers").

146

147

148

Sequins or spangles add a kinetic dimension to clothing and hangings; light glints from the small dots of metal as the wearer, or the onlooker, moves.

147, 148 Baby-carrying pads, details, Shui people, Guizhou, China. To the Shui, butterfly and bat images are protective figures. Prominent use of metal spangles; thick, padded layers; and the guardian butterfly's wide-spread wings suggest psychological and physical armor both visually and metaphorically.

149 *China poblana* (skirt, part of a set constituting a type of national dress for women), detail, Mexico. *Lentejuelas* (sequins) reached Mexico via Manila galleons, which carried luxury materials from China to Acapulco for distribution to Spain. Myths surround the origin of *china poblana*, but by 1920, the rural regional dress evolved to express rising nationalistic identity.

150, 152 *Kalaga*, details, Myanmar. *Kalaga* (Sanskrit for hanging) depicted Buddhist tales and astrological images hung in monasteries and aristocratic homes. Glittering surfaces were inspired by Indian and Thai court and theatrical dance costumes. Sequins are made of copper electroplated with zinc or nickel.

149

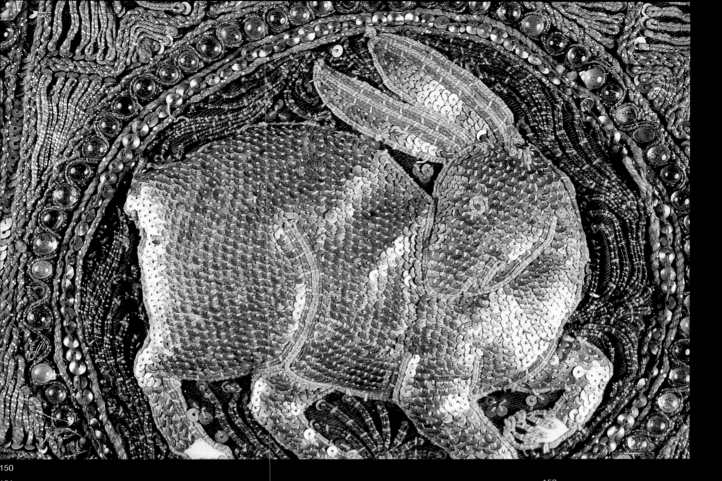

152

151 *Kain bidak* (shoulder cloth),
Pubian people, detail, Sumatra.
Pubian peoples of southwest
Sumatra, like others throughout
the island, used silk and metallic
goods to communicate their status
and to display the frequency of
their interaction with urban
centers. The shoulder cloth
utilizes motifs seen throughout
Southeast Asia, such as hooked
trees-of-life, *tumpal* (triangles),
and eight-pointed stars.

Haitian sequin arts

Vodou, the mysterious forces that govern the world and its people, seek to evoke the energy of its deities to heal and drive away evil. *Drapo* (prayer flags) and *rara* (ritual) tunics serve as flashing intermediaries to summon the gods of the Vodou pantheon.

153 *Majò jonk*, Rara Société Mystic 777. Vodou temples have their own sequin-dressed bands to perform and collect funds, led by the *Majò jonk*, who carries a baton and wears a sequinned chasuble, scarves, and short trousers.

154 Rara Etoile de Bethlehem, Haiti. Bands perform in rituals called *rara*. Chasubles are decorated with sequinned Vodou symbols and bird images, which are believed to help the *Majò jonk* see what lies ahead in the band's pre-Easter six-week trips in their regions.

155 *Drapo* Vodou, Haiti. *Drapo* (prayer flags) focus the worshippers' attention on the deity represented. Glinting light summons the deity and symbolizes the transition from present reality to the metaphysical. Serpents represent Damballah, the creator, and the heart, Ezili, the female deity of love and mercy.

156 *Drapo* Vodou, detail, Haiti. Aida Wedo, the female creator spirit, is depicted as a rainbow fanning out from the sacred waterfall. Vodou sequins are inspired by Napoleonic court garments and military regimental flags.

153

154

155

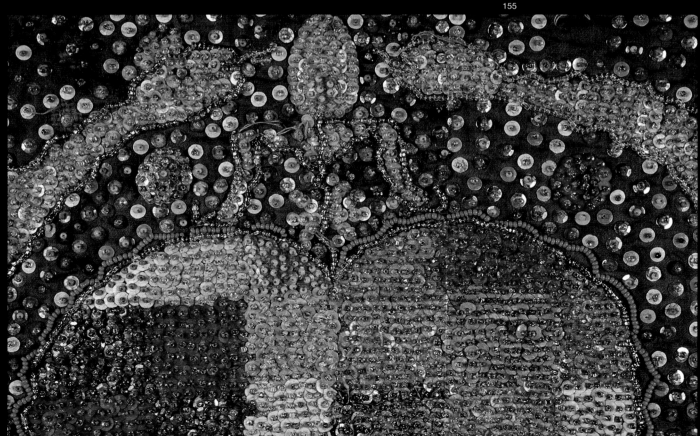

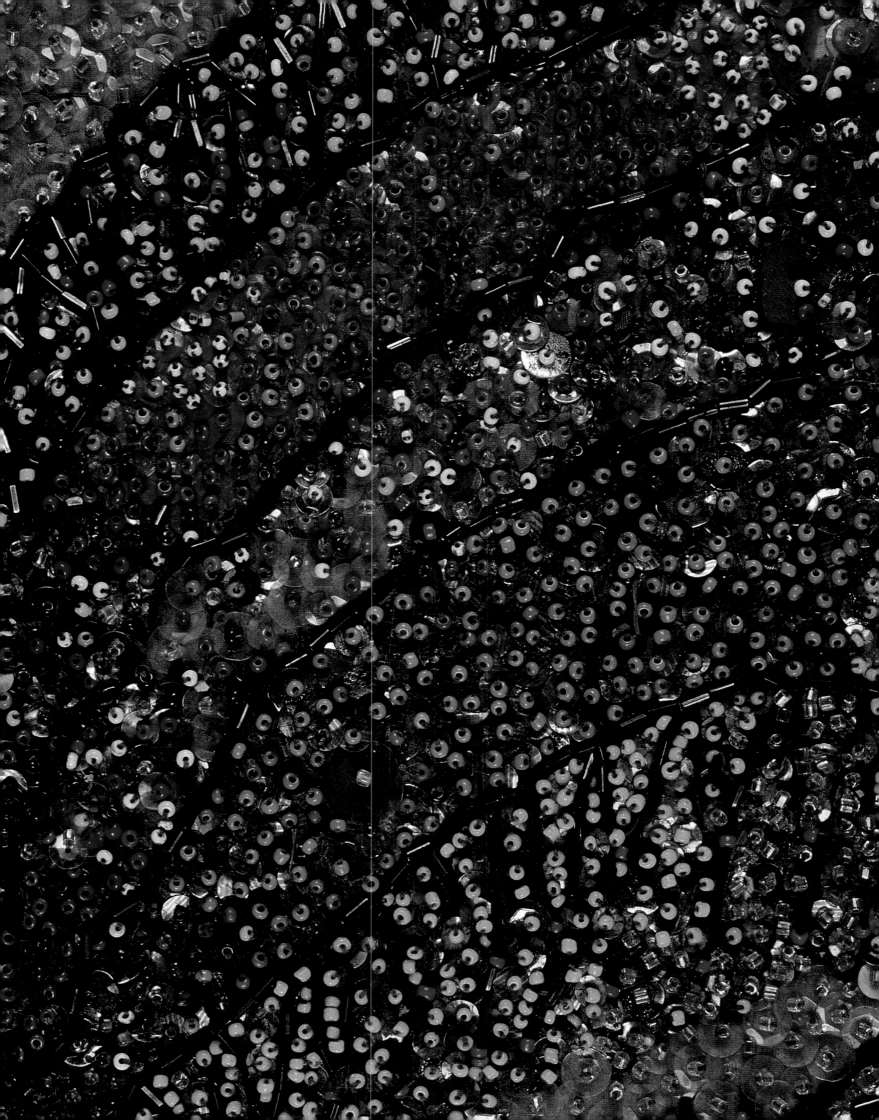

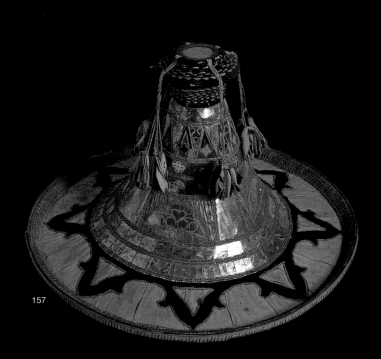

157

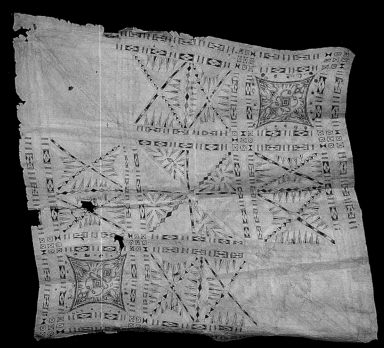

158

159

160

161

Glimmer from head to toe

Mica, pyrite, and hematite are naturally reflective minerals found throughout the world. Pieces or ground particles could be stitched or glued onto textiles and elements of dress to reflect the sun and firelight. The minerals sometimes added ritual meaning, while other uses were purely to delight.

157 *Sarau*, Flores, Indonesia. In equatorial areas, large decorative *sarau* (sun hats) sheltered wearers from the beating sun and sudden rains. Farmers and fishermen often used mica, for its reflective, heat-diverting properties. Women's hats were turned up, and men's had tassels and flaring brims.

158, 159 *Siga*, and detail, Toraja, Sulawesi. Sun-reflecting mica was glued with Nompi tree sap to the headwrappers, *siga*, of the highest-ranking men. Hierarchical buffalo horn designs and frigate birds indicated headhunting accomplishments, fertility, and the upper world of the sun.

160 *Rumal*, Kutch, Gujarat, India. Viscous castor-oil-based *roghan* was poured from a stylus onto cloth in patterns. Mica particles were then scattered over the damp lines to create *rumal*, a glittering ceremonial square cloth. The lotus/solar motif imitates more time-consuming, regional embroidery, but the glisten is unique.

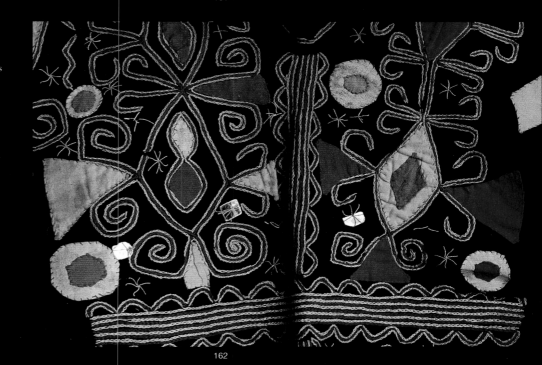

162

163

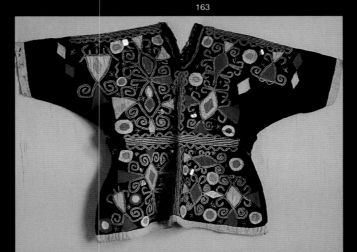

162, 163 *Halili*, and detail, Toraja, Gimpu region, Sulawesi. Shiny materials and motifs on womens' *halili* (cloth upper-body garments) were connected to headhunting, the sun, and the upper heavens. The back was most highly embellished, with cloth appliqué, tin foil, metal strips, and shaped mica slabs or glitter.

165

164

167

Mineral, metal, and magic

Shimmering light-reflecting hematite and polished metal mirrors were often sacred and magical. Hematite was highly valued, and widely traded among the Aleut and Koniag peoples of Alaska. Ground hematite was applied to hunting bags, and used for face paint, while whole pieces were used in charms attached to hunting boats. Hematite's precise symbolic meanings are unknown.

164 *Ak-fju-dat*, Aleut, Alaska. Men's personal bags (*ak-fju-dat*) often carried hunting supplies and were frequently painted with ground hematite. Many were made for sale to foreigners after Russian contact; perhaps the hematite was an eye-catching novelty. The sacred character of hematite may have added meaning to the bags.

165, 166 Cap, and detail, Aleut or Koniag, Alaska. Certain hats had visors and headbands inspired by Russian sailors' caps. Caribou hair and sinew were worked into the seams. The Aleut people painted their foreign-influenced caps red or black, and both Aleut and Koniag used glittering hematite.

167 *Ak-fju-dat*, Aleut, Alaska. Sewing, tobacco, and hunting-gear pouches used imaginative seam treatments, paints, and natural glitter. Graphite black, brown ocher, and vermilion powder came from China through the Russian-American Company after 1850.

168 *Quyay*, Mongolia. Shamans' ritual, self-sustaining power clothing, *quyay* ("armored dress"), contains elements necessary for their supernatural work. Large overlapping, polished bronze and copper mirrors, *toli*, provide protective armor by catching light, reflecting, and revealing. Mirrors contain a shaman's mount on which he travels to the supernatural world; they also help to scare away evil spirits.

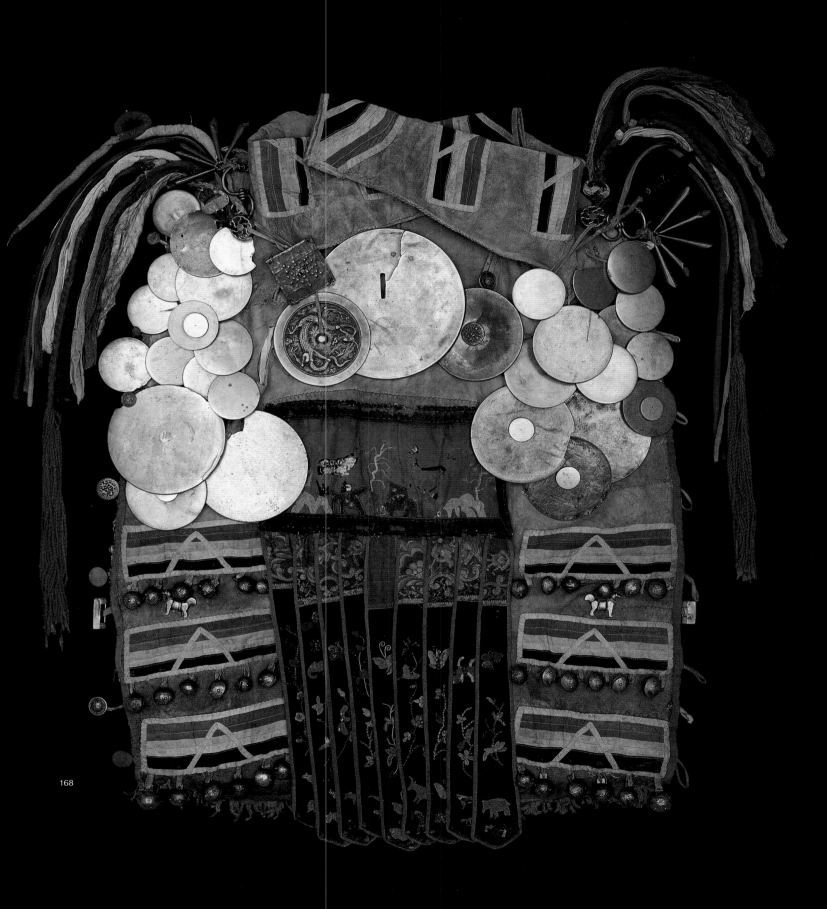

168

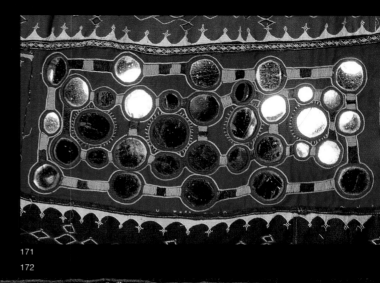

170

171

172

The language of mirror embroidery

Mirror embroidery is made in rural India, Pakistan, and Afghanistan. The reflective surfaces suggest glinting water and evoke ancient solar worship.

169 *Khoya*, detail, Kanebi people, Kutch, Gujarat, India. This *khoya* (cradle cover), made from *khaddar* (handspun, handloomed cotton), is covered with auspicious motifs. The rhomb-shaped patterns topped with trident or peacock's footprint motifs protect the baby.

170 Chandrakala Rathod Naik, a Bombay newspaper publisher, wears traditional mirror-covered Banjara dress. The set consists of a headcover and mirrored border, called *mathravati*, a *choli* (blouse), which is tied at the back, and a full, gathered skirt.

171 Skirt section, Banjara people, India. Huge convex mirrors, typical of Banjara work from Andhra Pradesh state, are exuberantly worked with appliqué and embroidery in this glittering skirt panel.

172 Cushion cover, detail, Mutwa people, Kutch, Gujarat, India. The Mutwa are one among a number of Muslim clans living in the northern area of Kutch; their work is notable for its use of small mirrors and tiny stitches.

173 *Dharaniyo*, detail, Ahir people, Kutch, Gujarat, India. Rounded flower shapes in white and yellow typify the embroidered textiles of the Ahir people. Stylized parrots and a goddess figure in a *toran* (doorway hanging) shape further imbue the textile with fertility and good luck.

173

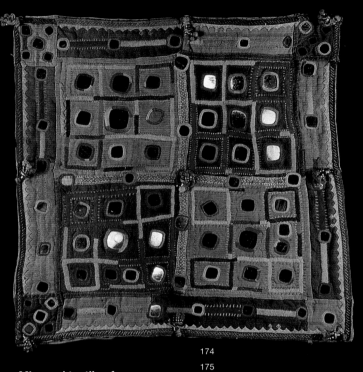

174
175

176

Mirrored textiles for the home

Women embroidered textiles for their daughters' dowries, to grace the home, to store or protect possessions, and for ritual purposes. Settled people tended to make decorative objects, while nomadic people made functional items. Dowry textiles were often made in sets consisting of *torans* (doorway hangings); *chaklas* (squares); *rumal* (ceremonial squares); quilts; *dharaniyo* (quilt covers); and *kothelo* (storage bags).

174, 175 Banjara *chakla* or *rumal*, and Vaniya *chakla* or *rumal*, detail, India. *Chaklas* or *rumal* were made for decorative or ceremonial uses as offerings to deities, or as food or gift covers. Stitches, color schemes, motifs, and mirror sizes reveal the communities from which cloths originate. Both Banjara and Vaniya women made mainly geometric patterns, but the Vaniya and Mahajans used untwisted *hir* (silky floss).

176, 177 *Kothelo*, Rajput people, and *kothelo*, detail, Rabari people, Kutch, India. Many sizes and types of bags were worn or used for storing personal possessions. Envelope-shaped bags called *bachakadiyo*, pillowcase-like sacks called *kothelo*, small rectangular market bags called *theli*, and drawstring purses called *vatwas* were all types of mirror-embroidered bag.

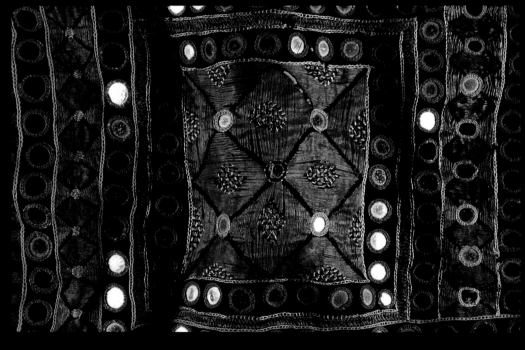

177

178

179

180

178 *Ganesha sthaphana* (household shrine), Kanebi people, Saurashtra, Gujarat, India. Bridal couples make their first offerings to the Hindu deity Ganesh, the elephant-headed bestower of good fortune. The temple-shaped shrine depicts him, his two wives churning buttermilk, and his steed, the rat, which can squeeze through the smallest openings to make things possible.

179 *Toran*, Rajput people, Rapar, Gujarat, India. *Torans* (doorway hangings) divide sacred space from profane and promote fertility and protection with their odd-numbered pointed pendants and dazzling mirrors. Rajput style utilizes numerous mirrors.

180 *Pardada*, Ahir people, Kutch, Gujarat, India. *Pardada* (Persian for curtain) are wedding hangings suspended at family compound entrances. Grooms touch the ceremonial hangings for luck in fertility and in respect for brides and their honor.

181 *Toran* and *sankia* in a Kutch home, Gujarat, India. Brackets, called *sankia*, and *torans*, as well as a mirrored storage chest strategically placed opposite the entrance, deflect malevolent forces from penetrating the space. *Torans* are no longer so commonly linked to protective functions, but they are still considered to be generally auspicious.

181

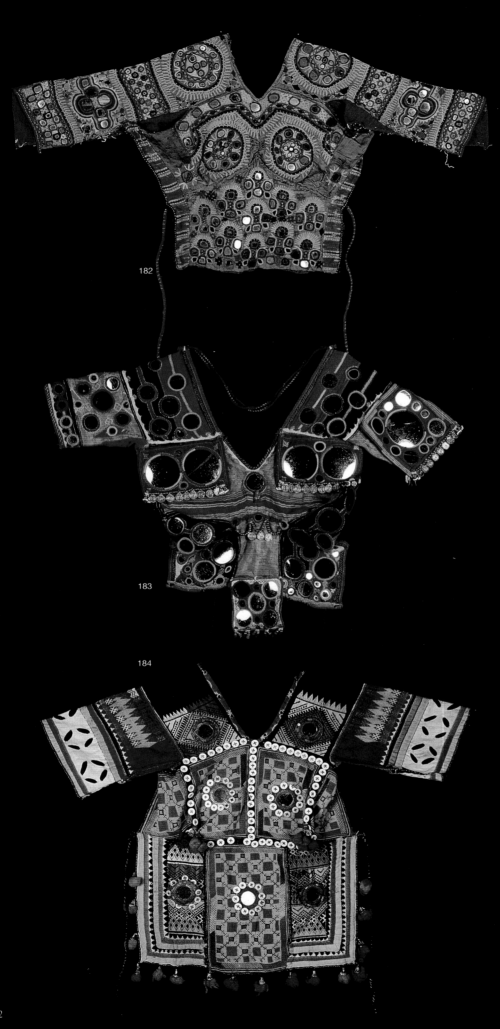

182

183

184

Women's mirrored dress

Festive and ceremonial mirrored upper-body garments, *kapada, kauchali*, or *choli*, were prominent in the desert regions of Pakistan, Rajasthan, and Gujarat in India until recent times. Colors, the elaborateness of the designs, the style of the garment, and embroidered or appliqué motifs communicated specific information about the wearer, such as age group, marital status, occasion, community affiliation, and religious background. The majority of these upper-body garments were tight-fitting and tied at the back. Some were embellished with novelty buttons or pieces of lead, an important metal to some Banjara groups. Banjara women living in southern India retained their three-piece sets of clothing, which typified the dress of Rajasthan. Pairs of mirrored flaps, *karya*, attached to Banjara *kapada* indicated marriage. Harijan women of northern Kutch wore longer blouse fronts, suggesting Muslim influence from Sind, Pakistan, compared to the short, tight, midriff-revealing *choli* (blouses) of Hindus. Some groups in Sind wear blouses with heavily encrusted shimmering surfaces for celebratory occasions; as they begin to wear out, such blouses are worn daily.

182 *Kapada*, Rabari people (?), Rapar, East Kutch, India.

183 *Kapada*, Banjara people, central India.

184 *Kapada*, Banjara people, central India.

185 *Kapada*, Banni Muslim or Sind, India/Pakistan.

186 *Guj* or *chola*, Lohana people, Thar Parkar, Pakistan.

187 *Kapada*, Rabari people (?), Gujarat, India.

188 *Guj* or *chola*, Lohana people, Thano Bula Khan, Sind, Pakistan.

185

186

187

188

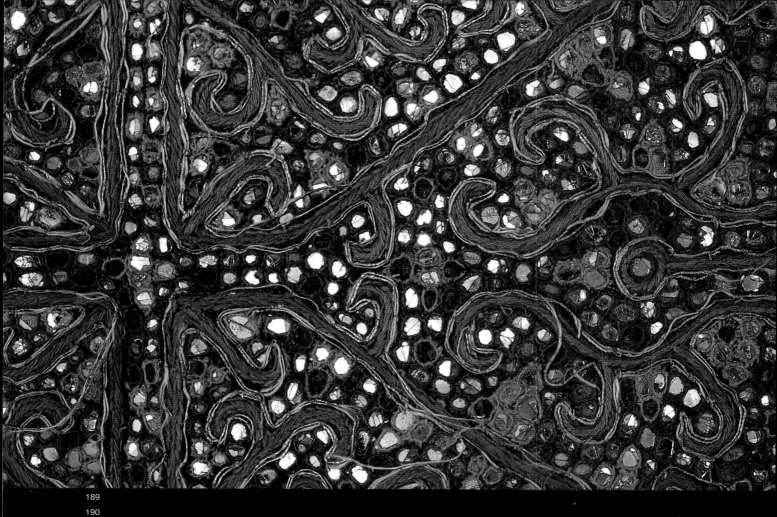

189
190

Mirroring wealth: Sumatra's shining cloths

Tapis (tube skirts) were embroidered with expensive imported materials and mirrors, called *cermuk*, which came from India. Indian mirrored cloths probably inspired glittering *tapis*. Some mirrors had metallic backings, while others glittered in green and gold tones, resembling golden pyrite or mica fragments.

189, 190 *Tapis*, details, Sumatra. *Tapis*, resplendent with embroidery and reflective *cermuk*, express a universal sense of delight, but are extremely heavy. Some weigh up to ten pounds.

191 *Tapis inu* panel, Paminggir people, Lampung area, southern Sumatra. *Tapis inu* alternates bands of handspun, ikat-dyed, woven cloth with heavily silk-embroidered strips showing traditional imagery redolent of ancient Dongson culture images from mainland Asia.

192 Jacket, front detail, Kauer people, southern Sumatra. Women's jackets were embellished before they were stitched together. Necklines were outlined with nassa shells and minute *cermuk* embroidery glinted along the front openings.

193 *Tapis*, detail, Kauer people, Sumatra. Unmarried women were expected to complete a *tapis* and jacket set prior to marriage. A young man frequently asked about his love interest's sewing progress as a subtle marriage proposal.

91

92

193

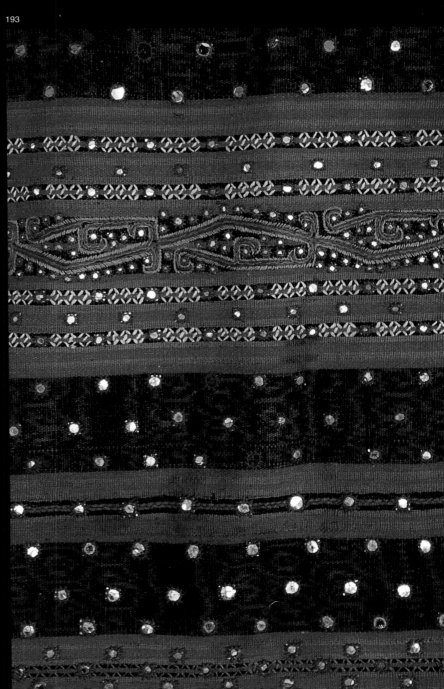

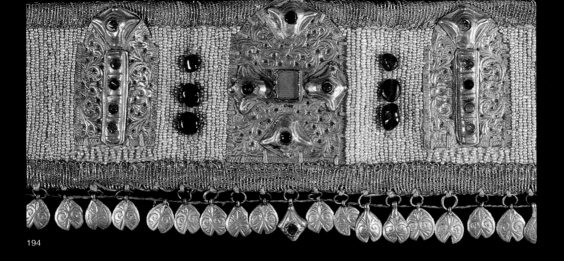

194

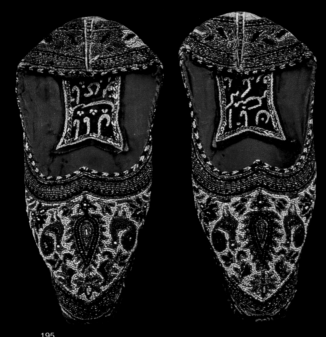

195

196

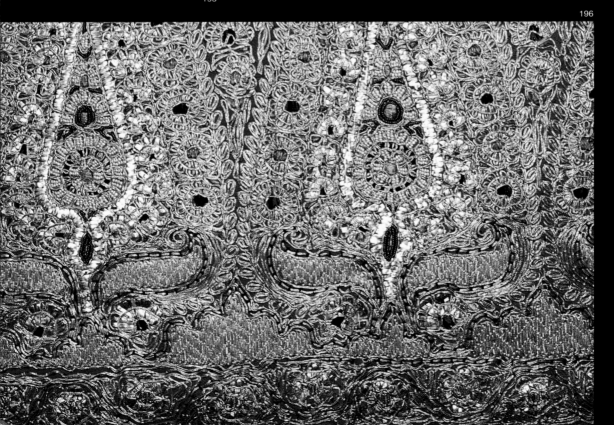

Natural beads

Long before the ancient Egyptians first made faience and, later, glass beads, people had fashioned bone, tooth, amber, pearl, and agate into items of personal adornment. The oldest known bead and perhaps one of the earliest exchange items was amber. Desire, trade, prestige, and colonial expansion were all inextricably linked to the sensuous, cool gleam of beads.

194 *Taj*, detail, Salé, Morocco. *Taj* (Persian for crown) typified the eclectic nature of Moroccan dress. Protective and showy natural seed-pearl strands and semi-precious stone *taj* diadems were tied over layered bridal headdresses or married women's festive headgear.

195 *Babouche* with Basra pearls, Persia. Long associated with beauty and luxury, Basra pearls from southeastern Iraq covered *babouche* (slippers). Glass-beaded peacocks were associated with royalty and the Persian court, and the cypress with longevity.

196 *Pashmina* shawl border, Rajasthan, India. Wealth and social power were expressed through extravagant materials like Basra pearls, beads made from emeralds, and pure gold and silk threads worked on ultra-fine *pashmina*, the wool of Himalayan goats. This example belonged to the Jaipur royal family.

Things of money: beads, trade, and prestige

After the sixteenth century, tons of glass beads were made in Europe for overseas trade. Wherever they were distributed, the beads made huge profits for traders and had an enormous effect on local economies, the ranking of objects of prestige, and concepts of value.

197 Tobacco pouch, Cheyenne or Arapaho, North America. Plainsmen carried long cylindrical bags with fringes for their tobacco and smoking gear. Horizontal band motifs reflect the transition from quillwork to glass beads.

198 Oba Ademuwagun Adesida II in beaded regalia and coral *ade* (crown), Yoruba, Nigeria, Africa. Beads are sacred to the Yoruba because their translucency transforms light and color. The Oba, the king, wears heavily beaded regalia as an emblem of his divine power.

199 *Jocolo*, detail, Ndebele, South Africa. Strong bead traditions in Africa arose from peoples that wore skins. Among Ndebele young women, *jocolo* (scalloped-bottom aprons) were associated with marriage. Their predominantly white beads kept beneficial spirits alert to protect the wearer.

200 *Na-ko-gun*, Inuit, Bering Sea, North America. *Na-ko-gun* (belts) displayed women's wealth in trade beads. Blue beads, which first came from Vitus Bering in the 1740s, were most favored; in the nineteenth century European beads were traded with Russians for furs.

197   198

199
200

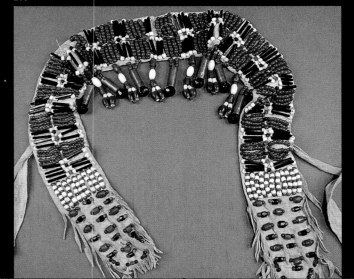

201

202

203

204

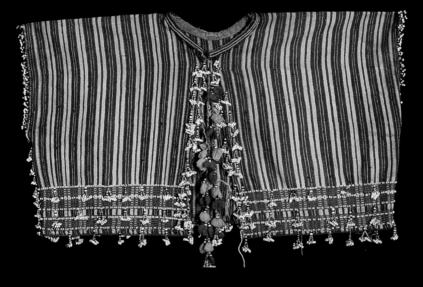

Speaking with beads

Glass beads greatly enhanced dress. Their hardness, durability, monetary and ceremonial value, and resulting prestige were all combined with concepts of protection. In Southeast Asia, beads took on almost supernatural powers due to intricate connections between social and economic class, ancestral blessings, and wealth. Sometimes, by social rank or accomplishment, people earned rights to wear certain images. Elsewhere, beads were less intricately intertwined with stratified societies.

201 *Kain manik*, detail, Maloh people, Sarawak. Maloh women's ceremonial beaded tube skirts, *kain manik*, represented their world and spiritual view. Beads reflected wealth, while *kakaletau* (guardians or ancestor spirits) and *kalang asu* (dragon-dog-like) animal motifs protected the wearer.

202, 204 *Maab* (man's upperbody garment), and *lufid* (woman's lower-body garment), detail, Gaddang people, Luzon, Philippine Islands. The Gaddang used beads stitched to characteristic striped garments to proclaim family wealth, prestige, and to announce young women's eligibility for marriage. Concepts of protection were associated with ornaments, which often visually commemorated successful warriors. Beads distributed throughout China were obtained in the Philippine Islands from the Spanish Manila galleons.

203 Toraja women, Buntalobo village, Sulawesi, Indonesia. Women wore *kandauré* (ceremonial bead ornaments with fringes in front) and girdles, called *sassang*, while dancing the *Ma'gellu* to honor ancestors at harvests and weddings.

205 Bridal fezs, Turkmen people, Keles and Surkun areas, Turkey. Beads and sequins brought amuletic protection to bridal hats or fezs. The fezs were topped with sequin-covered scarves, which further diverted the evil eye's attention from brides.

206, 207 Dress bodice, detail, and *phul*, Pushtun people, Afghanistan. The Pushtun people were related to ancient fire-worshippers, who viewed the sun as the ultimate source of life-force and dispeller of evils associated with darkness. In Persian antiquity, floral medallions and sun disks mingled to symbolize the sun's life-giving and protective properties. Therefore, glinting light from *phul* (meaning flower) and shiny beaded disks related to the sun's protection.

208 Kalash women wearing *shushut* (beaded headdresses), Chitral Valley, Pakistan. Every day Kalash women wear caps with long cascading trails of buttons, cowries, and beads. Not easily obtained, cowries and beads were purchased from the bazaar in Swat Valley, a four-day walk from Chitral.

205

206
207

208

Part Three:
Gifts from Nature

209 Pom-pom ties, Rajasthan, India. Beads, cowries, and iridescent green beetle thoraxes are threaded onto wool-yarn ties, which are worn in women's hair or belted at their waists.

Shells

We see shells as luminous, beautifully patterned, curiously shaped, wondrous objects from faraway places. All the things we love about them we share with people who lived thousands of years ago. Because shells were often shiny, iridescent, and durable, they were highly prized. During the Upper Paleolithic period, ivory and shell were among the most valued substances; shell jewelry has been found in cemeteries along the Rhine and Danube dating from 3000 BC.[1] Mediterranean shells were being traded over the Alps and into central Europe by the early second millennium BC, and nassa and cowrie shells were found in Old Kingdom and twelfth and twenty-fifth to twentieth-sixth dynasty Egyptian tombs.[2] A large number of these Egyptian tomb amulets were made of mother-of-pearl or sea shell, and may have been used to ward off *oculus fascinus*, the evil eye.[3]

Shells were valued for their beauty, but those of uniform size and hardness were monetized and traded thousands of miles away from their origins. Shells were second only to metals in popularity as currency.[4] Shell money was important in Africa, India, Asia Minor, and the Mediterranean, as well as in China, where taxes were paid with cowrie shells. Among the Yurok of northern California, tusk (dentalium) shells were valued as symbols of wealth, while the Pomo of central California used clam-shell beads as currency.

Cowries' durability, consistent size, and the difficulties they posed to fakers made them perfect for currency. There are over 180 species,[5] but only the yellow money cowrie, *Cypraea moneta*, and the ring cowrie, *Cypraea annulus*, have been used as money for many centuries. Arab traders brought cowries to Africa from the Maldive Islands off the coast of India, and the shells were transported by camel across the Sahara, and distributed into central and West Africa by river.[6] So many cowries were brought to Africa as ship ballast that their value as currency eventually collapsed.[7]

Some types of shell were believed to be able to repel evil, to assist with controlling forces of nature, to cure illness, and to promote fertility; many were used by sorcerers, healers, and priests. Some shells with their semen-like color associations alluded to water, rain deities, and rain-making. Others acted as powerful metaphors, because of their various physical attributes. If horizontal, cowries resemble eyes; if vertical, they resemble the female genitalia. Because mollusks can disappear inside their shells, their homes have been regarded as mysterious and were frequently associated with the womb. Cross-sections of exponentially expanding spiral shells, such as the chambered nautilus, symbolize regeneration and never-ending energy.

The use of whole shells or shell pieces in dress was more than just decorative. Some peoples, like the Bagobo and Bilaan of the Philippine Islands, believed that, when cut and attached to clothing, closed circular forms of shell created protective barriers of shining light. To others, shell disks suggested the moon, and evoked its powers and associations.

In sunlight, the flash of iridescent mother-of-pearl shell could suggest lightning. The Pomo of central and northern California associated abalone's luster with the god Thunder Man, who wore an abalone coat that created thunder when it shook and lightning when he blinked.[8]

Tinkling or rattling shell pieces made sounds that scared away malevolent forces, and shells' hardness and durability, when added to clothing, contributed to its beauty and prestige. Extra labor, money, and supplies were required to acquire large amounts of shell elements. If the shells were scarce, or only the élite were permitted to possess them, their presence proclaimed elevated status and often, the wearer's closer connection to supernatural beings than other mortals.

As we have seen, shell embellishments, beads, and metal elements were considered by some peoples to be hard or male products which contrasted with soft, female goods, like textiles. Traditionally, males obtained or manufactured durable elements, while women prepared, dyed, and wove fibers into cloth. The hard and soft, or male and female, substances created a complementary union, which enhanced the symbolic value of the garment.[9]

Shells are home to mollusks, soft animals without spines. Seven different classes of mollusk produce enormous varieties of shell shapes, sizes, colors, and patterns. Mollusks live in fresh water, salt water, and on dry land. Some of those whose shells are widely used include bivalves, with two shell halves joined by a ligament; gastropods, which include cowries, conch, and garden snails; and scaphopods, or tusk shells, such as tooth shells and dentalium.[10]

The mollusk has a fleshy covering called the mantle, which makes the shell that protects its invertebrate body. Through the mollusk's blood, liquified calcium carbonate is secreted between the mantle and its existing shell. Within moments the liquid crystallizes to form nacre, or shell. Mollusks produce three different crystalline forms of lime: calcite, aragonite, and zaterite. Aragonite is the heaviest form of lime; when laid down in thin sheets, it produces nacre, or iridescent mother-of-pearl.[11] However, not all shells produce iridescent linings. Mollusks vary their appearance through the use of either pigments or physical refraction from light rays. Pigments are manufactured and deposited into the liquid shell material through glands along the mantle. As with beetle elytra and many feathers, the optical effect of iridescence is caused by the principle of interference: iridescent coloration like that seen in abalone and pearl-producing mollusks results from the reinforcement, weakening, or elimination of light waves by numerous layers of nacre.[12]

Shells have had an enormous effect on many cultures. They were integral to economic, social, and political values, and often contributed religious and symbolic significance. Shells functioned in all these complex ways in parts of Africa. Some were covered with gold leaf, or gilded brass. Among the Akan people, red cockle shells from the Canary Islands were highly valued and traded for gold.[13] The Asante prized clam shell, while others in central and southern Africa accumulated *mpande*, or cross-sections of conus shells. In Angola, these disks were stitched onto leather straps that hung down the wearer's back.[14] Like nautilus shells, conus shells were believed to possess magical powers because of their spiral shapes. In the sixteenth century, Arab slave traders used them as currency in Africa, and later, they were imitated by white glass disks made in Bohemia.[15] Conus was also widely used in Mauritania, where disks and whorls from their tips were frequently notched and incised, before being made into ornaments to adorn the body and hair.[16]

In Central Asia, tiny conch shells were associated with rain-bringing rituals and fertility,[17] and incorporated into tassels and used on domestic bags. Similar practices were seen in Afghanistan, Pakistan, and western India, where tiny olive shells (oliva) were attached as embellishments to dowry embroideries, perhaps to promote fertility. There is indeed an ancient history to the use of shells, perhaps for their meanings related to regeneration and new life: cowries were imported from Central Asia and buried with other treasures in fifth-century BC Scythian underground chambers in Pazyryk.[18] Among the Turkmen of Central Asia, cowries were used by females only, to protect their fertility: the shells were worn by newborn infants immediately after birth, and by young girls until they eventually married and had children of their own. The shells symbolized women's wombs, because new life is generated from within.[19]

Among the nine indigenous peoples of Taiwan, including the Atayal, Bunan, Paiwan, and Yami, shells and shell disks were worn on dress. These groups practiced headhunting at one time, and each dressed distinctively. The wealthy, or those who had earned the privilege, wore shell ornaments. Shell-disk bandoliers were restricted to the highest-ranking chiefs and their women, and functioned as a tally of heads taken.[20] Many Naga groups from northeast India, who were also formerly headhunters, used conch shells and cowries to indicate accomplishments and high status, too.

Many shell varieties, especially rare or luminous ones, were used by Oceanic peoples to display wealth and status. Any refinement of shells into useable forms further enhanced their value. Shells like the giant clam (Tridacna sp.), the pearl (Margaritifera sp.), and the nassa (Nassarius sp.) generally required some work, and were frequently used as currency. Nassa and cowries were sliced or ground to flatten their arched backs, and then strung onto strings to be transformed into money. Since clam shells were extremely hard and only simple bamboo tools with abrasive stone or sand were available, much labor was required to cut and drill them.

Other economic uses of shells included competitive gift exchanges. In Papua New Guinea, more than ten types of shells were part of the system of value: some particularly prized for their color and sheen included green turban shells, Turbo marmoratus, and gold pearl oysters, Pinctada maxima, from which gold pearl crescents were made. At Moka, the ceremonial exchange ceremony of the Melpa people of Mount Hagen in highland Papua New Guinea, men earned social rank by giving away their wealth, which included highly prized pearl shells of red and yellow-orange hue. Big Man status was indicated by breastplates composed of bamboo sticks which represented tallies of shell sets given away.[21]

Shells and shell pieces with brightly luminous coloration are important in North America too. Among northern Californian Native Americans, spiritual wealth is expressed through regalia which contains the spiritual essence of the natural materials utilized. Wealthy individuals, through their virtuous living, obtain the financial means to accumulate ceremonial dress and accessories. Therefore, it is their obligation to hold dances, so that the living spirits within the regalia can also dance.[22]

Along the northwest Pacific coast, abalone was favored for its iridescent nacre. The blue-green abalone, *Haliotis fulgens*, of southern Californian waters was preferred to paler pink northwest coast varieties[23] and the brighter shells were traded over great distances. The Haida and Tlingit peoples used pieces of abalone inlay in food dishes, boxes, and regalia, and wore ceremonial clothing with platelets of abalone shell or mother-of-pearl shell buttons.[24] Other Native American groups accumulated dentalium and clam-shell money to convey wealth, while the small, beige, and brownish shells of the marginella and oliva groups were worn in regalia for their shininess. White, beige, and purple quahog, hard-shell clam from *Mercenaria mercenaria*, was cut, drilled, strung into wampum (money made from rows of shell disks strung onto flat belts), and traded widely across America.[25]

Among ancient Andean peoples, the shell of *Spondylus princeps*, the thorny oyster, was sacred and often found in élite burials. Red and pink *Spondylus* sp. were treasured more than emeralds, for their colorful shells were hard to collect and difficult to work due to their nasty spines.[26] Shell disks were traded at least 1,000 miles from the coasts of Ecuador, Colombia, and Panama where the shells were found, into the Nazca valley of Peru.

Mother-of-pearl buttons, like shells, have been widely employed for decorative and protective purposes rather than just as closures. White or even colorful plastic buttons were often utilized alongside beads and coins, as their bright, reflective surfaces were believed to be effective in combating the evil eye. Disks, buttons, and other shapes were cut from the nacrous or mother-of-pearl lining of *Margaritifera margaritifera*, salt-water pearl oysters, and freshwater pearl mussel shells like *Lucina* sp. or *Anodonta* sp. In the nineteenth century, shells of a Mississippi clam, *Quadrula ebena*, yielded large amounts of shell buttons in the United States.[27] At one time, mother-of-pearl shell was more valuable than pearls, and the cost of harvesting the expensive material led to artificial mother-of-pearl. Lucite, an acrylic resin, was commonly cast into button-shaped molds. Made of white opaque material swirled into translucent, these plastic buttons were marketed around the world and appeared in dress and adornment after the 1950s.

With their hard, shiny surfaces and mysterious, glowing interiors, it's not surprising that shells capture our imaginations. Surplus goods have been sacrificed for them, great distances have been traveled to obtain them, and lives have been risked to harvest those living in deep waters. Inventive techniques and hours of labor have been expended to fashion shells into useable items. For all this beauty, we must thank the mollusks that made magic by transforming calcium carbonate and water into luminous shells.

Seeds and Fibers

Nature's genius has produced countless shapes, sizes, and patterns of seeds and useful vegetable fibers. With their ingenious designs, seeds drifted, floated, or hitchhiked into new environments. Humans carried them into the realm of personal adornment. The consistently sized, indehiscent, or hard-shelled seeds of the Leguminosae family were widely used for decorative purposes.[1] Seeds were usually free, and easy to harvest; they could be quickly transformed into either lively surface additives when dried and stitched to cloth, or noise-makers when strung and suspended.

Because seeds germinated into new plants, they were commonly associated with fertility, reproduction, and metamorphosis. Some bright or shiny seeds and vegetal materials maintained their luster or shine for many years; these represented life-force and vitality. Molucca beans and nickernuts from *Caesalphinia bonduc* and *Guilandina crista*[2] were shiny gray seeds that often floated thousands of miles across oceans.[3] Talismans were made from the nuts, because they had traveled so far by sea and remained intact throughout their long journeys.[4]

Whether simply to delight the senses or to address the spirit world, seeds have been important in producing elements of sound in dress.[5] When tethered or clustered into dangles, they made tinkling and rattling noises and their aural potential was frequently employed in clothing, headdresses, and adornment to be worn at important ceremonies and festivals.

Aromatic plants and seeds were sometimes associated with repelling evil, promoting fertility, or providing restorative healing powers. Beads were made from many kinds of sweet-smelling plant seeds and resins. Cloves, for example, were believed to ward off evil. In parts of Mali, soft myrrh resin was threaded onto strings to make beads.[6] Some Californian Native Americans used dark, slightly glossy juniper berries, *Juniperus* sp., for ornaments and fringes in ceremonial dress; the berries were a valuable trade item which originated in the Mount Shasta area of northern California. If left next to anthills, the berries would be eaten out and hollowed by the ants.[7] Juniper was fragrant, but it was also regarded as medicinal: baskets of *Juniperus phoenicea* or *Juniperus drupacea* berries were frequently found in ancient Egyptian tombs, and the aromatic seeds were often used in the mummification process.[8]

Some seeds were extremely glossy and hard, and were therefore commonly used for beads, buttons, and ornaments. The black seeds of the candlenut tree, *Aleurites molucanna*, were especially lustrous and gem-like. The soap berry, *Sapindus saponaria*, also produced dark, gleaming seeds.[9] The ivory-nut palm or vegetable ivory, *Phytelephas macrocarpa*, of South America is edible, until its ripened seeds become too hard; then they are made into buttons. In contemporary fashion, ecologically minded designers use vegetable ivory buttons instead of plastic. Even the endocarp, the shell surrounding the coconut seed, is cut into buttons and polished to a shine.[10] The kernel of the *dhom* palm, which has a dark outer surface and a light inside, was carved and incised to create contrasting designs between the outer and inner layers; bead disks were made from other types of nut palm shells, too, which were polished with wet sand until they glistened. Among the Yoruba of Nigeria, the thinnest palm disks were highly prized for the skill required to make them.[11] The seeds of the sago palm, *Cycas revoluta*, were worn in Papua New Guinea, where the plants were highly prized as food,[12] and "glossy brown sheets of the sago palm" were chain-stitched as decorations onto baskets made in Sulawesi in Indonesia.[13]

Other edible seeds, such as pine nuts, were strung like beads and used in dress. The pointed ends of the hulls were ground flat, so that the nuts could be perforated. Hard, shiny nuts of digger pine, *Pinus sabiniana*, and knob-cone pine, *Pinus tuberculata*, were commonly used by northern Californian Indians. When knob-cones were heated, small black nuts rolled out; these were used as beads.[14]

Shiny red abrus, *Abrus precatorius*, is nicknamed crab-eye or rosary bean. These seeds are commonly used in adornment, but if their outer shells are broken, they are poisonous.[15] Because dried abrus seeds and those from the locust tree, *Ceratonia siliqua*, have a consistent weight (about three grains in the Indian jewelers' system), they have been used to weigh precious gemstones and gold. Indian goldsmiths still use an ancient system even though weights and standards were established in 1956.[16] The word carat is derived from the use of *Ceratonia* sp. seeds as weights.[17] Abrus seeds were often embedded into surfaces with natural adhesives. Some groups from Papua New Guinea stuck them into hard-drying glue coated onto vegetable fiber pectoral shields, which were then worn in battle. The seeds were also used decoratively in the Philippines, in India, and in Africa.

Some of the commonest seeds used by people throughout Asia are Job's tears, *Coix lacryma-jobi*, and related species from the grass family. The Latin name *coix* descends from the Greek word *koix*, for a reed-leafed plant. The plants require long, hot summers in order to flower, and the seeds mature in the fall. Job's tears seeds are round or elongated, and range in coloration from white to blue-gray to gray-brown; they are commonly strung into beads, and their hard forms make pleasant noises when strung into clusters. Some peoples, such as the Akha of northern Thailand and Myanmar, turn them white by placing them in the embers of fires for up to two weeks.[18] In Papua New Guinea, widows from the Mendi area wore huge necklaces of Job's tears, whose accumulated mass was sometimes up to thirty pounds. After each prescribed period of mourning the widow would discard one strand, until all the Job's tears necklaces were gone.[19]

As well as seeds, numerous other parts of plants are useful for embellishment and decoration. Some plant fibers, like the outer leaves of bamboo shoots or dried orchid vines, are naturally shiny or brightly colored. Others, like pandanus leaves, become shiny when smoked over a fire and burnished. Sleek golden grasses are used to manufacture personal adornment. Dried grasses are plaited, twisted, or combined with other materials like wax or mud. *Darbha* grass, *Demostachya bipinnata*, has sacred connotations in India, because it is believed by Hindus to have been the first plant created by the gods. *Gajia*, ornaments made of shiny grass, are worn by Bhil and Garasia tribal women of Rajasthan and Gujarat. Other types of grasses, wheat stalks, and rice stalks are frequently used as well. To some, grass ornaments were sacred; to others, the color of dried straw imitated precious gold.[20] In Niger, women sometimes wear golden ornaments of baked clay and golden-colored straw, which is nicknamed "Timbuktu gold." Sometimes, the shiny yellow straw is combined with beeswax and formed into ornaments that are so realistic that they are often mistaken for gold.[21]

Personal adornment commonly featured bamboo of the family Bambusoidea. Beads made from small-diameter bamboo tubes become quite shiny as they are worn. In Irian Jaya, Indonesia, the Dani people wear polished bamboo beads,[22] while in the Mount Hagen area of Papua New Guinea, bamboo breastplates called *omak* are worn as emblems of prestige by high-ranking men.[23]

One of the most vibrant vegetable fibers is made from numerous species of wild orchids. Their brilliant, glossy yellow fibers have frequently been combined with darker, duller vegetable substances, like coconut, which provide a foundation and contrast with the brighter, shiny orchid fibers. Personal adornment with yellow orchid stems was prevalent in Nagaland in northeast India, as well as throughout Melanesia. Naga groups utilized yellow orchid straw, called *ayi-khwo*, in their personal adornment because it was naturally brilliant and would not fade. Wild orchid stems were gathered, pressed, dried, cut into strips, and incorporated into personal ornaments. To the Naga people, their permanence was probably a visual representation of soul-force.[24]

Dried wild orchids were also combined with other natural materials throughout Melanesia. There, clothing was unknown until foreigners arrived, but adornment with vegetal fibers and natural materials was prevalent. Belts and tight-fitting armlets were worn, and people frequently stuck fresh leaves or even smoking gear in them.[25] Fern stems from *Gleichenia genera*, rattan, and coconut fiber contrasted with the yellow orchid stems.[26] While armlets and belts made of disks of clam shell or thorny oyster shell were used in ritual exchanges and as currency, vegetable fiber elements of dress were probably used in ordinary circumstances by the less wealthy. For variety, some plant fibers, such as rattan cane, were dyed. A red dye was obtained from the root of *Morinda citrifolia*, and the dyed cane was sprinkled with coconut juice to make it glossy. Then the shiny dyed fibers were plaited with bright yellow and dull brown plant materials.[27]

Throughout the world, people have found an extraordinary variety of creative uses for plants and seeds. Nature provides the ingredients, and human ingenuity transforms the raw materials into glossy and bright surfaces achieved with the simplest processes.

Feathers

Small patches of molten metallic bronze, displays of mesmerizing emerald, and flits of shocking turquoise momentarily glimpsed among thick vegetation are among the most elusive and dazzling gifts of nature. Brilliant and iridescent feathers have fascinated humans for millennia. Countless diverse cultures have invented ingenious ways of fashioning the functional materials that enable birds to fly, to fill out their forms, to keep themselves warm, and to make themselves beautiful.

Although it is hard to imagine soft shimmering-feathered birds' scaly-skinned origins, numerous fossils record their reptilian ancestry. The oldest fossilized feathers were found in a Bavarian quarry from which limestone blocks were cut to make lithograph stones. The 140-million-year-old specimen had a lizard-like tail and skull, but also had flight feathers just like the birds of today. Aptly, the species was named *Archaeopteryx lithographica*.[1]

Fine, insulating down feathers, contour feathers, wing coverts, and tail feathers or *retrices* come from over 8,600 species of birds in numerous different colors, patterns, and textures. Each has unique design potential. Feathers can be tethered individually or attached to long strings and then overlapped, glued flat, gathered into tufts, or combined into mosaics. The tips can be cut at angles, and the barbules, the feathery parts branching off from the vane, can be serrated or cut away leaving just the quill.[2]

Feathers are used to communicate visually social, political, economic, aesthetic, and spiritual concepts. Some cultures use them to construct self-identity and to show attachment to a group, while others use feathered objects as political tools and emblems of social status. Feathers are used to enhance beauty and sexual attraction, and, in many societies, rare, precious, colorful, or fragile feathers enhance the worth of other objects.[3]

Among most peoples, iridescent and brightly colored feathers, especially red ones, have been associated with wealth and supernatural powers because of the intensity, the brilliance, and the rarity of their colors. And because certain species possess unusual behaviors as well as the ability to fly, birds and their feathers are associated with the spiritual or supernatural. Perhaps the wearer absorbs a bird's unusual powers by wearing its feathers. Shamans have symbolically associated themselves with birds and their feathers: birds see everything from their aerial perspective, and assist with healers' or visionaries' trips to other worlds, serving as intermediaries with other levels of reality.

In North America, native peoples use feathers in all aspects of life. Living things are regarded within the totality of the universe, so feathers connect wearers with their cosmos. Feathers possess special powers and carry the bird's spirit, sweeping away illness, helping to communicate with the spirit world, and signaling accomplishments in battles.[4]

Feather arts mirror the cultures of over 120 South Amerindian groups in the Amazon Basin by conveying gender, the wearer's community, and frequently social status. Feathers are worn at important events like name-giving rituals, youth initiation rites, funerary practices, and feasts related to harvests. The wearer is spiritually strengthened by adornment with the products of the sacred feather arts.[5]

In ancient Peru, intricate feathered garments, hangings, and items of personal adornment were manufactured as offerings to gods, war chiefs, rulers, and, to provide a pleasant afterlife, to the high-ranking deceased. Feathers formed part of the taxation system, and the production and distribution of feather garments, as with other luxury textiles, was highly regulated. Feathers were believed to possess magical properties and to reflect the sun and the realm of the gods. Plumes were also used to cast spells over enemies, to foretell the outcomes of battles, and for other forms of magic.[6]

In Oceania, feathers were important for many peoples to express status, wealth, and beauty. In highland Papua New Guinea, the wearing of feathers promoted vitality and assisted in sexual attraction, for the beauty of the birds was transferred to the wearers. Plumes from various birds of paradise linked prestige and wealth to benevolent blessings from ancestors.[7] In Hawaii, feathers were used to distinguish between social ranks, and only the highest-ranking men made and wore feather capes, '*ahu'ula*, and helmets; women used feathers to make lei garlands, fans, and small objects.[8] The Maori brought elements of their Polynesian heritage, including social rank and dress privileges, when they migrated to New Zealand in around AD 800.[9] The climate there was too cool and damp for garments made of *tapa* cloth, so *Phormium tenax*, flax fiber, and flax with feathers were used for clothing high-ranking individuals. Women used pigeon, parrot, kiwi, and hawk feathers to make sacred feather cloaks, which expressed status.[10]

Feathers are composed of keratin, a tough protein similar to hair or nails.[11] Birds' colorings are determined through heredity and the types of follicles from which the feathers grow. Colors are produced chemically, by pigments present within the keratin, or structurally, by the reflection of light from the feathers' surface structures. In chemical pigment coloration, the surface absorbs all the colors of the spectrum contained in white light except for the color itself which is reflected and therefore seen. Chemical substances are present in the pigments which cause only certain light rays to be reflected. Most chemical pigment colors, like browns, blacks, and some reds and yellows, fade after the death of the bird or animal. Iridescent colors, however, do not, as they are created by the feathers' physical structure.[12]

Vibrant iridescent effects are caused by the scientific phenomenon called interference, which results from different types of structures in the surface layers of feather tissues. Most iridescent colors are greens, blues and violets, and their brilliance and purity are unmatched by any pigment. Interference occurs when beams of light from the same source meet, scatter, and diffuse as they pass through tissues and hit sub-microscopic physical structures. Wavelengths of equal amplitude reinforce or weaken each other, while wavelengths of different colors frequently neutralize one another, causing only certain wavelengths to be reflected in greater magnitude.[13] Since there are no colors brighter than interference colors, iridescent feathers are highly valued and often believed to be sacred.

Numerous universal, archetypal stories exist about how birds obtained their colors. Some peoples believed that iridescent or brilliant feathers were the sun transformed. Many myths involved the sun, a fire, or a battle between an evil serpent and birds of the world. Some stories told of birds that had bathed in the blood of the slain serpent and were instantly turned red; birds that touched some part of the evil creature became rust or green. In other legends, birds that flew close to the sacred sun or a sacred fire turned red, yellow, or black from contact with flames, heat, or smoke.[14]

Birds with appealing plumage are found all around the world, although those with the most arrestingly beautiful feathers live in tropical climates. Some birds are brilliantly colored all over their bodies, while others have only small patches of iridescent plumage or grow just a few bright feathers. Iridescence is found in tanagers, cotingas, hummingbirds, peacocks, kingfishers, and quetzals, to name just a few; brilliantly colored feathers are produced by toucans, parrots, and macaws, amongst others.

Feathers were obtained in numerous ways. Some birds molted annually, and their feathers were simply gathered; other birds were hunted for food, and their feathers were saved. Sadly, the feathers of some species were so prized that they were hunted to extinction. Some birds were kept as pets, while others were captured, plucked, and released. Some feather colors were altered through various treatments, including heat. In *tapirage*, the artificial coloring of feather growth on a bird, poisonous toad secretions or toad's blood were applied to the bird's skin to alter the color of its new feathers.[15]

Deeper-colored birds, like grackles and starlings, produce iridescent feathers or plumage with a glossy sheen. The pelagic cormorant, *Phalacrocorax pelagicus*, is a drab, black-brown sea and freshwater bird; related to the pelican family, it has metallic green-violet, iridescent throat patches which Alaskan people made into parkas and other garments.

Some of the most vibrant of all bird species are cotingas, members of the Cotingidae family. Some males are shocking blue, red, or violet, while the "Cock-of-the-Rock," another member of the family, is bright orange-red. The *Cotinga cotinga* male from the Amazon has intense blue feathers all over his body. Blue and violet colors have longer wavelengths and scatter light more than shorter-wavelength reds, thus appearing more brilliant.[16]

Hummingbirds, the family Trochilidae, are living jewels. Usually glittering green or blue with brilliant iridescent patches of violet, red, gold, or copper at the head, throat, or breast, these birds' beauty, swiftness, miniscule size, and agility are fascinating. Depending on the angle at which they are viewed, hummingbird feathers change color: at one moment they look black, and at another, they flash iridescent golden copper or violet. Hummingbird feathers overlap like shingles or tiles, and only the tips produce the brilliant colors, so Inca feather artists placed overlapping hummingbird feathers at twenty-one, forty, or sixty-five degree angles in mosaics to maximize the iridescence.[17]

Electric-blue feathers come from several species of kingfisher, in the family Alcedinidae. Kingfishers are found around small streams and shores, and in rainforests. Frequently they have shocking blue backs and reddish bellies, but some are brown or light green. The Eurasian kingfisher[18] is especially bright. Called *fei-ts'ui*[19] in China, these radiant blue to violet feathers were used in jewelry and headdresses. Han dynasty accounts described the splendor of a royal bedchamber with dazzling, electric-blue kingfisher-feather tapestries and bedspreads covered with pearls.[20] Kingfisher feathers were prominently worn in Chinese court ornaments and in bridal crowns, but at the beginning of the twentieth century, commoners were given permission to wear small kingfisher ornaments as hair combs. By the 1930s, the enormous demand for feathers exceeded supply and caused the extinction of the Eurasian kingfisher in China. Feathers of the Indian kingfisher were substituted, but their feathers were not as brilliant as the original *fei-ts'ui*.[21]

The members of the parrot, Psittacidae, family, some of the largest of bird species, are an important source of feathers in the Amazon Basin. The Hyacinthe macaw, *Anodorhynchus hyacinthinus*; the blue and yellow macaw, *Ara ararauna*; the scarlet macaw, *Ara macao*; the red and green macaw, *Ara chloroptera*; and many others provide brilliant long tail feathers and contour feathers. Interestingly, ninety percent of green parrot feathers are structurally blue, with just enough yellow pigment to make them appear green.[22] Macaws are associated with the sun for their dazzling colors and radiating tail feathers. Red macaw feathers are believed to be too "hot" for the average person to work with, and if worn, were usually attached to a frame to extend them away from the skin.[23]

Perhaps because of its huge bill, the toucan, of the family Ramphastidae, has strong mystical associations. Toucan feathers and bodies are widely used in adornment among peoples of the Amazon Basin. Mostly black, with a few bright red and yellow rump and breast feathers, the birds are probably valued more for their powers than their beauty.

Universally acknowledged as one of the most beautiful of all birds is the peacock, *Pavo cristatus*, of the family Phasianidae. A mature male's train contains about 200 iridescent ocelli, eye feathers, which can be fanned out into a hypnotically dazzling display to attract peahens.[24] His neck and head are brilliant blue-green; the color, "peacock blue," has taken his name. Adult peacocks molt and grow new feathers in seven-month cycles. Billions of particles are required annually to create the physical structure of the feathers, which enable us to see the peacock's iridescent colors.[25] Peafowl are indigenous to Southeast Asia, where they are associated with auspicious meanings. According to legend, they are capable of swallowing poisons without harm, and so their feathers are often used on Buddhist altars to symbolize the eradication of spiritual poisons.[26] Peacock-feather quills are used in headdresses, the ocelli are made into numerous articles, and even individual feather barbules are stripped from the quill and used in embroidery and weaving.

Rivaling the peacock for sheer splendor is the Himalayan or Monal pheasant, also known as the Impeyan pheasant, *Lophophorus impeyanus*, whose gleaming, iridescent copper-gold feathers are often associated with molten metal or the embers of a fire.[27] The males are almost entirely iridescent with shimmering green heads, copper neck patches, violet and shocking turquoise backs, and emerald-green undersides.

In contrast to the metallic appearance of Impeyan pheasants, quetzals, of the family Trogonidae, the sacred birds of the Mayas and Aztecs, are known for their shimmering, frosty appearances. The Quetzal's green feathers are structurally iridescent gold-green to blue-green, and their soft appearance is caused by a lack of interlocking barbules on the contour feathers. Some quetzals have bright red or yellow breasts, which contrast with their emerald bodies. Of thirty-six species of Trogonidae, fifteen live in the Americas from southern Mexico to northern Argentina. Resplendent quetzals, the red-breasted *Pharomachrus mocino*, were believed to be the personification of Quetzalcóatl, the plumed serpent god and patron of the arts worshipped by the Mayans and Aztecs. Quetzals later became the national emblem of Guatemala. Only the highest Mayan and Aztec élite were permitted to wear the long glittering plumes of quetzals, which were made into royal headdresses.[28] Each male bird grows four tail feathers approximately twelve inches long which were harvested at the birds' molt to be used in feather regalia.

People found decorative potential, too, in bird quills, porcupine quills, grasses, maidenhair fern stems, and even dyed corn husks.[29] Collectively called quillwork, decorative applications of these materials were favored in North America.[30] The raised dimensions and frequently shiny surfaces of these materials provided relief from monotone hides and leather.

Porcupines are found in North America, Europe, and Asia. About fifteen species of the prickly rodent of the Hystricidae family exist, and their bodies are covered with up to 30,000 sharp, rigid quills; the finest come from the animal's belly, while the tail produces the largest. Contrary to popular belief, porcupines do not throw their quills. If threatened, they either raise them up, roll into a ball, and wait for the attacker to impale itself, or charge backwards into the enemy.[31] In Southeast Asia, porcupine needles can be up to nine inches long. Some tribal women use them in weaving to lift warp or weft threads, and the sharp points are also useful for pulverizing medicines.

In North America, quills were a trade item, as porcupines are not indigenous throughout the entire continent. Numerous techniques existed for working with quills, and they were also used to shorten or extend feathers or hair tufts. Feather shafts and porcupine quills were flattened between the teeth, then dyed with mineral and vegetable materials. They were spliced to make seemingly continuous lengths, and were inserted around and over sinew stitches.[32] Quills, and later beaded bands, were often worked along the shoulders and sleeves of hide shirts. Women created quillwork from designs handed down from older generations or made their own patterns. Some designs were protective, while others were decorative. When glass beads became available, decorative work incorporating them substituted older quillwork techniques, because beadwork was quicker and required less preparation.

From exquisite quills to fragile feathers, human lives are greatly enriched by these gifts from the birds. The kaleidoscope of color available in the feather arts is truly remarkable and resplendent. And for a material as light and delicate, iridescent feathers possess irrefutably strong powers. Perhaps it is our own enduring fascination with flight, or our love of beauty and allure. Whatever the reason, feather arts are a soaring tribute to the worldwide appeal of light-reflecting dress and personal adornment.

Beetle Elytra

Young Pwo Karen girls wearing bright red shawls thrown over one shoulder dance as fringes sparkle and tinkle—their celebratory costumes with coins, bells, beads, and brilliant-green beetle elytra are worn for funeral gatherings. An Angami Naga warrior from northeast India prepares for a Feast of Merit wearing ear rosettes made of gleaming bright-green beetle wing and fringes of scarlet hair. In Mughal times, a Jaipur noble's prized *patka* (sash) flashed in the sunlight, resplendent with gilded metallic work and accents of iridescent blue-green-violet beetle elytra. The Shuar people of Amazonia collect and save iridescent greenish-violet wing covers of enormous beetles, which they incorporate into many kinds of personal adornment. Fashionable Victorian ladies swept through ballrooms with dresses, shawls, and fans embellished with glittering, verdant touches of exotica from distant lands. These are just a few examples of interesting, imaginative textiles and ornaments which use natural, metallic-looking beetle elytra for embellishment.

Beetles literally fly through the pages of history. The use of live or deceased beetles in personal adornment has appeared in many places around the world. Scarab or dung beetles seem miraculously to emerge as adults from underground chambers, and have therefore been associated with the sun and the eternal renewal of life. A brilliant metallic-green beetle was even found embalmed in a tomb at Thebes.[1] Some produce glowing light and are used as decorations in hair or attached to clothing. Living bejeweled beetles have been worn and kept as pets in India, Sri Lanka, and Mexico.[2]

Beetles have two sets of wings. The hard outer wing covers, called elytra, are of extremely lightweight and sturdy chitin; these are lifted out of the way while the insect flies using its true wings. The brilliant metallic coloration of the elytra is caused by interference, which occurs because of the physical structure of the chitin. The seemingly magical coloration of metallic beetles has made them perennially fascinating.[3] Since the elytra are hard and their vibrant color is permanent, decorative uses for them abound.

At one time, great quantities of shining green buprestid, or jewel, beetles were used in textiles and ornaments. Myanmar was the chief market and distribution point, but these days Bangkok is a center for buprestid wings. Beetle elytra were sent to Calcutta, from where they were further distributed for the embellishment of table linens, shawls, fans, and clothing.

The oldest documented example of the use of beetle elytra is the Tamamushi Shrine in Japan, which dates from AD 650. The shrine's name is derived from the Japanese name for a kind of green beetle, *tamamushi*.[4] The iridescent wings are placed under bronze filigree ornaments on the shrine. A later tradition dating from 1690–1730 is seen in Indian miniature painting from the Basohli School, in which bits of iridescent beetle elytra are glued to paintings to suggest emeralds.[5]

A strong folk tradition with the use of beetle elytra exists in India, where entire beetle wings, wing pieces, or even beetle thoraxes have been incorporated into clothing and ornaments. Some of the objects which incorporate them include handmade rural jewelry, camel decorations, belts, *rumal* (ceremonial squares), garments, dolls, playthings, decorative fans, and *torans* (hangings placed over doorways from northwest India).

Some of the finest and most elegant examples of beetle-wing work were created during the Mughal era, when expensive costume accessories and garments with small pieces of beetle elytra and heavily worked precious metal were worn, perhaps to imitate more expensive emeralds or to create a rare color not achieved through enameled jewelry. Many of these belonged to royalty, or were treasured gifts awarded for service or as signs of favor. In extremely competitive times, where great pressure was exerted upon artisans to create unique designs, Mughal textiles using beetle elytra satisfied a craving for novel and innovative pieces.

The Naga groups of northeast India use dress to communicate information about an individual's bravery, wealth, rank, and accomplishments in achieving certain social obligations. Embellishment on garments is linked to traditional lifestyles and cultural values.[6] A link exists between social status and the privilege of wearing beetle elytra in several Naga societies. Females assume the right to wear certain decorations based upon their husbands' or fathers' accomplishments. Women's wrap skirts and breast cloths are embellished with rows and fringes of beetle elytra and other elements, and men wear earrings and cloaks embroidered with a fringe of green beetle elytra on festive occasions.[7]

By capturing heads, the locus of life-giving energy, the Naga believed that an inherent psychic force could be harnessed for personal benefit, as well as for the benefit of the entire group. Soul-force, called *aren*, is also connected to the fertility of humans, livestock, crops, and therefore, with survival.[8] Since metallic-looking beetles display intensely vibrant colors which last after their death, the privilege of wearing their elytra probably expresses this soul-force.

Beetle bodies and wing covers are used by various groups in Papua New Guinea too, where the intricate interconnectedness of beauty, wealth, and spirit are expressed through personal adornment. Many ornaments are believed to contain a kind of magic, which helps their wearers to seem more powerful, attractive, and successful than others. Brightness and luster are important in achieving these goals; bright materials, such as orchid straw, red flowers, feather plumes, shells, and iridescent beetles are particular favorites. Wearing something bright not only expresses wealth, but attracts it, too.[9]

Shuar groups, who occupy parts of the Amazon extending into northeast Ecuador, were once traditional head-taking cultures, known for the beauty and variety of their personal adornment. Their use of bright tropical bird feathers, shiny seeds, and iridescent beetle elytra serves psychic as well as decorative functions, for the raw materials used in their ornaments contain mystical associations. Shuar ornaments are essential to the wearer's personality and express wealth, well-being, status, and soul-power. Furthermore, dress and ornament strengthen the wearer and protect against mysterious influences.[10]

Shuar ornaments are treated with great respect. Some are worn every day, but the use of others is strictly regulated. Both sexes wear earrings, but other ornaments are gender-specific. At dances and ceremonies, for example, special adornments must be worn because wearers enter into a relationship with the spirits.[11]

In Asia, in northern Thailand and Myanmar, the Karen are a large group of hilltribe people whose several social subdivisions are manifested by distinctions in their traditional dress. Certain groups of Pwo Karen use beetles to embellish clothing and useful objects. On festive occasions, both boys and girls wear their finery. Funerals are the most festive times of all: the purpose of the gathering is as much for boy to meet girl as it is to send the spirit of the deceased to the afterworld. In three-day-long ceremonies, people come together to sing, to dance, to form friendships, and to court.[12] For festivities, girls have special hairstyles and wear special dresses and singing shawls embellished with fringes of tinkling beetle wing covers.

In Europe, Charles Germain de Saint-Aubin, the eighteenth-century embroiderer to the King of France, tells of embroidered clothing which used parts of iridescent insects.[13] And extravagant French ball gowns of the 1860s used profuse amounts of butterflies and beetles.[14] Imported by the East India Company, muslin dresses decorated with beetle elytra first appeared in England in the early nineteenth century. By the middle of the century, Europeans were collecting souvenir objects composed of unusual materials such as iridescent feathers, hummingbirds, and beetle elytra, similar to curiosities on display in the 1851 Great Exhibition in London. Changing tastes and values have caused the production of exotic export curios to cease, but in some tribal areas the use of beetle elytra for personal adornment still continues. This little-known aspect of embellishment—the marriage of human imagination with the iridescent beauty of an insect—is a fascinating chapter in the rich history of expertly crafted and innovative textile and personal adornment traditions.

210 Singing shawl, detail, Pwo Karen people, northern Thailand. Young unmarried men and women wear the most ornaments at funerals. The tinkling sounds of beetle elytra, coins, and bells on young women's long singing-shawl fringes help to send the deceased safely to the afterworld.

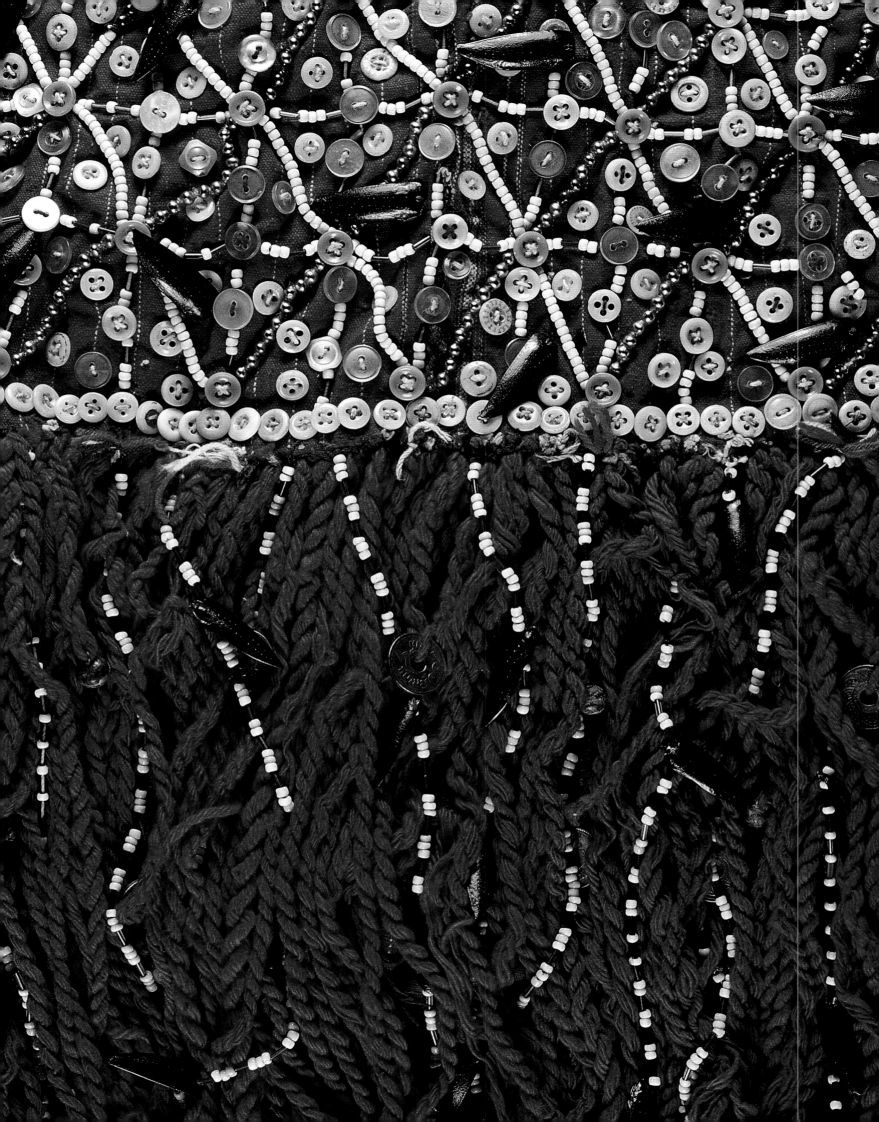

The shell trade

Shells—portable, durable, and gleaming, and often distributed far from their origins—increased the value of objects through economic or ritual and symbolic meaning. The labor involved in harvesting, grinding or cutting them into useful shapes further enhanced objects' worth.

211 *Phulia*, Banjara people, central India. Banjara brides wear padded head rings, *indhoni*, for carrying ceremonial water pots. The *phulia* (flaps) prevent water from splashing the women's necks, and cowrie shells symbolize femininity and fertility.

212 *Aeeweenuk*, Chugach people, northwest Pacific coast. *Aeeweenuk* (men's spruce root hats) were embellished with much-traded dentalium (tusk shell) and blue-green vivianite pigment. The outer part of the root of *Picea sitchensis* was shiny, so it was used for visible areas.

211

212

213

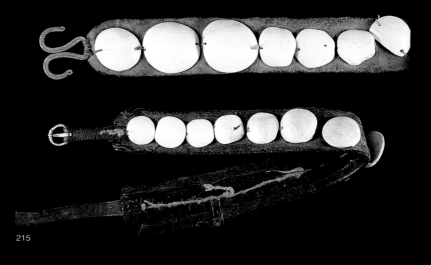

215

216

213 Pouch, Inuit, Alaska. Dentalium and abalone were trade items that reflected wealth. The Nootka group traded in tusk-like shells; the longest, and therefore the most valuable, came from secret deep-water beds.

214, 216 Stormy Rojas, a Yurok northern California Native American, wears her regalia, *yafus*, after dancing in the all-night Brush Dance healing ceremony; and detail of a *tantaaz* (apron) and *yafus'iish* (backwrap). Hupa, Yurok, and Karok medicine women and unmarried girls dress in heavy ritual garments consisting of a *tantaaz* (apron) and a *yafus'iish* (backwrap), weighing up to forty pounds. Abalone, oliva, clam shell, obsidian, coins, beads, juniper berries, and pine nuts are some of the highly valued substances attached to the fringes with beargrass and maidenhair fern. Regalia is sacred, because spirits are inherent in the materials.

215 Milking strap, central Tibet. Women used milking-strap hooks to secure milk pails. Chank shell, *Turbinella*, from the Bay of Bengal was traded far inland and associated with the Hindu deity Shankar or Shiva.

214

217

218

219
220

White shell buttons and cowries

White luminescent shells and shell buttons are associated with the moon and femininity, or with maleness when equated with water, rain, and fertility.

217, 220 Child's hat and *jumlo* (woman's full-skirted upper-body garment), Indus Kohistan, Pakistan. Central Asian-inspired sun disks, trees-of-life, and ram's horn motifs worked in darning stitch are found in textiles from northwest frontier Pakistan, due to trade between the regions.

218, 219 *Asherah nahuak* (wedding *qaftans*), details, Siwa oasis, Egypt. Siwa was an ancient pilgrimage site for worshippers of Amun Ra, the Sun God. Women wear T-shaped dresses embroidered in sunburst designs in the colors of ripening dates, with mother-of-pearl buttons from ancient Arabian Sea pearl industry sites. On the third day of the wedding, brides don white or black *asherah nahuak*, and certain customs are enacted to protect against *jinn* (evil spirits). *Salwar* (trousers) with embroidered bottoms, needleworked shawls, and talismanic silver jewelry complete the dress.

221 Man's shirt, Kiembara region, Burkina Faso. White cowries were connected to spiritual beliefs and were also currency. Nineteenth-century Europeans flooded Africa with cowries and deflated their value; thereafter they were used as surface embellishment on prestige dress and dance costumes.

222 Madame Agbonavbare, a healer priestess, wears a ritual garment, an *abaigho*, covered with cooling, curing cowrie shells and metal elements. In Nigeria, white shells are symbols of wealth and are also associated with Olokun, the god of the sea connected to material wealth and fertility.

223 Nyim Kot a Mbweeky III in prestige dress, Kuba people, Zaire. The wearing of *lapash* (cowrie) regalia is restricted to those of royal lineage, or those of sufficient political or social power; the shells are intricately linked to wealth, prestige, and the Kuba ancestor-god Woot, who comes from the sea.

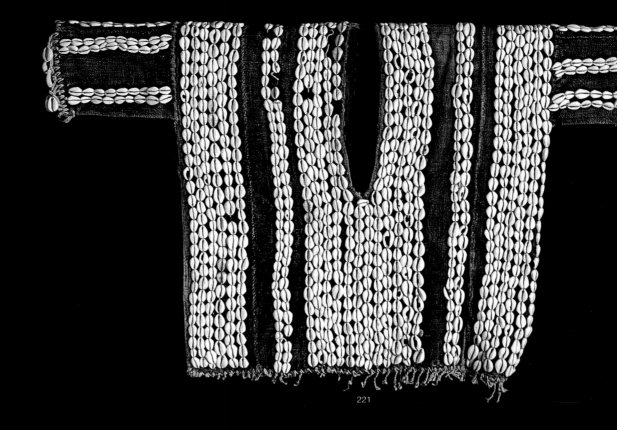

221

222

223

141

224
225

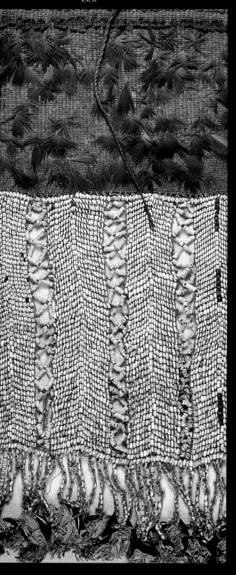

226
227

Oceanic and Southeast Asian peoples have access to a multitude of shell shapes, colors, patterns, and sizes, matched by myriad methods of utilizing their beauty.

224 *Heva*, Tahiti. The *heva* (mourning costume for élite funerals) was deliberately frightening and conspicuous with its noise-making components. The apron tinkled with up to 2,500 mother-of-pearl shell dangles, while the wearer carried a rattle or shell clappers.

225 *Bak*, Admiralty Islands. High-status men and women wore *bak* (display loincloths) made of valuables like giant clam shells, which were difficult to cut into disks, and highly esteemed red feathers. Men from the Solomon Islands and New Ireland Islands traded the disks for food.

226 *Kain buri*, Maloh or Kayan people, Sarawak. *Kain* (tube skirts), encrusted with beads and nassa shells, were important to the ritual lives of their makers, because the hardness of beads and shells imbued the cloths with almost magical qualities which were passed on to the wearer.

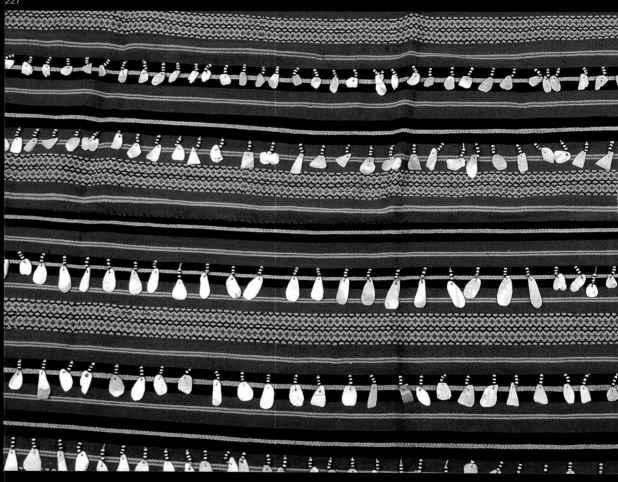

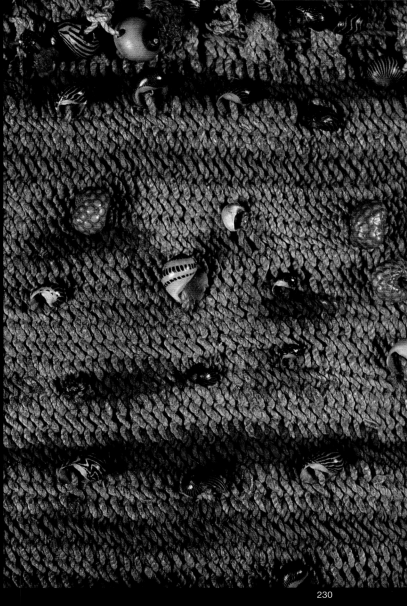

228
229

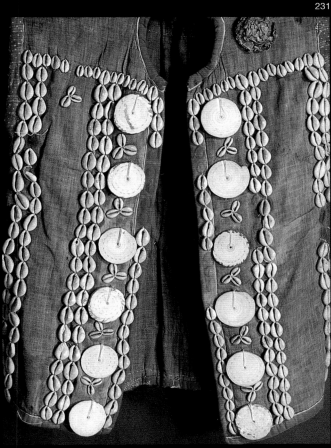

230
231

227 *Saya*, Southern Kalinga people, Luzon, Philippine Islands. Southern Kalinga women wore backstrap-loomed, striped lower-body garments, *saya*, that reached to the knees. Women with surplus rice crops could afford to embellish festive *saya* with mother-of-pearl pieces tied to short, beaded strings.

228 Man's status dress, Zaparo people, Ecuador. Dress with rare and valuable elements from vast trade networks proclaimed high status. Luminous hard-shelled clam disks of the *Anadonta* sp. or Lucinidae families, bird bones, feathers, seeds, beetle wings, monkey teeth, and human hair completed the ensemble.

229 *Umpak*, woman's garment with *kalati*, Bilaan or Bagobo people, Mindanao, Philippine Islands. *Kalati* (closed circles of mother-of-pearl), named after KiLat, the god of lightning, gave magical protection.

230 *Kon kamban*, detail, Kirau, Papua New Guinea. *Kon kamban* (small, netted bags made from shredded vegetable fiber) were frequently decorated with playful seeds and shells. Worn by men over the shoulder or chest, they were used for carrying personal possessions such as tobacco.

231 *Sapé buri*, Murot people, Sarawak/Borneo. The *sapé buri* (vest) was embellished with sliced cowries and conus cross-sections, called *ba'oulam*. *Conus leopardus* was considered dangerous for its potentially fatal sting, so wearing the shell may have signified bravery or transformation.

232
233

Job's tears

Hard, durable, and free, Job's tears seeds (*Coix lacryma-jobi*) come from plants in the grass family. When mature, Job's tears seeds are round, but when young and edible, the seeds are soft and elongated. Colors range from light-blue gray to brown, but the Akha of northern Thailand and Myanmar place Job's tears seeds in embers to turn them white.

232, 234, 235, 236 Details of women's dress, Sgaw Karen, northern Thailand/Myanmar. The short upper-body garments of married Sgaw Karen women are distinguished by Job's tears seed-work on black-colored cloth. Elongated, immature seeds are favored, and the insides are pulled out to create the hollow beads. Seeds are combined with embroidery and stitched into geometric patterns. The pattern names describe the geometric shapes created with the seeds, but there is perhaps a connection between the use of young seeds and women's fertility, as seed-work blouses are only worn by married women.

233 Woman's headdress, Akha people, Myang Payap area, northern Thailand and northeastern Myanmar. Once married, Akha women wear elaborate headdresses, whose distinctive shapes and combination of materials indicate the wearer's community. Some are armor-like, with massive amounts of metal ornaments, while others amass strings of Job's tears seeds and dyed chicken-feather tassels.

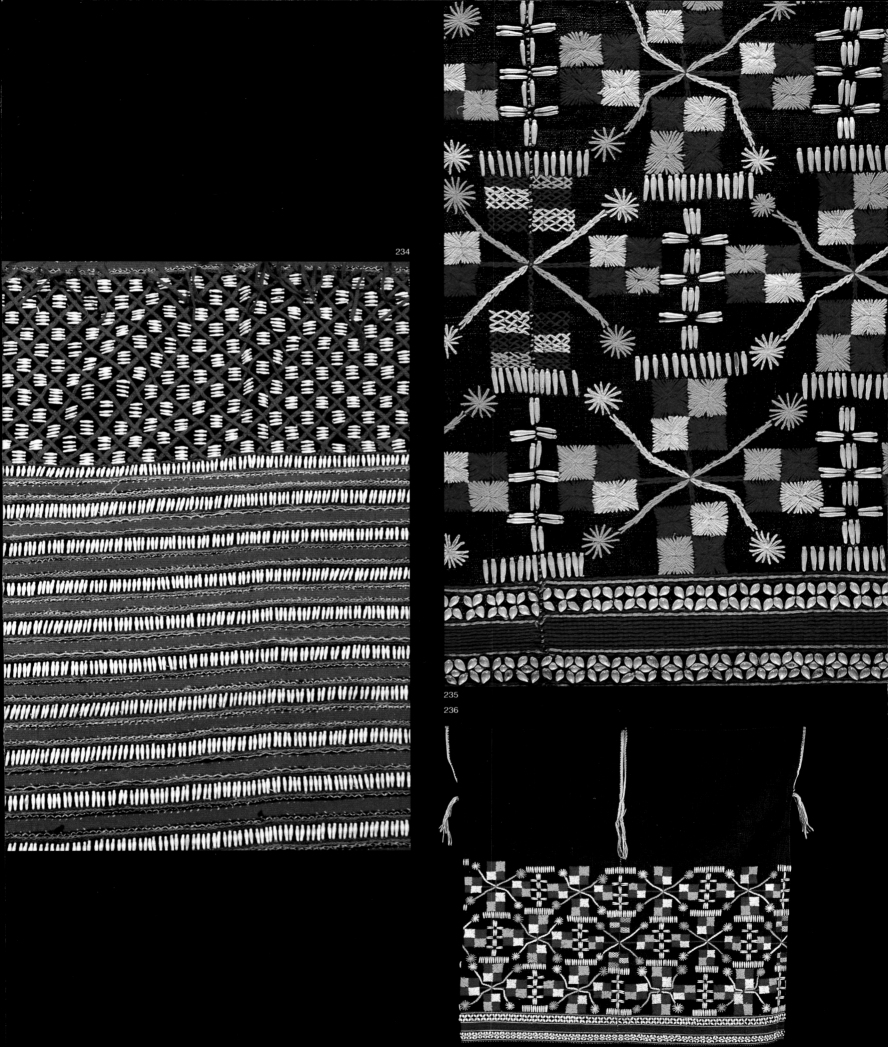

234

235

236

237

238

239

Vibrant and shiny plant products

People have used many light-reflecting plants and seeds for personal adornment. Some vegetable fibers are naturally sleek and shiny, or turn brilliant yellow when dried. Glossy seeds, when pressed into resins or pierced and strung, create natural beads. Sometimes the permanent shine and brightness of these materials is connected to harnessing life essence.

237, 238 *Aba obi* (unmarried women's belts), and *gwaro'a adiadi* (armbands), Admiralty or Solomon Islands. People wore varieties of belts and armbands punctuated with *adi* (bright orchid vines) and cane fibers dyed red with *Morinda citrifolia*. M-shaped designs represented frigate birds, while other patterns related to tattoo designs which boys and girls received prior to marriage. Similar designs and bands were found throughout Melanesia, showing lively trade and exchange.

240

242

241

243

239 Mandarin undergarment, China. Short, hollow bamboo beads were netted into underwear to keep silk garments from clinging to the skin in hot weather. Officials were required to wear silk-lined dress in July, and the underwear made the robes cooler.

240 *Ukunch*, Shuar, Ecuador. An *ukunch* (bandolier) made from either tiny strung *nupish* seeds or small insect larvae was the privilege of shaman healers or chiefs, worn to impress and reinforce status and soul-force at big festivals.

241 *Luhupa*, Tangkhul Naga people, northeast India. *Luhupa* headdresses, worn on important tribal occasions, use shiny, non-fading *Abrus precatorius* seeds, hornbill feathers, and human hair to communicate warriors' social status and accomplishments.

242 *Tagauza*, Aguaruna/Shuar people, Ecuador. Shiny seeds, *nupi* or *ahoaj*, were employed by many Amazon Basin Indian groups. Being very hard, the seeds were excellent noise-makers and as such were frequently suspended from men's *tagauza* (diadems).

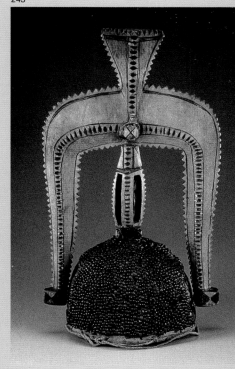

243 Headdress, Koro people, Nigeria. The ruby-like seeds of *Abrus precatorius* were commonly pressed into resin or other sticky natural substances. The seeds, like other products of nature, brought elements of the untamed wild into the headdress's meaning.

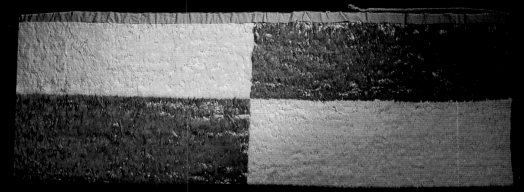

244

245

Feather wealth

Some objects of wealth are durable, like gold, but feathers' fragility, rarity, brightness, and iridescence make them especially valuable. Humans have invented countless ways of expressing complex social, spiritual, and economic concepts with beautiful plumage, from whole bird skins to fluffy down, sturdy plumes, or tiny feathers.

246

247

244 Hanging, Chuquibamba, south coast, Peru. As early as 2000 BC, élite people wore feather tunics and headdresses, while color-blocked hangings ornamented buildings. Feathers were first tied to long strings, called *hilaras*, then stitched onto cloth in overlapping rows.

245 Huli man in everyday wig, highland Papua New Guinea. The dark wig contrasts with shocking blue *yagama* (bird of paradise) feathers to convey contrasting pairs of opposites that transform the wearer into an idealized state of being.

246 Reproduction of Moctezuma's *quatzalapanecayotl*, Mexico. Only the highest-ranking Aztecs wore male quetzal tail feathers, associated with the creation and culture-bringing god, Quetzalcóatl. The *penoche* or *quatzalapanecayotl* headdress contains over five hundred shimmering plumes.

247 *Tavau*, Santa Cruz Island, Admiralty Islands. Lustrous, bright red feathers from the honeybird, *Myzomela*, were glued to hibiscus fiber to make *tavau*, coils of currency up to thirty feet long used for funerary displays and in formalized systems of negotiation for bride price.

248, 249 *Kahu* kiwi, details, Maori, New Zealand. Maori women twined individual kiwi and iridescent blue bush pigeon feathers under the weft of flax fiber capes, *kahu*. Feather cloaks were a sign of high social status in Maori society; rain cloaks, flax tag cloaks, and plain twined cloaks were worn by most.

250

251

252

The colors of the rainbow: Amazonian feather arts

Feather ornaments are often specific to an Amazon Basin group and identify the wearer's clan. Ornaments are used to mark transitions to adulthood, to indicate accomplishments and status, and to make people attractive. Feathers carry spiritual associations, and are often made into highly esteemed gifts.

250, 252 Birdskin armband, Haumbiza people, and *muha patai* (headband), Shuar people, Ecuador. Toucans are believed to possess magical power, and their bodies and those of other birds, such as the brilliant blue cotinga, are suspended from headbands, waist ornaments, and armbands worn at feasts by powerful men. Perhaps the wearing of toucans reflected sufficient power and soul-force to harness the birds' supernatural powers.

251 Hair tubes, Wai Wai people, northern Brazil. Feathers were assembled in symbolic order of the birds' habitats in the forest. Dark plumes of birds living on the forest floor were tied at the bottom, with colorful bird feathers from the forest canopy tied higher.

253 *Etsemat*, Shuar, Ecuador. When Shuar men entered adulthood, they earned the right to wear *etsemat* (feathered headbands). Red and yellow toucan feathers and electric-blue cotinga feathers, called *secha*, protected the wearer from malevolent spirits in dangerous circumstances.

254 *Rembe-pipo*, Urubu-Kapoor people, Amazon Basin. The *rembe-pipo* (labret) is part of a requisite set worn only by men. The lower lip ornament is a mosaic of cotinga and iridescent violet hummingbird feathers attached with beeswax to a scarlet macaw tail feather.

255 Chief's festive feather dress, Guarani people, Paraguay. The Guarani chief's special-occasion feather dress, with diadem, apron, and two armlets, contrasts with his minimal everyday dress.

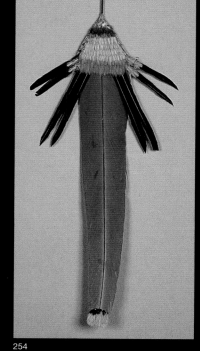

253

254

255

256 Wristlet, Guaicurú people, Paraguay. Wristlets, made from feathers tethered to handmade string, are worn in pairs as part of a festive dress set. Because so many feathers were needed to make it, this type of dress clearly proclaimed the wearer's wealth and stature.

257 Headdress, Shuar, Ecuador. Iridescent beetle elytra and hard, shiny *tucum* seeds made delightful sounds as the wearer walked. Each element with its accompanying soul-force enhanced the wearer's sense of well-being, pride, and identity.

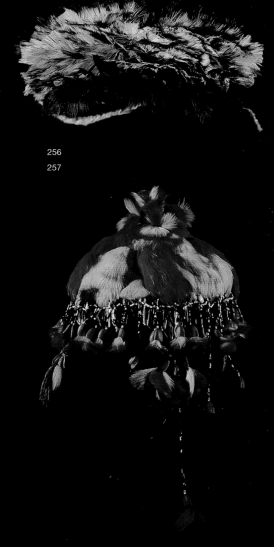

256

257

151

feather arts

Bright and iridescent feathers were used for many aspects of Native Americans' lives. Some feathers were prized as wealth, while others were believed to carry special powers associated with aspects of birds' behavior. To some, lustrous bird skins were sources of soft, delightful warmth.

258, 259 Child's pelagic cormorant parka, and pelagic cormorant neck patch parka, detail, Koniag, Alaska. Parkas made from the neck patches of the iridescent pelagic cormorant, *Phalacrocorax pelagicus*, require up to one hundred and forty birds. In warm weather, or on special occasions, the radiant feathers were worn facing out, while in cold weather the feather side was worn on the inside. Skins were sewn with whale or caribou sinew and ornamented with bits of trade cloth, white ermine fur, caribou hair, and even puffin beaks.

260 Headband of an *eem* with hummingbird pelts, Karok people, northern California. Female shaman-healers, *eem*, cured their patients through sucking, blowing tobacco smoke, and spitting out the disease. Hummingbirds are associated with healing because of their ability to hover and suck nectar.

261, 262 Treasure baskets, Pomo people, central and northern California. Feathered baskets were a form of wealth that transcended currency. Such lavish vessels marked important alliances, friendships, and prestige. Skilled women used *shi bu* (the three-stick coiled method), and inserted feather clusters as they stitched one coil layer to another.

Inuit, Alaska. The woman's *ak-fju-dat* (work-bag) was made from seal intestine and trimmed with iridescent cormorant neck feathers, unraveled worsted-wool trade cloth, and bits of down.

258

259

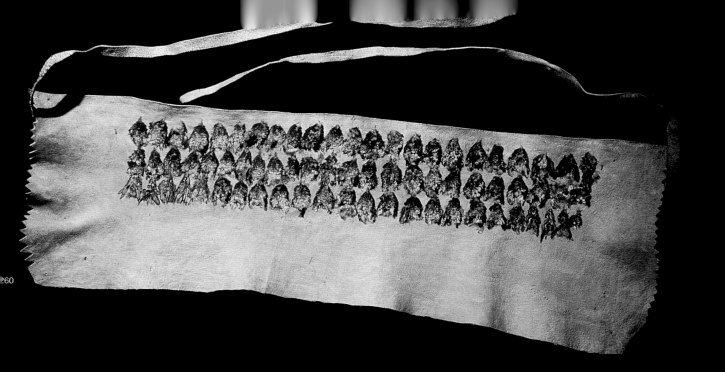

260

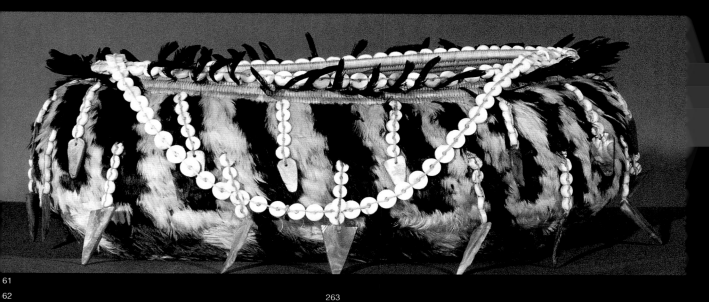

261

262

263

264

265

266

"Spreading the blue": peacock and kingfisher feathers

Some of the most widely utilized brilliant-colored and iridescent feathers came from peacocks and kingfishers. Feathers were stitched, appliquéd, woven, and glued to make objects for kings and queens, or for a couple dressed like royalty for their wedding day.

264 Dragon robe panel, China. This Ming Dynasty panel uses peacock feather barbules twisted onto thread and woven in interlocking tapestry technique, *kesi*. Since at least the fifth century, peacock-feather embroidery was called "spreading the blue."

265 *Fei-ts'ui* bridal ornament, China. Electric-blue feathers, called *fei-ts'ui*, of various Asian kingfishers were glued to cardboard, to imitate enamel *cloisonné*. Brides wore kingfisher headdresses, which became synonymous with happiness and prosperity.

267

266 *Fei-ts'ui* court headdress, detail, China. Magnificent headdresses with wicker, metal or papier-mâché frames covered with kingfisher feathers, pearl, and coral beads were worn by eighteenth- and nineteenth-century court ladies.

267 Fan, India. Created for Victorian tastes, this dazzling fan uses exotic peacock feathers from India and emerald-like beetle elytra from northern Thailand or Myanmar, which were distributed through Calcutta.

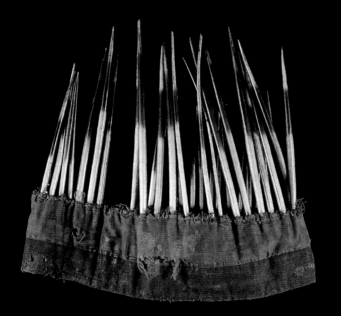

268

270
271

269

Feather shafts and quills

Many peoples explored the decorative potential of feather shafts and animal quills.

268 Porcupine quill hat of a Jhankri shaman, Tamang people, central Nepal. Quills and peacock feathers were part of the ritual equipment of *bompo* (healers), practicing Jhankrism, or shamanism, who frequently wore upward-pointing quill hats.

269 War shirt belonging to Kicking Bear, Band Chief of the Minneconjou of the Lakota Nation, North America. War shirts—earned and worn by the most distinguished Plains Indian leaders—told of warriors' accomplishments; porcupine quillwork at the shoulders may have been inspired by epaulets on military dress.

270 Porcupine hat, Myanmar. Quills are associated with magic and healing; porcupines and hedgehogs are believed to possess special powers.

271 Quillwork cuffs on gloves, Tanaina people, southern Alaska. The Tanaina and neighboring Athapaskan groups were known for their quill-embellished skin clothing, until glass trade beads replaced the women's elaborate work.

Beetles in court and courtyard

Shiny beetle bodies and hard outer wing-covers have been employed for decorative and symbolic purposes by numerous cultures. Some of the most colorful and widely used beetles come from the Buprestidae, or jewel beetle, group.

272
273

274

272 *Indhoni*, Rajasthan, India. Beetle thoraxes form a vibrant network suspended from an *indhoni* (a padded head ring) worn on top of the head to make carrying heavy water jars more comfortable.

273 Man's ceremonial wedding belt, detail, Banjara, southern India. The woman embroiderer included two pieces of beetle thorax like *shi-sha* (mirror rounds) into a ceremonial belt to be worn by her husband at their wedding.

274 *Rumal*, Soda Rajput people, India/Pakistan border. Beetle elytra cut into rounds are incorporated with a geometric peacock sitting in a tree. Triangular-shaped imagery and *soof* satin stitches are characteristic of the Soda Rajput people.

275 *Jama* bodice, detail, Jaipur, Rajasthan, India. This man's *jama* (dress-like garment with tight bodice and multi-paneled skirt) was encrusted with *gota* (flat silver-woven ribbon forms) and beetle elytra sequins, and worn by Maharaja Pratap Singh on his wedding day in 1790. Jaipur festive dress often combined large amounts of silverwork with beetle pieces.

276 *Butti* from *jama*, Mughal India. *Butti* (tiny floral bouquets) were created from emerald-like beetle elytra pieces, silk threads, and silver *badla* (flattened strips of metal). Some beetle pieces were punctured like sequins, while others were over-stitched in place.

277 Turban with beetle elytra and *zardozi* (gilded dimensional work on cloth), detail, Mughal India. Exquisite, costly Mughal-style *patkas* (sashes) and fish-scale motif turban cloths were often royal gifts, which projected the recipient's favor and position.

278 Shawl with beetle sequins and metallic thread work, detail, India. Woolen export shawls, popular in the late nineteenth century, were loomed in northern India and embellished in centers of beetle elytra embroidery such as Calcutta, Madras, and Delhi.

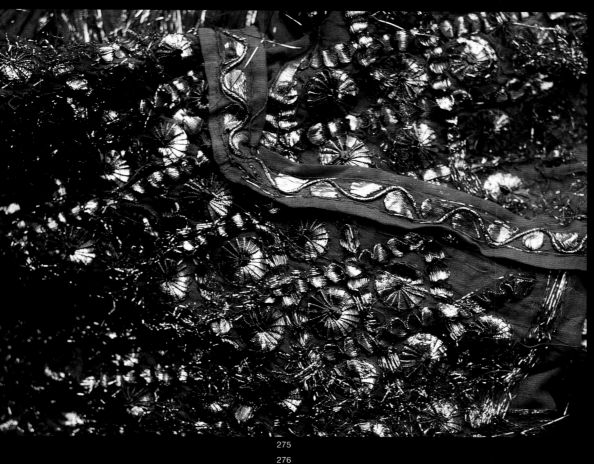

275
276

277
278

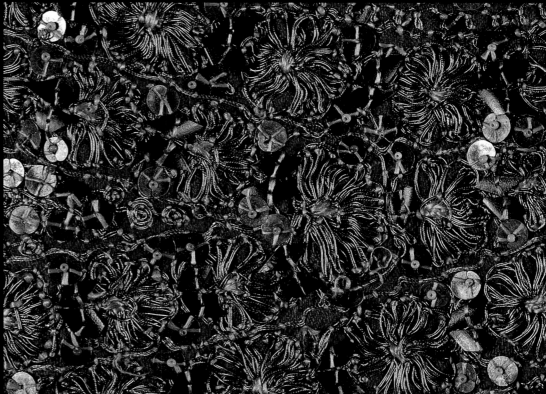

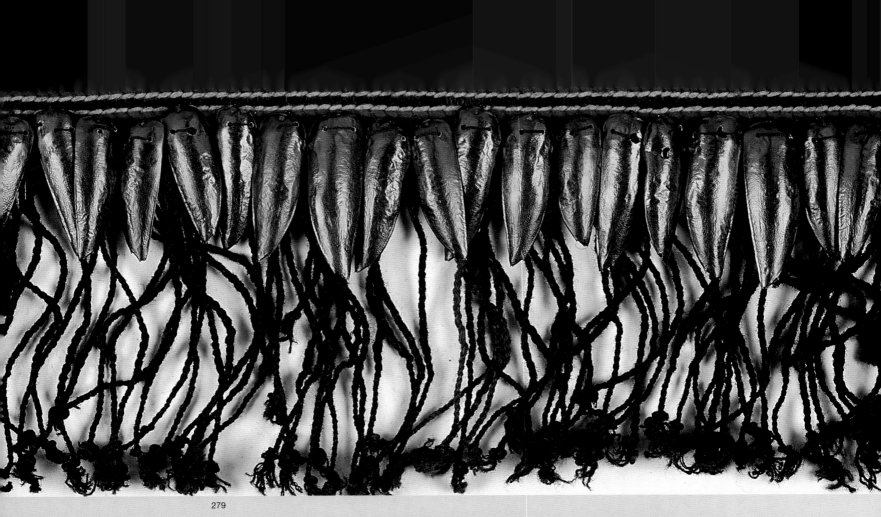

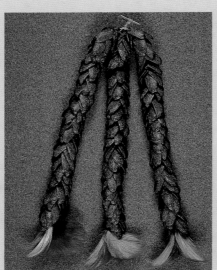

281
282

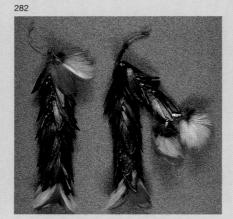

Headhunting and beetle adornment

Non-fading materials like brilliant orchid straw, shiny shells, animal teeth, and beetle elytra were favored ornaments of traditional headhunting communities because of the encapsulated life-force and vitality their non-fading colors conveyed.

279 Unmarried girl's wrapper, detail, Sema Naga people, Tsivikapotomi village, northeast India. Beetle-wing fringes from *Sternocera aquisignata* were symbolic and often indicative of the social rank and achievements of a girl's warrior father.

280 Ear ornament with beetle elytra and orchid straw, Naga, northeast India. This rare Naga ear ornament utilizes ever-brilliant beetle elytra, shiny yellow orchid straw, and bright red yarn to achieve its dazzling effect.

281, 282 *Akajik*, sideburn and ear ornaments, Aguaruna/Shuar people, Ecuador. Worn by both sexes, ear ornaments are made from *tuik*, densely punctured, curling wings from the scarab (*Chrysophora chrysoclora*), or huge *wauwau* (beetle wings) from *Euchroma gigantea* of the Buprestidae family. Toucan feathers are stuck on with wax. Amazon people consider adornments essential, since they contain beauty, power, and the energy of once-living things.

283 Beetle necklace, Papua New Guinea. Sago palms and sago palm beetles are an important food source for people living at lower altitudes, and the shells are highly valued for their shine. Beetles are enticed inside felled palms so that their larvae can be harvested and eaten.

284 Woman's upper-arm ornament, Shuar/Huambiza, Ecuador. The most valued ornaments were made from femurs of the oil bird (*Steatornis* sp.), called *tayu*, to express soul-force. *Tayu* birds roost in caves inhabited by dangerous jaguar spirits; only the powerful would dare to gather their bones.

285 A woman in Papua New Guinea wears a cane headband, decorated with green *Cetonniinae* sp. or *mormi* beetles, tied to her forehead; a towering headdress is attached to the headband.

286 Unmarried girl's breastcloth, detail, Zemi Naga people, Benroumi village, northeast India. Beetle wings and cowrie shells announce a girl's prestige within her community.

283
284

285
286

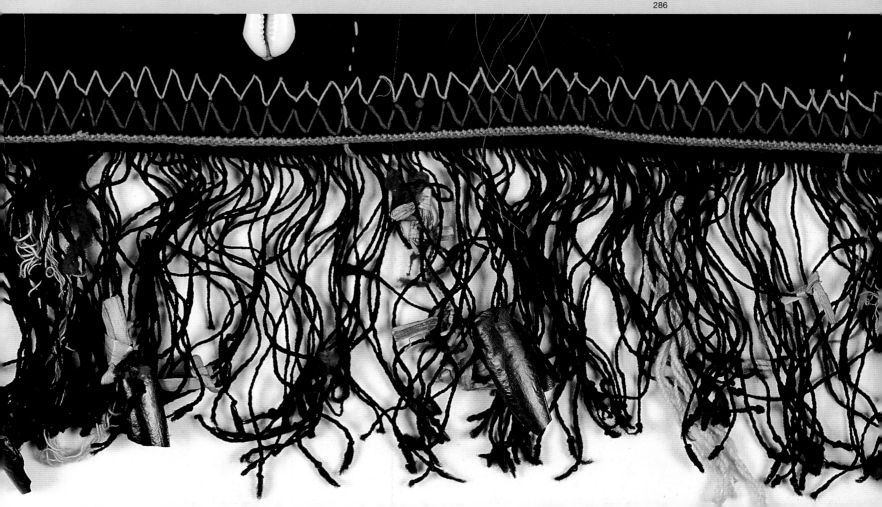

Change and the Making of the New

What has happened to the radiant textiles and ethnographic traditions illustrated and described in this book? Have they been elevated to art, or relegated to the past? Some have gone and others have changed and adapted over time. What is lost or gained when we leave the old and embrace the new? Among many peoples, the lives of the makers are so intertwined with their ceremonial hangings, personal adornment, and dress that they continue to make them in the same ways as before; many of the photographs in this book of people wearing shining cloth were taken within the last ten to fifteen years.

The word tradition is troublesome, for it implies that there is some ideal of how things should be, and evokes a sense of the loss of something that has been replaced by something less authentic, inferior, and modern.[1] But dress has never been fixed in time; it is a dynamic force driven by the way people redefine themselves in response to the social, economic, and political influences and upheavals around them.[2] Factors promoting change are numerous and complex and include influences from outsiders through trade, religious conversions, and imposed forms of government. Colonial governments flooded territories with cheaper mass-produced goods; the prohibition of headhunting forced many societies to seek new ways to achieve renewal, fertility, and social hierarchy; and India's independence in 1948, when princely states signed over their lands and rule to the new government, impacted on hundreds of years of artistic patronage for courtly textile products. Wars disrupt homes and lifestyles, and in refugee camps, missionaries and charitable and government programs encourage the production of needlework.[3] Shopkeepers and boutique owners often dictate design preferences based upon their ideas of what will sell, rather than allowing craftspeople to develop designs and images themselves.

Many hybrid styles have evolved, too, employing altered and re-created elements of "traditional" dress for foreign tastes, the result of tourism and the rise of manufactured souvenirs.[4] The concept of the textile souvenir might seem a modern phenomenon, as tourism currently leads the global economy, but it dates back to at least the eighteenth century, if not before: in the Americas, Alaskan peoples made clothing, amulets, and bags for sale to outsiders shortly after European contact;[5] several native North American groups crafted beaded goods to sell to strangers; and in the Amazon basin,

287 Contemporary sari, detail, woven by Pravin Parghi of Surendranagar, Gujarat, India. The well-known design of Gujarat's famous, high-status *patola* (a double silk ikat wedding sari) was given a new twist with traditional *patola*-patterned silk ikat weft threads combined with gilded *kalabatun* thread warps.

the Shuar and others created objects strictly for sale to foreigners. In Africa, beadwork objects were sold to Europeans in the early nineteenth century, as beading was an important economic skill taught by missionaries.[6]

Changing life-styles, too, have had an impact upon the production of textiles: many craftspeople have relocated to urban environments to seek employment or are attending school rather than continuing handicraft production. The escalating costs of luxurious materials like silk and gold thread have led to the introduction of new materials and processes for embellishing textiles, or to more limited production. In Morocco, for example, Fez's weaving industry has almost died out, as few can afford elaborate bridal dress; rather than purchasing many layers of garments, people today hire the required sets.[7]

Transitory and ever-changing fashions mirror peoples' self-identities.[8] Old forms of dress and textiles are rejected in favor of those that are more efficient, pleasing, and modern, those which incorporate new fibers, design solutions, dress styles, and forms of surface embellishment. Whether to escape negative associations and judgments others "read" from their dress, or to appear different from their elders, or simply to utilize the latest materials and motifs, the wearers of "traditional" dress help it to reinvent itself constantly. This energetic reflection of new ideas, materials, and motifs is clearly seen in present-day Guatemala, where three generations of Mayan women weavers create hand-loomed fabric and invent traditional dress or *traje*.[9]

Mid-twentieth-century artificial materials made a dramatic impact, much as synthetic dyes did in the nineteenth century. Through the perfection of Lurex in the 1950s, and the rise of imitation gold leaf and bronze pigments, cheaper materials became widespread.[10] In Africa, for example, Lurex has been embraced to satisfy "a deeply embedded aesthetic of shininess."[11]

As much as we love glittering cloth embellished with natural or man-made materials, it is important to remember that there has been, and continues to be, a dark side to the shine—the human cost of its production. Throughout the world, European quests for gold brought greed, exploitation, colonialism, and the collapse of local economies. Even today, many *zardozi* artisans in India and Pakistan work long hours under miserable conditions for poor pay and are often cheated by middlemen. As the world races rapidly towards universal clothing styles, it is important to cherish and support textile artisans and to remember that handmade items are produced not by a machine, but by somebody.

Since the dawn of humanity, tremendous energy and imagination, coupled with every conceivable light-reflecting material, have been harnessed to capture the gleam of the sun, the moon, and the stars. Gold or Lurex, silk or polyester, the shine is what delights us, and because it never dims, it gives us hope. Glittering things are not essential to the body's survival, but they are perhaps the key to the nourishment of the soul.

Endnotes

Introduction: Glittering Journeys through Time
(pp. 6–16)

1 Singh, 1993, p. 126.
2 *Ibid.*, pp. 10–11. Singh addresses gender associations with the sun and moon. The male sun and female moon/water idea is sometimes reversed so that fire is seen to come from within the earth and rainwater is associated with semen.
3 Erikson, 1993, p. 27.
4 Dubin, 1987, p. 141.
5 Gittinger, 1979, and Maxwell, 1990, discuss gendered pairs of opposites.
6 Till and Swart, 1997, p. 54.
7 Rossi, 1986, and Rossi, 1992. Hers are the seminal writings on the subject.

Part One: Silks and Surfaces
SILK
(pp. 26–29)

1 The history of silk in the world is a huge topic; many books are dedicated exclusively to the subject. Recommended reading includes: Burnham, 1959; Marinis, 1994; and Scott, 1993.
2 Gilroy, 1868. See pp. 159–161 for a detailed account of attempts to raise spiders commercially for silk.
3 Baker, 1995, p. 41.
4 Wilson, 1979, p. 186.
5 Stone, 1987, pp. 33–34.
6 Much has been written about the Silk Road. For some varying perspectives, the following books may be of interest. For information on the early twentieth-century archaeological raids in Central Asia, try Hopkirk, 1980. From the perspective of the raiders, look at Stein, 1971: Stein conducted three expeditions in Central Asia. Albert von Le Coq also explored there: see Le Coq, 1928. Other references include: de Khanikoff, 1965, which contains interesting mentions of silk chapans and silk cultivation, caravans, and imports; and Furber, 1976, for the expansion of Europe into Asia, colonialism, and economic impact.
7 See Guy, 1998, pp. 14–15.
8 Burnham, 1959, p. 2.
9 Hanyu, 1992, pp. 11–12.
10 Kalter, Pavaloi, and Zerrnickel, 1993, pp. 211, 214–216.
11 See Reynolds in Pal, 1991, p. 106.
12 Baker, 1995, p. 25.
13 Kalter, Pavaloi, and Zerrnickel, 1993, p. 214.
14 *Ibid.*, p. 211.
15 Oz, 1950, p. 25.
16 Baker, 1995, p. 86.
17 *Ibid.*, p. 113.
18 Scott, 1993. See pp. 134–148, 202, 211 for Safavid silks.
19 Like the histories of the Silk Road and of silk weaving, many books explore the subject of textiles from these regions thoroughly. The reader is referred to: Fischer, 1979; Gittinger, 1979; Gittinger, 1982; Guy, 1998; Kahlenberg, 1977; and Maxwell, 1990.
20 Kartiwa, 1986, p. 2.
21 *Ibid.*, p. 4.

DYES AND TREATMENTS
(pp. 29–32)

1 Harvey, 1996, p. 92.
2 Krishna, 1966, p. 15.
3 Irwin and Brett, 1970, p. 11.
4 Harvey, 1996, p. 92.
5 Fitz-Gibbon and Hale, 1997. All these processes are described on p. 169.
6 Gittinger, 1979, p. 153 and Maxwell, 1990, p. 320. Maxwell describes the process and depicts a woman using a shell to calender cloth.
7 Conway, 1992, p. 79.
8 Cole, 1913, plate xxiv. Cloth is shown being polished with a large cowrie shell.
9 Benedict, 1916, p. 70.
10 Buck, 1957, pp. 183–186.
11 Minnich, 1963, p. 202.

12 Baker, 1995, p. 117, and Wills, 1883, p. 333.
13 Balfour-Paul, 1977, p. 43.
14 Rossi, 1992, p. 64.
15 Rossi, 1990, pp. 22–23. Rossi lived in China and has written and published extensively about the various dyeing techniques of some of China's ethnic minorities.
16 Eicher, 1976, p. 77.
17 Balfour-Paul, 1977, pp. 4–7.
18 Ibid., pp. 94–95.
19 Ibid., p. 91. Balfour-Paul cites a report, "Foreign Office Annual Series," #2203, January 1899, J.S.D.C., vols. xiv and xv, Bradford, 1899, which states that gum arabic had been used in Yemeni and Saudi Arabian indigo processes at least one hundred years before.
20 Kaudern, 1944, pp. 167, 439.
21 Garner, 1979, p. 15.
22 Biebuyck and Van Den Abbeele, 1984, p. 176.
23 Hepner, 1935, p. 216.
24 Conway, 1992, pp. 145–146. A lacquered pha chet noi cloth from the Chiang Mai court is depicted on p. 145.
25 Mato, 1987, p. 37.
26 Ibid., pp. 162–169, describes the entire process, but doesn't explore the meanings of the shiny sap.

Part Two: Materials from the Earth
GOLD
(pp. 50–55)

1 Marx, 1978, pp. 11–22.
2 Garrard, 1989, p. 110.
3 Lechtman, 1984, pp. 56–63, explains the metallurgical processes.
4 Ibid., p. 63.
5 Oppenheim, 1949, pp. 172–193. See pp. 182–185 for line drawings of historic carvings with representations of platelets on garments.
6 Ibid., p. 181.
7 Marx, 1978, pp. 68, 74.
8 Rolle, 1980, pp. 47–51.
9 Anikia, 1983, p. 89.
10 Rolle, 1980, p. 53.
11 See Marazov, 1998, for new information.
12 Baker, 1995, pp. 13, 53.
13 Clark, 1986, pp. 54–56.
14 Hsi, 1991, p. 78.
15 Xun and Chunming, 1987, p. 76. In the reign of Empress Wu Zetian, embroidered robes appeared with different designs to distinguish civil officials from military ones, thereby establishing Ming and Qing Dynasty rank badges.
16 Kennedy, 1990, and Minnich, 1963, are full of interesting stories about competitive dress.
17 Krishna, 1966, p. 11. Numerous ancient references to the use of gold in ancient Indian mythic and historical times are cited.
18 Kartiwa, 1986, pp. 4–6.
19 Kahlenberg, 1977, p. 8.
20 Ibid., p. 25.
21 Guy, 1998, p. 55.
22 Leigh, 1993, p. 178.
23 Ibid., pp. 179–181.
24 Guy, 1989, p. 49.
25 Guy, 1998, p. 11.
26 Gittinger, 1982, p. 31.
27 Richards, 1983, pp. 231–238.
28 Garrard, 1989, p. 40.
29 Ibid., pp. 46–54, for Bowdich's descriptions of gold objects on display.
30 Lechtman, 1984, p. 63.
31 Moseley and Feldman, 1978, pp. 15, 18.

SILVER, OTHER METALS, AND SEQUINS
(pp. 56–60)

1 Mack, 1988, p. 14.
2 Untracht, 1997, p. 278.
3 Schletzer, 1984, p. 65.
4 Chaussonnet, 1988, p. 213. Chaussonnet talks about women "reinforcing the transformational relationship between" humans and animals.
5 Forbes, 1950, p. 201.
6 Ogden, 1982, p. 23.
7 Forbes, 1950, pp. 582–582.
8 Clark, 1986, pp. 62.
9 Ogden, 1982, p. 28.
10 Herbert, 1984, pp. xxii, 3.
11 Fisher, 1993, p. 152.
12 Randhawa, 1996, pp. 77–78.
13 Maddin, Wheeler, and Muhly, 1977, p. 35, 38.
14 Ogden, 1982, pp. 28–30.
15 Maddin, Wheeler, and Muhly, 1977, p. 46. Old tin ingots were analyzed.
16 See Schienerl, 1982, p. 16 for magical properties of adornment.
17 Tucci, 1974, p. 34, and Liu, 1983, p. 59.
18 Holmberg, 1922, pp. 18–19.
19 Ibid., pp. 7–8. Holmberg discusses the purposes of Shaman's dress: to camouflage and distract spirits, as well as to offer armor-like protection.
20 Bliss, 1982, p. 12.
21 Gifford, 1958, p. 5.
22 Ibid., pp. 76–77. Gifford also describes Italian amulets made of silver, which were powerful because of the metal's association with Diana, goddess of the moon.
23 Schletzer, 1984, p. 20. See this book for an incisive description of the Turkmen world view seen through their metalwork and embroidery.
24 Jewellery, 1988, p. 13. Interestingly, in Anakhita's early origins, she was a solar goddess, but over time many solar deities became male, and female deities became associated with water, the earth, and fertility.
25 Parker, 1984, pp. 169–170.
26 Ives, 1954, pp. 26, 29.

MINERALS
(pp. 60–63)

1 Hanyu, 1992, pp. 11, 23–24, 263.
2 Lucas, 1948, p. 297.
3 Ogden, 1982, p. 102.
4 Yoshioka, 1980, pp. 6, 81.
5 Watt, 1972, pp. 510–513.
6 See Rivers, 1996ii, for a complete description of the khadi print process.
7 Kooijman, 1963, pp. 18, 27. See also Kaudern, 1944.

8 Gilroy, 1868, p. 392.
9 Shams, 1987, p. 1.
10 Wilson, 1979, p. 30.
11 Anderson, 1981, p. 116–117.
12 Ogden, 1982, p. 104.
13 Rudenko, 1970, p. 207.
14 *Ibid.*, p. 95.
15 Lang, 1994i, p. 6.
16 *Ibid.*, p. 6.
17 Anderson, 1981, p. 126.
18 Ray, 1981, pp. 12, 19.
19 Black, 1982, p. 50.
20 Ray, 1981, p. 12.
21 *Ibid.*, p. 19.
22 *Ibid.*, p. 23.

MIRRORS
(pp. 63–67)

1 McAlister, 1995, p. 309.
2 Schmidt, 1971, p. 67.
3 Kaeppler, 1978, p. 100.
4 Singh, 1993, pp. 10–11.
5 Jacobson, 1995, p. 182.
6 Evans-Pritchard, 1972, p. 45.
7 Coss and Moore, 1990, pp. 367–380.
8 Roche, Courage, and Devinoy, 1985, p. 11.
9 Schifter, 1983, pp. 3–5.
10 V'avra, 1954, pp. 13–16.
11 Roche, Courage, and Devinoy, 1985, p. 41.
12 See Rivers, 1993ii, pp. 66–67, for images and description of the mirror-making process.
13 Elson, 1979. Elson conducted the pioneering study of this region.
14 Frater, 1989. See her article for images and meanings of embroidery by the Rabari, a group that continues needlework traditions.
15 Graham, 1992, p. 154.
16 Frater, 1995, pp. 77–109.
17 Maxwell, 1990, p. 413.
18 Gittinger, 1979, p. 79.
19 *Ibid.*, p. 84.
20 Maxwell, 1990, p. 257.

BEADS
(pp. 68–72)

1 Clark, 1986, p. 3.
2 Dubin, 1987, p. 19. Both Dubin,

1987, and Erikson, 1993, discuss the correlation of eyes and eyesight to eye beads and the resulting attraction to beads.
3 Erikson, 1993, pp. 134–139.
4 Dubin, 1987, p. 22–26.
5 *Ibid.*, p. 21.
6 Lucas, 1948, pp. 54–55.
7 Benedict, 1991, p. 37.
8 Ogden, 1982, p. 131.
9 Lucas, 1948, p. 53.
10 Dubin, 1987, pp. 33, 38.
11 Rolle, 1980, p. 60.
12 Nanavati, Vora, and Dhaky, 1966, p. 65.
13 Clark, 1986, p. 5.
14 Dubin, 1987, p. 42.
15 Dunsmore, 1978, p. 3.
16 Dubin, 1987, pp. 79–83.
17 Maxwell, 1990, p. 137.
18 Rodgers, 1985, pp. 117–119.
19 Clark, 1986, p. 84.
20 Kunz and Stevenson, 1908, p. 308.
21 Hose and McDougall, 1912, vol. 2, pp. 124–125.
22 Munan-Oettli, 1983, p. 95.
23 Dubin, 1987, pp. 307–308.
24 *Ibid.*, p. 312.
25 *Ibid.*, p. 30.
26 Francis, 1990, p. 104.
27 Untracht, 1997, p. 74.
28 Borel, 1994, p. 41.
29 Clark, 1986, p. 30.
30 Ryder, 1969, pp. 270–271.
31 Dubin, 1987, p. 45.
32 Clark, 1986, p. 69.
33 Baker, 1995, p. 17.
34 Kunz and Stevenson, 1908, pp. 319–320.
35 Untracht, 1997, p. 335.
36 Lucas, 1948, p. 56.
37 Dubin, 1987, p. 43.
38 Lucas, 1948, pp. 209, 214.
39 Dubin, 1987, p. 106.
40 *Ibid.*, p. 111.
41 Carey, 1991, p. 8.

Part Three: Gifts from Nature
SHELLS
(pp. 122–125)

1 Clark, 1986, p. 8. Burial jewelry was made from *Spondylus gaederopus* mussel shell.

2 Ogden, 1982, p. 121.
3 Schienerl, 1982, p. 20, and Safer and Gill, 1982, pp. 51, 140, 141.
4 Safer and Gill, 1982, p. 49.
5 Abbot and Dance, 1973, p. 97.
6 Ryder, 1969, p. 61.
7 Richards, 1983, p. 253. See this source for a historical account of African exchange systems.
8 Safer and Gill, 1982, pp. 71, 139.
9 This concept of contrasting or complementary opposites to express metaphors has been cited in other chapters. See also Gittinger, 1979; Maxwell, 1990; and Strathern, 1971.
10 Safer and Gill, 1982, p. 18.
11 Abbot and Dance, 1973, p. 12.
12 Simon, 1971, pp. 67–77, 105–109. See this source for diagrams and explanations of iridescence and the mechanics of light.
13 Garrard, 1989, p. 72.
14 Safer and Gill, 1982, pp. 97–98. The conus species used included *Conus leopardus*, *Conus betulinus*, and *Conus prometheum*.
15 Gordon and Kahan, 1976, p. 11.
16 Liu, 1995, p. 29.
17 Harvey, 1996, p. 44.
18 Schletzer, 1984, p. 50.
19 *Ibid.*, p. 50.
20 Ryotaku and Keiji, 1985, pp. 9–11.
21 Safer and Gill, 1982, p. 62.
22 Margolin, 1994, p. 9.
23 Safer and Gill, 1982, p. 71.
24 See Jensen and Sargent, 1993, for old and new robe designs and the history of shell buttons.
25 Orchard, 1975, p. 20. See pp. 71–87 for information on wampum.
26 Oro del Peru, 1978, p. 15.
27 Kunz and Stevenson, 1908, p. 271.

SEEDS AND FIBERS
(pp. 126–128)

1 Armstrong, 1991, p. 69.
2 Quinn, 1934, p. 65.
3 See Gunn and Dennis, 1976, for details of the history and folklore of floating seeds, and scientific

information on them. Many have been used in jewelry and adornment.

4 Quinn, 1934, p. 65.
5 See Needham, 1967, for the percussive use of natural materials.
6 Gordon and Kahan, 1976, p. 8.
7 Margolin, 1994, p. 11. Margolin interviewed Maria Tripp, a Californian regalia-maker.
8 Lucas, 1948, p. 357.
9 Armstrong, 1991, p. 69.
10 Ibid., p. 68.
11 Gordon and Kahan, 1976, p. 8.
12 Strathern, 1993, p. 18.
13 Kaudern, 1944, p. 253.
14 Schenck and Gifford, 1949–1952, pp. 378, 379.
15 Templeton, 1965, p. 13. If the seed has a black spot, it is called a rosary bead; if the stem is connected to the red part of the seed, it is known as a crab-eye seed.
16 Untracht, 1997, pp. 284–285. See chart on p. 285 for traditional Indian goldsmiths' weights.
17 Kunz and Stevenson, 1908, p. 322.
18 Paine, 1990, p. 244.
19 Strathern, 1993, p. 139. Pages 3, 98, and 99 depict women wearing Job's tears necklaces.
20 Untracht, 1997, p. 27.
21 Garrard, 1989, p. 26.
22 Borel, 1994, p. 211.
23 Ibid., p. 211.
24 Untracht, 1997, pp. 53–58.
25 Guppy, 1887. The dress of people from the Solomon and Admiralty Islands is described throughout the book. See especially p. 132.
26 Phelps, 1976, p. 224.
27 Ivens, 1927, pp. 382–383.

FEATHERS
(pp. 129–133)

1 Cavagnaro, 1982, p. 34.
2 Art de la plume, 1985, pp. 14–16, covers diverse feather-arts techniques.
3 Rabineau, 1979, explains the use of feathers to convey concepts around the world.

4 Koch, 1977, pp. 11–14.
5 See Mekler, 1992, for information, images, and maps of the Amazonian area.
6 Reid, 1986, p. 9.
7 Rabineau, 1979, p. 21.
8 Ibid., p. 27.
9 Phelps, 1976, p. 21.
10 Pendergrast, 1987, pp. 106–107.
11 Simon, 1969, pp. 35–41.
12 Ibid., p. 78.
13 Simon, 1969, and Simon, 1971.
14 Pressman, 1991, for legends and interpretations of bird colors.
15 Reina and Pressman, 1991, p. 114.
16 Simon, 1971, pp. 50–57.
17 Anders, 1970, p. 50.
18 Perrins and Middleton, 1985, p. 266: Alcedo atthis, Eurasian kingfisher. Hartman, 1980, states that Alcedo atthis is extinct in China, but not in northern and eastern Australia, Tanzania, England, and parts of the United States.
19 Boyer, 1995, p. 215, specifies the Chinese name.
20 Hartman, 1980, p. 75.
21 Ibid., p. 75.
22 Simon, 1971, p. 61.
23 Furst, 1991, p. 94.
24 Perrins and Middleton, 1985, p. 141.
25 Simon, 1971, pp. 116–125.
26 Newark, 1983, p. 74.
27 Cavagnaro, 1982, p. 49.
28 Estranda, 1991, p. 125.
29 Hail, 1980, p. 46.
30 Koch, 1977, p. 35.
31 Lekagul and McNeely, 1978, p. 488.
32 Koch, 1977, pp. 36–40.

BEETLE ELYTRA
(pp. 134–136)

1 Cowan, 1865, p. 30.
2 Curran, 1945, p. 187.
3 Simon, 1971, pp. 68–77, for explanations of interference and iridescence.
4 Asuka, 1974, pp. 40–48. The shrine is depicted on p. 47.
5 Kandalavala, 1982, pp. 14–16.

6 Jacobs, 1990, is an invaluable resource for the ethnographic background and images of diverse Naga material culture.
7 Hodson, 1921, p. 25.
8 Barbier, 1985, p. 19.
9 Strathern, 1971, pp. 170–172. See this work for the complex system of dark and bright contrasts.
10 Shuar ornaments are covered in Karsten, 1923; Karsten, 1935; and Stirling, 1938.
11 Karsten, 1923, p. 427.
12 Marshall, 1922, pp. 167, 193–209.
13 Saint-Aubin, 1983, p. 56.
14 Armstrong, 1976, p. 61.

Epilogue: Change and the Making of the New
(pp. 161–162)

1 See Clifford, 1987, for responses to early twentieth-century anthropologists' concerns about vanishing ethnographic traditions, the "salvage paradigm."
2 See Tarlo, 1996, for examples of changing dress responding to societal change in India.
3 Cohen, 1983, pp. 1–34.
4 See Graburn, 1976, introduction, for tourism and its impact on indigenous arts and crafts.
5 Ray, 1981, p. 71.
6 Carey, 1991, p. 33.
7 Mackie, 1992, pp. 88–93.
8 Rivers, 1998ii, pp. 74–75.
9 Schevill, 1997.
10 Higgins, 1993, pp. 81–83.
11 Picton and Mack, 1995, p. 12.

Notes to the Illustrations

1   Shaver, 1966, pp. 28, 222.
5   See Gittinger, 1982, p. 71.
6   See Garrard, 1989, pp. 88, 104.
7   See McNaughton, 1982, p. 55.
8   See Rossi, 1986, and Rossi, 1988i.
11 See Forelli and Harries, 1977, p. 56.
12 See Kroeber, 1953, p. 254, for ceremonial uses.
14 See Jackson, 1997.
15, 16, 17 See Garrett, 1990, p. 30.
18 Fitz-Gibbon and Hale, 1997, p. 169.
19, 20 Yuchi and Shizhao, 1985, pp. 55–56.
21 See Rossi, 1988ii, p. 33, for the complete process.
22 See Bokhara, 1967–1968, p. 68, for the origin of the term.
23 See Clothings, 1985, p. 53.
25 See Conway, 1992, p. 98, for trade and textiles in Siam and Khmer kingdoms.
26 Irwin and Hall, 1973, p. 73–74.
27 Lebeuf, 1970.
28 See Hitkari, 1980, for regional styles and types of phulkari.
29 See Dhamija, 1964, p. 48b. Dhamija spells the word heer.
30 Wilson, 1990, p. 44.
31 See Meng, 1987, p. 72, for types of bridal hangings.
32 See Dhamija, 1988, p. 37 for ari (tambour-needle) worker information.
Intro (p. 38) Harvey, 1996, p. 93.
35 Fitz-Gibbon and Hale, 1988, p. 14, and Fitz-Gibbon and Hale, 1997, p. 174, for baghmal processes.
37 See Fitz-Gibbon and Hale, 1988, p. 14, for qanawaz details.
38 See Weir, 1989, p. 38, for Syrian ikat details.
39 See Kalter, Pavaloi, and Zerrnickel, 1993, pp. 201, 216, 219.
40 See Naenna and Phanichphant, 1993, p. 43, and Naenna and Perangwatthanakun, 1990ii, for Tai subgroups, textiles and dress.
41 Myers, 1989, p. 131.
42 See Reynolds in Pal, 1991, p. 106, for Chinese tribute silks in Tibet.
43 Burnham, 1959, describes rong weaving processes.
44 See Nomura, 1914, p. 9, for the history of nishiki weaving.
45, 47 Scott, 1993, p. 184, states that bizarre silk designs were made from 1690–1730, while Arizzoli-Clementel, 1990, p. 76, dates them from 1695–1710.
Intro (p. 44) See Rossi, 1986, p. 42 and Rossi, 1988i.
48 Benedict, 1916, pp. 68, 69, 74.
49 Hitchcock, 1989, p. 19.
50 Baker, 1995, p. 135.
51 Fumin and Yaohua, 1988, p. 21.
52 Yuchi and Shizhao, 1985, pp. 80–81.
53 Rossi, 1990, pp. 22–23.
54 Thompson, 1971, p. 18/3.
55 Tuareg wedding, Agadar. See Rasmussen, 1991, pp. 105–114, for men's and women's headcoverings.
56 See Beckwith and Van Offelen, 1993, p. 119, for embroidery patterns; pp. 174–175 for dances when tunics are worn; and pp. 177–178 for images of tunics in yaake dances.
57 Ecke, 1977, p. 51. The earliest lacquered leather dates to the twelfth century BC.
58 Garner, 1979, p. 19.
59 Mato, 1987, pp. 40–41, 169, 188.
60 Pritchard, 1984, pp. 32–40.
61 Balfour-Paul, 1997, pp. 132, 136.
62 Kooijman, 1963, p. 103, and Kaudern, 1944, p. 236.
63, 64 Chee, 1989, p. 25.
66 See Maxwell, 1990, pp. 257–260.
Intro (p. 76) See Rivers, 1996ii, for gold print in Asia.
72 Zung, 1964, p. 72, depicts a military woman wearing an apron with pointed pendants in the play Yu-ching-tao-jen.
73 See Guy, 1989, p. 52; Gittinger, 1982, pp. 26–27, 114–133; and Hope, 1990, p. 51, for Indian trade cloths.

75　See Gittinger, 1982, p. 155, and Conway, 1992, p. 11, for sixteenth-century pillar with patterns similar to Indian-made textiles.

76　See Anon, 1888, p. 6.

Intro (p. 79)　Books like Rodgers, 1985, and Schneider and Weiner, 1989, provide excellent background in ways cloth and elements of dress reinforce realms of power and wealth.

78　Scarce, 1987, pp. 46, 52.

81　See Olson, 1960, p. 2, for uses and Newark, 1961, p. 44, for Chinese brocades in Tibet.

82　Gittinger and Lefferts, 1992, p. 350. The authors cite Constance Wilson, "State and Society in the Reign of Mongkut, 1851–1868: Thailand on the Eve of Modernization," PhD dissertation, Cornell University, 1970.

83　Lefferts, 1988, p. 81, examines Thai linguistics and concepts of divinity and leadership. See Gittinger and Lefferts, 1992, p. 164, for netted wire technique.

84　See Hanyu, 1992, p. 20, for records of ancient looped pile weaving.

85　Gion Matsuri, 1993, and Gonick, 1994. Guy, 1998, pp. 174–175, explains the history of Gion Matsuri cloths related to trade.

86　Takemura, 1991, p. 153. The couple's embroidered robes suggest the Noh play *Takasogu*, written by Zeami Motokiyo.

88　Minnich, 1963, pp. 282, 352.

89　Takemura, 1991, p. 172, and Hays, 1998. Passing the Dragon's Gate signified passing exams required for entrance into Chinese government positions. The figure riding the carp was probably Sugawara Michizare, an early Heian Dynasty Japanese court figure and poet writing in Chinese around 845–903. Michizare, holding a scroll, became the Shinto tutelary deity of learning and scholarship.

90　See Nomura, 1914, and Till and Swart, 1997, pp. 55–63, for a historical overview of *kesa*.

91　Dhamija, 1995, p. 6.

92　See Lynton, 1995, p. 178–179.

93　Marriage of Kartikeya Shodhan to Naina Shodhan in 1992, Ahmedabad, Gujarat, India.

94　Dhamija, 1995, p. 76.

95　See Kalter, Pavaloi, and Zerrnickel, 1993, pp. 152–153, 155, for similar garments.

96　Maxwell, 1992, pp. 68, 72, fig. 64. The wearing of headcloths arrived with Islam.

98　See Leigh, 1993, pp. 181–182, for the use of luxurious textiles to create idealized states of being and to express concepts of paradise among the Acehnese.

99　Dalrymple, 1984, p. 93. See Maxwell, 1992, p. 49, for the term.

100　Term from Dalrymple, 1984, p. 94. The origin of the gold thread term is my suggestion.

101　Summerfield, 1991, p. 7–9.

102　Garrard, 1989, p. 72.

103　See Micaud, 1970, p. 40. Stabb, 1998, says the *dohlja* synthesizes Andalusian gold work from Spanish Jews, Roman Byzantine tunics, orphrey bands from ecclesiastical garments, and metallic ribbons woven in Lyons, France.

105　Mackie, 1992, p. 92. Besancenot, 1990, p. 147, for *hizam* illustration.

106　Mackie, 1992, p. 89, for *menbar* and Besancenot, 1990, p. 206, for *qosba del rib* and other layers.

107　Stone, 1985, pp. 84, 105, 161; Celebration, 1982, p. 126.

109　Tucci, 1974, pp. 34–36. *Khyungs*, Garuda-like half-man, half-eagle figures, were sacred to pre-Buddhist Bonpo and Hindu worshippers.

110　Moseley and Feldman, 1978, p. 42. Depletion silvering processes were developed by the Moche people around 100 BC to AD 800. See Lechtman, 1984, pp. 59–60, for processes.

112　Spring and Hudson, 1995, pp. 92–93.

114　The Old Medina district of Marrakesh.

116　For Turkmen clothing details, see Lobacheva, 1989, p. 119, and for the nine required gifts see Schletzer, 1984, p. 52.

118　Turkmen Festival, Turkey, 1994. See Bacon, 1966, for historical overview prior to Soviet rule.

119　See Nolan-Muzzy, 1989, p. 66.

120　See Rivers, 1995iii, p. 14.

121　See Arnoldi and Kraemer, 1995, p. 30, and Griaule, 1951, pp. 159–160.

122　See Goswamy and Krishna, 1993, pp. 27–35.

123　Johnstone, 1985, p. 21, and *pestemal* term from Berry, 1932, p. 354.

124　Rivers, 1998i, p. 23. Women never wore black or navy except on Kali Chaudas, the day before Diwali, when the goddess Kali was worshipped.

125　See Ambalal, 1987, pp. 163–164, for months Kartika Shukla 9 and Shravana Krishna 10.

126　See Minnich, 1963, pp. 159, 349, for historical references to *hakama*, and Dalby, 1993, p. 232, for imagery and color meanings.

127　See Rivers, 1996ii, p. 4.

128　Clothings, 1985, pp. 38–41, depicts similar jackets.

129　Solyom, 1984, p. 29.

130　See Rock, 1992, p. 106, figure 6.27, and p. 119. See also Pal, 1992, p. 106.

131　Conway, 1992, pp. 100, 111. Colored backgrounds were selected for the day of the week; purple was associated with Saturday.

132　See Forelli and Harries, 1977, pp. 44–45. See also Picton and Mack, 1979, p. 67.

133　Yohe, 1981, p. 114.

141, 144, 145　See Gunay, 1986, p. 58, for complete dress depicted.

143　Marriage information in Gunay, 1986, pp. 10–11, 47, and bridegroom details in Tansug, 1985, p. 18.

146　Turkmen Festival, Turkey, 1994, in Gunay, 1986, p. 11.

147, 148　Garrett, 1990, p. 66. The *ma-wei* technique is described in Guochang and Rossi, 1985.

149 See Mozzi, 1987, p. 207, for numerous legends, and Dewar, 1963, p. 16, for Asian trade in sequins.

152 See Fraser-Lu, 1982; Lowry, 1974, p. 25; and Drower, 1995, p. 42.

Intro (p. 102) Thompson, 1995, p. 102, defines Vodou and, on p. 107, discusses ritual dotting. Blier, 1995, p. 83, outlines the history of Vodou from West Africa.

153 *Majò jonk*, Rara Société Mystic 777, Charpentier, Haiti. See Tselos, 1996, pp. 61–63, for origins of the dress.

154 Rara Etoile de Bethlehem, Cabaret, Haiti. See Tselos, 1996, p. 59.

155 See Girouard, 1994, pp. 22–23, for Vodou symbolism and interpretations.

156 Polk, 1995, p. 327.

157 See Juynboll, 1922, part II, p. 51, and plate 4.

158 Kooijman, 1963, pp. 20–39.

160 See Rivers, 1995ii, pp. 42–57, for information on *roghan*.

161 Rudenko, 1970, p. 209, says one pair had fifty-four pyrite crystals.

162 See Kaudern, 1944, pp. 236, 240–247, 260–264, for regional variations to *halili*.

165 See Varjola, Averkieva, and Liapunova, 1990, pp. 182–183, and Black, 1982, p. 160, for seam treatments.

167 See Varjola, Averkieva, and Liapunova, 1990, p. 187.

168 Hansen, 1993, p. 155. Armor concepts are discussed in Heissig, 1980, p. 17.

Intro (p. 109) See Frater, 1989, pp. 46–53.

169 See Elson, 1979, p. 37, for Kanebi information.

170 See Fisher, 1993, p. 149, for dress indicating marriage, such as *karya* (flaps added to married women's *kapada*).

171 See Rivers, 1993ii, p. 68. This group is also referred to as Lambadi.

172 See Frater, 1993ii, p. 103.

173 See Elson, 1979, pp. 26–27, and Frater, 1993ii, p. 91.

Intro (p. 110) See Elson, 1979, pp. 16–19, 24.

174 See Dhamija, 1988, p. 41.

175 See Irwin and Hall, 1973, pp. 83–84.

176 See Elson, 1979, p. 30. A Rajput *dharaniyo* with the same motifs is depicted on p. 23.

177 See Frater, 1995, pp. 68, 78. The triangular-shaped motif, *deri*, symbolizes a temple.

178 See Hacker and Turnbull, 1982.

179 Rivers, 1996i, p. 94–97.

180 See Rivers, 1996i, pp. 86–97.

181 Pramat, 1987, p. 344.

Intro (p. 112) See Elson, 1979, for similar *kapada* of many ethnic groups. See Frater, 1993ii, pp. 68–70, 74–83 for regional embroidery styles.

Intro (p. 114) Gittinger, 1979, pp. 80, 113.

189 Kahlenberg, 1977, p. 27.

192 Gittinger, 1979, p. 65.

193 Gittinger, 1979, p. 84.

194 Baker, 1995, p. 111, and Besancenot, 1990, pp. 10, 140–145.

195 The first part of a poem inside the right shoe reads, "The dust under your feet is brighter than the sun," and in the left, "Those who deny it, tell them to bring the sun and compare." Below, the shoemaker signed, "May I sacrifice my life for the dust under your feet." Translation by Perry Dehghan, data sheet, The Bata Shoe Museum, Toronto.

197 Hail, 1980, p. 188, and Orchard, 1975, pp. 104–152.

198 See Fagg, 1980, p. 40, for bead regalia set.

199 Peoples who produced cloth usually did not embellish clothing with beads; Carey, 1986, pp. 31–37. Young girls wore beaded panels called *ghabi* over pleated skirts. Older girls' aprons, *pepetu*, increased in length and width. Once engaged, girls wore scallop-bottomed aprons, *jocolo*.

200 Fitzhugh and Crowell, 1988, p. 48, and Francis, 1994, Appendix 1, p. 341.

201 See Hose and McDougall, 1912, p. 235, for *kalang asu*, dragon-dog-like patterns and meanings.

202 Rodgers, 1985, p. 238, for Luzon and Sarawak ornaments.

203 Toraja wedding dancers, Buntalobo village, Sulawesi, Indonesia. See Taylor and Aragon, 1991, pp. 186–187. *Sassang* is depicted in Solyom, 1984, p. 16.

204 See Schurz, 1959.

205 See Gunay, 1986, pp. 11, 56, for Surkun and Keles caps.

206 See Bellew, 1880, p. 62, for Persian peoples.

207 See Singh, 1993, pp. 240, 242, for sun worship and rosette images.

208 See Askari and Crill, 1997, pp. 133–134, for Kalash women's dress.

210 The ends of singing shawls employed three- or four-pointed stars or diamond-shaped motifs, which may be related to similar patterns found in funeral-game sticks and grids. See Marshall, 1922, pp. 200–201.

211 See Fisher, 1993, p. 155. Also see Rose, 1992.

212 See Varjola, Averkieva, and Liapunova, 1990, p. 218, for Chugach details, and Ray, 1981, p. 20, for pigments.

213 See Varjola, Averkieva, and Liapunova, 1990, p. 74, for trade information and Drucker, 1965, p. 151, for Nootka details.

214 See Lang, 1994ii, p. 21, for *yafus* details, and pp. 11–12 for dance cycles.

215 Left-opening chank shells in particular were associated with Shiva. Abbott and Dance, 1991, p. 210. See Newark, 1961, p. 66, for description of milking-strap hook by Carter Dean Holton.

Intro (p. 141) Money cowries were associated with all of the Yoruba water-gods, as well as Obatala, chief of the white gods and creator of life, and Orisha Oko, the god of agriculture and fertility of the earth. Safer and Gill, 1982, pp. 135–136.

217 Askari and Crill, 1997,
pp. 111–138 for Swat, Chittral,
and Indus Valleys textiles.

218 See Spring and Hudson, 1995,
p. 53, and Rusch and Stein, 1988,
fig. 20, for complete dress and
jewelry.

219 Fakhry, 1973, p. 7, for Siwa
information, and Rugh, 1986,
p. 75, for the relationship of
starburst designs to solar worship.

220 White beads, called *shong*, come
from Swat: Askari and Crill,
1997, p. 130.

221 See ch. 3 of Anderson and
Kreamer, 1989, for water spirits
and natural materials.

222 Rosen, 1998.

223 Nyim Kot a Mbweeky III on
a state visit to a subject village,
Zaire, 1970. See Cornet, 1982,
p. 187, for cowrie regalia, and
Safer and Gill, 1982, pp. 96–97.

224 Edge-Partington, 1969, vol. 1,
p. 27, and Kaeppler, 1978,
pp. 125–127.

225 Information on *bak* in Borel,
1994, p. 207, and on clam shell in
Poulsen, 1970, p. 41.

227 Vanoverberg, 1929, pp. 218–220.

228 Celebration, 1982, pp. 70–71.

229 Rodgers, 1985, p. 243, and
Benedict, 1916, pp. 117, 130,
136.

230 Lewis, 1951, pp. 132–135, and
Edge-Partington, 1969, vol. 2,
p. 190.

231 Solyom, 1984, p. 17, and Munan-
Oettli, 1983, p. 93, for *Conus
leopardus* sting.

Intro (p. 144) Paine, 1990, p. 144.

233 Seed-work details in Campbell,
1978, p. 143.

237 Burt, 1990, p. 5.

238 Ivens, 1927, pp. 84–85, for images
and Speiser, 1923, plates 36, 74,
76, 77 for patterns.

239 In Mandarin-ruled China, the
Board of Ritual dictated the day
when warm weather robes and
headgear were exchanged for
those of cool weather: Dickinson
and Wrigglesworth, 1990,
pp. 63–64.

240 Bianchi, 1978, called the element
of dress *ukunch*.

241 See Untracht, 1997, p. 53 and
Jacobs, 1990, pp. 22, 229.

242 Bianchi, 1978, named the nut
nupi. Needham, 1967, p. 606,
called the seed *ahoaj*. Ivens, 1927,
p. 383, described a similar seed,
Terminella catappa or *Terminella
canarium* nut. The Lega of eastern
Zaire used a similar nut called
maseza: see Biebuyck and Van
Den Abbeele, 1984, pl. 34.

244 Reid, 1986, p. 9.

245 See Strathern, 1971, p. 171, for
paired opposites and Strathern,
1993, p. 138, for *yagama*, meaning
to fly.

246 See Anders, 1970, p. 54.

247 See Davenport, 1962, pp. 101–
102, and Phelps, 1976, p. 226.

248, 249 Kiwis, *Apteryx* sp. are
members of the ostrich group,
while blue feathers come from
the bush pigeon, *Hemiphaga
novaeseelandiae*. See Fischel, 1951.

250, 252 Karsten, 1935, p. 389.

251 Roe in Braun, 1995, pp. 60–61.

253 See Harner, 1972, pp. 112, 130,
for headband information.

254 Ribeiro, 1957, p. 109, depicts
an Urubu-Kapoor man's complete
feather ornament set being worn.
See Roe in Braun, 1995, p. 92,
for *rembe-pipo* (labret).

255 Celebration, 1982, p. 214.

257 See Art de la plume, 1985, p. 64.

258 Ray, 1981, pp. 52–54.

259 Laughlin, 1980, p. 55.

260 Lang, 1994ii, p. 19.

261, 262 See Purdy, 1902, pp. 24–26,
and Allen, 1972, for basketry
techniques.

264 Hanyu, 1992, p. 35.

265, 266 See Hartman, 1980, p. 76.

267 Untracht, 1997, p. 45.

268 Biebuyck and Van Den Abbeele,
1984, p. 168.

269 Gubernatis, 1978, pp. 10–12.

270 See Hail, 1980, p. 68, for
information on warshirts. On
p. 69, Hail cites Clark Wissler,
"Costumes of the Plains Indians,"
a 1975 reprint of *Anthropological
Papers*, American Museum of
Natural History, New York,
vol. 17, parts 2 and 3, 1915 and
1916, p. 103, for the theory that

Native American quillwork at the
shoulders was inspired by military
epaulets.

271 Varjola, Averkieva, and
Liapunova, 1990, p. 103.

273 See Graham, 1992, p. 154,
for kinds of Banjara ceremonial
embroideries.

274 See Frater, 1993ii, p. 78.

275 See Singh, 1979, p. 67.

276 See Dar, 1982, pp. 37–49, 52,
for Mughal influences in Indian
dress.

277 See Chopra, 1954, pp. 210–228.

278 See Rivers, 1993i, p. 16, and
Gostelow, 1983, p. 247.

279 Untracht, 1997, p. 60, states that
beetles encapsulate the souls of
Naga ancestors.

280 For diverse ear ornaments see
Jacobs, 1990, p. 231.

281 Von Hagen, 1937, p. 201.

282 Bianchi, 1978, pp. 57–60, 79–80,
228.

283 Strathern, 1971, p. 172.

284 Karsten, 1935, p. 92 and pl. XIII,
and Stirling, 1938, p. 102.

285 O'Hanlon, 1993, p. 15.

286 Hodson, 1921, p. 25, and Mills,
1979, p. 25.

287 The Salvi family of Patan,
Gujarat, have woven *patola* for
many centuries. Mr. Parghi
learned *patola*-tieing from
Chotilal Salvi, but the use of
kalabatun threads is his own
innovation for modern but
traditional wedding saris.

Bibliography and Sources

Abbott and Dance, 1973
Abbott, R. Tucker and S. Peter Dance, *Shells in Color*, The Viking Press, New York, N.Y., 1973.

Abbott and Dance, 1991
Abbott, R. Tucker and S. Peter Dance, *Compendium of Seashells*, Charles Letts and Co., London, 1991.

Allen, 1972
Allen, Elsie, *Pomo Basket Making*, Naturegraph Publishing Inc., Happy Camp, Calif., 1972.

Ambalal, 1987
Ambalal, Amit, *Krishna as Shrinathji: Rajasthani Paintings from Nathdvara*, Mapin Publishing, Ahmedabad, 1987.

Anders, 1970
Anders, Ferdinand, "Minor Arts," *Artes de Mexico*, vol. 17, no. 137, 1970, pp. 46–67.

Anderson, 1981
Anderson, Frank J., *Riches of the Earth*, Winward Publishing, New York, N.Y., 1981.

Anderson and Kreamer, 1989
Anderson, Martha G., and Christine Mullen Kreamer, *Wild Spirits, Strong Medicine: African Art and the Wilderness*, The Center for African Art, New York, N.Y., 1989.

Anikia, 1983
Anikia, Andrei Vladimirovich, *Gold: The Yellow Devil*, International Publishers, New York, N.Y., 1983.

Anon, 1888
Anonymous, "The Industries of the Punjab," *Journal of Indian Art*, vol. 2, nos. 17–24, 1888.

Aragon, 1991
Aragon, Lorraine V., "Sulawesi," in Taylor and Aragon, 1991, pp. 173–199.

Arizzoli-Clementel, 1990
Arizzoli-Clementel, Pierre, *The Textile Museum*, Musées et Monuments de France, Lyons, 1990.

Armstrong, 1976
Armstrong, Nancy, *Victorian Jewelry*, Macmillan, New York, N.Y., 1976.

Armstrong, 1991
Armstrong, Wayne P., "Beautiful Botanicals: Seeds for Jewelry," *Ornament*, vol. 15, no. 1, 1991, pp. 66–69.

Arnoldi and Kreamer, 1995
Arnoldi, Mary Jo, and Christine Mullen Kreamer, *Crowning Achievements: African Arts of Dressing the Head*, UCLA Fowler Museum of Cultural History, Los Angeles, Calif., 1995.

Art de la plume, 1985
L'Art de la plume: Indiens du Brésil, Musée d'Ethnographie, and Musée Nationale d'Histoire Naturelle, Geneva and Paris, 1985.

Askari and Crill, 1997
Askari, Nasreen, and Rosemary Crill, *Colours of the Indus*, Merrell Holberton and the Victoria & Albert Museum, London, 1997.

Asuka, 1974
"Asuka Buddhist Art: Horyu-Ji," *Heibonsha Survey of Japanese Art*, vol. 4, transl. by Richard L. Gage, Weatherhill and Heibonsha, New York, N.Y., and Tokyo, 1974.

Bacon, 1966
Bacon, Elizabeth E., *Central Asians Under Russian Rule*, Cornell University Press, Ithaca, N.Y., 1966.

Baker, 1995
Baker, Patricia L., *Islamic Textiles*, British Museum Press, London, 1995.

Balfour-Paul, 1997
Balfour-Paul, Jenny, *Indigo in the Arab World*, Curzon Press, Surrey, 1997.

Barbier, 1985
Barbier, Jean-Paul, *Art of Nagaland*, The Barbier-Müller Collection, Geneva, and Los Angeles County Museum of Art, Los Angeles, Calif., 1985.

Barrett, 1907–1910
Barrett, S. A., "Pomo Indian Basketry," *American Archaeology and Ethnology*, vol. 7, 1907–1910, pp. 134–245.

Basilov, 1989
Basilov, Vladimir N., *Nomads of Eurasia*, Natural History Museum of Los Angeles County, Los Angeles, Calif., 1989.

Beckwith and Van Offelen, 1993
Beckwith, Carol and Marion Van Offelen, *Nomads of Niger*, Abradale Press, Harry N. Abrams, Inc., New York, N.Y., 1993.

Beer, 1970
Beer, Alice Baldwin, *Trade Goods: A Study of Indian Chintz*, Smithsonian Institution, Washington, D.C., 1970.

Bellew, 1880
Bellew, Surgeon-Major M. W., *The Races of Afghanistan*, Thacker, Spink and Co., Calcutta, 1880.

Benedict, 1916
Benedict, Laura Watson, "A Study of Bagobo Ceremonial Magic and Myth," *Annals of the New York Academy of Sciences*, vol. 25, 1916, pp. 1–308.

Benedict, 1991
Benedict, Burton, *Money: Tokens of Value from Around the World*, ex. cat., Lowie Museum of Anthropology, University of California, Berkeley, Calif., 1991.

Berry, 1932
Berry, Burton Yost, "Old Turkish Towels," part 1, *Art Bulletin*, vol. 14, 1932, pp. 344–358.

Besancenot, 1990
Besancenot, Jean, *Costumes of Morocco*, with a preface by James Bynon, Kegan Paul Intl., London and New York, N.Y., 1990.

Bhushan, 1959
Bhushan, Jarmila Brij, *The Costumes and Textiles of India*, Taraporevala, Bombay, 1959.

Bianchi, 1978
Bianchi, Cesar, *Mundo Shuar*, series C, no. 10, "Los Adornos," Centro de Documentacion, Investigacion y Publicaciones, SUCNA, Ecuador, 1978.

Bianchi, 1982
Bianchi, Cesar, *Artesanias y Tecnicas Shuar*, Ediciones Mundo Shuar, Ecuador, 1982.

Biebuyck and Van Den Abbeele, 1984
Biebuyck, David P., and Nelly Van Den Abbeele, *The Power of Headdresses*, The Leopold III Foundation for Exploration and Conservation, Brussels, 1984.

Black, 1982
Black, Lydia T., *Aleut Art*, Aleutian/Pribilof Islands Association, Anchorage, Alaska, 1982.

Blier, 1995
Blier, Suzanne Preston, "West African Roots of Vodou," in Cosentino, 1995, pp. 61–87.

Bliss, 1982
Bliss, Frank, "Bahriyan Jewelry and Its Relation to the Nile Valley," *Ornament*, vol. 6, no. 2, 1982, pp. 10–14, 44.

Bokhara, 1967–1968
Bokhara, cat. no. 39, The Israel Museum, Jerusalem, 1967–1968.

Borel, 1994
Borel, France, *The Splendor of Ethnic Jewelry*, transl. by I. Mark Paris, Harry N. Abrams Inc., New York, N.Y., 1994.

Boyer, 1995
Boyer, Martha, and Ida Nicolaisen, ed., *Mongol Jewelry*, Thames and Hudson, London and New York, N.Y., 1995.

Braun, 1995
Barbara Braun, ed., and Peter G. Roe, *Arts of the Amazon*, Thames and Hudson, London and New York, N.Y., 1995.

Buck, 1957
Buck, Peter H., *Arts and Crafts of Hawaii*, Special Publication 45, Bernice P. Bishop Museum, Bishop Museum Press, Honolulu, Hawaii, 1957.

Burnham, 1959
Burnham, Harold, *Chinese Velvets*, Occasional Paper 2, Royal Ontario Museum, University of Toronto Press, Toronto, 1959.

Burt, 1990
Burt, Ben, "Kwara'ae Costume Ornaments," *Expedition*, vol. 32, no. 1, 1990, pp. 3–15.

Campbell, 1978
Campbell, Margaret, *From the Hands of the Hills*, Media TransAsia, Hong Kong, 1978.

Carey, 1986
Carey, Margaret, *Beads and Beadwork of East and South Africa*, Shire Ethnography Publications, Aylesbury, 1986.

Carey, 1991
Carey, Margaret, *Beads and Beadwork of West and Central Africa*, Shire Ethnography Publications, Aylesbury, 1991.

Cavagnaro, 1982
Cavagnaro, David, *Feathers*, Graphic Arts Center Publishing Co., Portland, Oreg., 1982.

Celebration, 1982
Celebration: A World of Art and Ritual, Smithsonian Institution Press, Washington, D.C., 1982.

Chaussonnet, 1988
Chaussonnet, Valerie, "Needles and Animals: Women's Magic," in Fitzhugh and Crowell, 1988, pp. 208–226.

Chee, 1989
Chee, Eng-Lee Seok, *Festive Expressions: Nonya Beadwork and Embroidery*, National Museum, Singapore, 1989.

Chopra, 1954
Chopra, P. N., "Dress, Textiles and Ornaments during the Mughal Period," *Proceedings of Indian History Congress*, 15th Session, Calcutta, 1954, p. 210–228.

Clark, 1986
Clark, Grahame, *Symbols of Excellence*, Cambridge University Press, Cambridge, 1986.

Clifford, 1987
Clifford, James, "Of Other Peoples: Beyond the Salvage Paradigm," in Hal Foster, ed., *Discussions in Contemporary Culture*, Bay Press, Seattle, Wash., 1987.

Clothings, 1985
Clothings and Ornaments of China's Miao People, Cultural Palace of Nationalities, Beijing, 1985.

Cohen, 1983
Cohen, Eric, "Dynamics of Commercialized Arts: The Meo and Yao of Northern Thailand," *Journal of National Research Council of Northern Thailand*, vol. 15, no. 1, 1983, pp. 1–34.

Cole, 1913
Cole, Fay-Cooper, *The Wild Tribes of Davou District, Mindanao*, History Publication 170, vol. 12, no. 2, Field Museum of Natural History, Chicago, Ill., 1913.

Conway, 1992
Conway, Susan, *Thai Textiles*, British Museum Press, London, 1992.

Cornet, 1982
Cornet, Joseph, *Art Royal Kuba*, Edizioni Sipiel, Milan, 1982.

Cosentino, 1995
Donald J. Cosentino, ed., *Sacred Arts of Haitian Vodou*, UCLA Fowler Museum of Cultural History, Los Angeles, Calif., 1995.

Coss and Moore, 1990
Coss, Richard G., and Michael Moore, "All That Glistens: Water Connotations in Surface Finishes," *Ecological Psychology*, vol. 2, no. 4, 1990, pp. 367–380.

Cowan, 1865
Cowan, Frank, *Curious History of Insects*, J. B. Lippincott & Co., Philadelphia, Pa., 1865.

Curran, 1945
Curran, C. H., *Insects of the Pacific World*, Macmillan, New York, N.Y., 1945.

Dalby, 1993
Dalby, Liza Crinfield, *Kimono: Fashioning Culture*, Yale University Press, New Haven, Conn., and London, 1993.

Dalrymple, 1984
Dalrymple, Ross Elizabeth, "Gold Embroidered Ceremonial Sarongs from South Sumatra," *Arts of Asia*, vol. 14, no. 1, 1984, pp. 90–99.

Dar, 1982
Dar, S. N., *Costumes of India and Pakistan*, D. B. Taraporevala Sons & Co., Bombay, 1982.

Davenport, 1962
Davenport, William, "Red-feather Money," *Scientific American*, vol. 206, no. 3, 1962, pp. 94–104.

De, 1910
De, B. N., *A Monograph on the Wire and Tinsel Industry in the Central Provinces*, Government Press, Nagpur, 1910.

de Khanikoff, 1965
de Khanikoff, Nikolas, *Bokhara: Its Amir and People*, transl. by Baron Clement A. de Bode, James Madden Publishers, London, 1965.

Dewar, 1963
Dewar, John, "The China Poblana," *Quarterly*, Los Angeles County Museum, vol. 2, no. 2, 1963, pp. 16–19.

Dhamija, 1964
Dhamija, Jasleen, "Survey of Embroidery Traditions," *Marg*, vol. 17, no. 2, 1964, pp. 11–68.

Dhamija, 1988
Dhamija, Jasleen, "Embroidery,"

The India Magazine, vol. 8, no. 9, 1988, pp. 32–41.

Dhamija, 1995
Dhamija, Jasleen, ed., *The Woven Silks of India*, Marg Publications, Bombay, 1995.

Dickinson and Wrigglesworth, 1990
Dickinson, Gary, and Linda Wrigglesworth, *Imperial Wardrobe*, Bamboo Publishing Ltd., London, 1990.

Drower, 1995
Drower, Sara, "Kalagas: The Golden Tapestries of Burma," *Piecework*, no. 12, 1995, pp. 4–44.

Drucker, 1965
Drucker, Philip, *Culture of the North Pacific*, Chandler Publishing Company, San Francisco, Calif., 1965.

Dubin, 1987
Dubin, Lois Sherr, *The History of Beads*, Harry N. Abrams, Inc., New York, N.Y., 1987.

Dunning, 1970
Dunning, John S., *Portraits of Tropical Birds*, Livingston Publishing Co., Wynnewood, Pa., 1970.

Dunsmore, 1978
Dunsmore, Susi, *Beads*, Occasional Paper no. 2, The Sarawak Museum, Kuching, 1978.

Ecke, 1977
Ecke, Tseng Yu-ho, *Chinese Folk Art II*, University of Hawaii Press, Honolulu, Hawaii, 1977.

Edge-Partington, 1969
Edge-Partington, James, *An Album of the Weapons, Tools, Ornaments, Articles of Dress, Etc. of the Natives of the Pacific Islands*, Holland Press, London, 1969. Reproduced from the original three volumes dated 1892, 1895, and 1898.

Eicher, 1976
Eicher, Joanne Bubolz, *Nigerian*

Handcrafted Textiles, University of Ife Press, Nigeria, 1976.

Elson, 1979
Elson, Vickie G., *Dowries from Kutch*, UCLA Museum of Cultural History, Los Angeles, Calif., 1979.

Erikson, 1993
Erikson, Joan Mowat, *The Universal Bead*, W. W. Norton and Co., New York, N.Y., 1993.

Estranda, 1991
Estranda, Elsa, "El arte plumario," *Caminos del Aire*, Mexicana Airlines, 1991, pp. 119–125, 128.

Evans-Pritchard, 1972
Evans-Pritchard, Sir Edward, ed., *Peoples of the Earth*, vol. 14, Danbury Press, Danbury, Conn., 1972.

Fagg, 1980
Fagg, William, *Yoruba Beadwork: Art of Nigeria*, Rizzoli, New York, N.Y., 1980.

Fakhry, 1973
Fakhry, Ahmed, "The Siwa Oasis," *The Oases of Egypt*, vol. 1, The American University in Cairo Press, Cairo, 1973.

Fakhry, 1974
Fakhry, Ahmed, "Bahriyah and Farafra Oases," *The Oases of Egypt*, vol. 2, The American University in Cairo Press, Cairo, 1974.

Fischel, 1951
Fischel, Walter G., "Maori Textile Techniques: Clothing," *Ciba Review*, no. 84, 1951, pp. 3034–3059.

Fischer, 1979
Fischer, Joseph, ed., *Threads of Tradition: Textiles of Indonesia and Sarawak*, Lowie Museum of Anthropology, University of California, Berkeley, Calif., 1979.

Fisher, 1993
Fisher, Nora, ed., *Mud, Mirror, and Thread*, Mapin Publishing, Ahmedabad, 1993.

Fiske, Pickering, and Yohe, 1981
Patricia L. Fiske, W. Russell Pickering, and Ralph S. Yohe, eds., *From the Far West: Carpets and Textiles of Morocco*, The Textile Museum, Washington, D.C., 1981.

Fitz-Gibbon and Hale, 1988
Fitz-Gibbon, Kate, and Andrew Hale, *Ikats: Woven Silks from Central Asia*, Basil Blackwell Publications, Oxford, 1988.

Fitz-Gibbon and Hale, 1997
Fitz-Gibbon, Kate, and Andrew Hale, *Ikat: Silks of Central Asia*, Laurence King Publishing, London, 1997.

Fitzhugh and Crowell, 1988
Fitzhugh, William W., and Aron Crowell, eds., *Crossroads of Continents: Cultures of Siberia and Alaska*, Smithsonian Institution Press, Washington, D.C., 1988.

Forbes, 1950
Forbes, R. J., *Metallurgy in Antiquity*, E. J. Brill, Leiden, 1950.

Forelli and Harries, 1977
Forelli, Sally, and Jeannette Harries, "Traditional Berber Weaving in Central Morocco," *The Textile Museum Journal*, vol. 4, no. 4, 1977, pp. 41–60.

Francis, 1990
Francis, Jr., Peter, "Beads in the Philippines," *Arts of Asia*, vol. 20, no. 6, 1990, pp. 97–107.

Francis, 1994
Francis, Jr., Peter, *Beads of the World*, Schiffer Publications, Atglen, Pa., 1994.

Fraser-Lu, 1982
Fraser-Lu, Sylvia, "Kalagas," *Art of Asia*, vol. 12, no. 4, 1982.

Frater, 1989
Frater, Judy, "In the Language," *El Palacio*, vol. 94, no. 3, 1989, pp. 44–53.

Frater, 1993i
Frater, Judy, "Rabari Dress," in Fisher, 1993.

Frater, 1993ii
Frater, Judy, "The Elements of Style," in Fisher, 1993.

Frater, 1995
Frater, Judy, *Threads of Identity*, Mapin Publishing, Ahmedabad, 1995.

Fumin and Yoahua, 1988
Fumin, Zhang, and Lin Yoahua, *A Study and Analysis of Chinese Miao Costumes*, China House Gallery and China Institute of America, New York, N.Y., 1988.

Furber, 1976
Furber, Holden, *Rival Empires of Trade in the Orient, 1600–1800*, University of Minnesota Press, Minneapolis, Minn., 1976.

Furst, 1991
Furst, Peter T., "Crowns of Power: Bird and Feather Symbolism in Amazonian Shamanism," in Reina and Kensinger, 1991, pp. 92–109.

Garner, 1979
Garner, Sir Harry, *Chinese Lacquer*, Faber and Faber, London, 1979.

Garrard, 1989
Garrard, Timothy F., *Gold of Africa: Jewellery and Ornaments from Ghana, Côte d'Ivoire, Mali and Senegal*, Collection of Barbier-Müller Museum, Prestel Publishing, Munich, 1989.

Garrett, 1990
Garrett, Valery M., *Children of the Gods: Dress and Symbolism in China*, Hong Kong Museum of History and Urban Council, Hong Kong, 1990.

Gifford, 1958
Gifford, Edward S., Jr., *The Evil Eye: Studies in the Folklore of Vision*, Macmillan and Co., New York, N.Y., 1958.

Gilroy, 1868
Gilroy, Clinton G., *Pastoral Life and Manufacture of the Ancients*, William H. Starr, New York, N.Y., 1868.

Gion Matsuri, 1993
'93 *Gion Matsuri*, English translation by Maria Messina, Gion Matsuri Rengokai Foundation, Kyoto, 1993.

Girouard, 1994
Girouard, Tina, *Sequin Artists of Haiti*, Contemporary Arts Center of New Orleans, New Orleans, La., 1994.

Gittinger, 1979
Gittinger, Mattiebelle, *Splendid Symbols: Textiles and Tradition in Indonesia*, The Textile Museum, Washington, D.C., 1979.

Gittinger, 1982
Gittinger, Mattiebelle, *Master Dyers to the World*, The Textile Museum, Washington, D.C., 1982.

Gittinger and Lefferts, 1992
Gittinger, Mattiebelle, and H. Leedom Lefferts, Jr., *Textiles and the Tai Experience in Southeast Asia*, The Textile Museum, Washington, D.C., 1992.

Gonick, 1994
Gonick, Gloria Granz, "The Conversion of Chinese Court Robes into Japanese Festival Hangings," in *Contact, Crossover, Continuity*, Proceedings of the Fourth Biennial Symposium of the Textile Society of America, Inc., Los Angeles, Calif., 1994, pp. 67–79.

Gordon and Kahan, 1976
Gordon, Albert S., and Leonard Kahan, *The Tribal Bead*, Tribal Arts Gallery Inc., New York, N.Y., 1976.

Gostelow, 1983
Gostelow, Mary, *Embroidery*, Arco Publishing, New York, N.Y., 1983.

Goswamy and Krishna, 1993
Goswamy, B. N., and Kalian Krishna, *Indian Costumes in the Collection of the Calico Museum of Textiles*, vol. V, Historic Textiles of India, Calico Museum, Ahmedabad, 1993.

Graburn, 1976
Graburn, Nelson, *Ethnic and Tourist Arts: Cultural Expression from the Fourth World*, University of California Press, Berkeley, Calif., 1976.

Graham, 1992
Graham, Joss, "Banjara Embroidery," *Embroidery*, Embroiderers' Guild, Surrey, vol. 43, no.3, 1992, pp. 154–156.

Griaule, 1951
Griaule, Geneviève, "Le Vêtement Dogon, confection et usage," *Journal de la Société des Africanistes*, Centre National de la Recherche Scientifique, Paris, vol. 21, no. 1, 1951, pp. 151–162.

Gubernatis, 1978
Gubernatis, Angelo de, *Zoological Mythology*, vols. 1 and 2, Arno Press and New York Times Book Co., New York, N.Y., 1978.

Gunay, 1986
Gunay, Umay, *Historical Costumes of Turkish Women*, Middle East Video Corporation, Turkey, 1986.

Gunn and Dennis, 1976
Gunn, Charles R., and John V. Dennis, *World Guide to Tropical Drift Seeds and Fruit*, Quadrangle/New York Times Book Co., New York, N.Y., 1976.

Guochang and Rossi, 1985
Guochang, Lu, and Gail Rossi, *Precious Place: Minority Costume and Textiles of Guizhou China*, ex. cat., San Francisco Craft and Folk Art Museum, San Francisco, Calif., 1985

Guppy, 1887
Guppy, H. B., *The Solomon Islands and Their Natives*, Swan Sonnenschein, Lowrey and Co., London, 1887.

Guy, 1989
Guy, John, "Sarasa and Patola: Indian Textiles in Indonesia," *Orientations*, vol. 20, no. 19, 1989, pp. 48–60.

Guy, 1992
Guy, John, "Indian Textiles for the Thai Market: A Royal Prerogative," *The Textile Museum Journal*, The Textile Museum, Washington, D.C., vol. 31, 1992, pp. 82–96.

Guy, 1998
Guy, John, *Woven Cargoes: Indian Textiles in the East*, Thames and Hudson, London and New York, N.Y., 1998.

Hacker and Turnbull, 1982
Hacker, Katherine F., and Krista Jensen Turnbull, *Courtyard, Bazaar, Temple: Traditions of Textile Expression in India*, ex. cat., University of Washington and University of Washington Press, Seattle, Wash., 1982.

Hail, 1980
Hail, Barbara A., *Hau, Kola!: The Plains Indian Collection of the Haffenreffer Museum of Anthropology*, Brown University, Rhode Island, R.I., 1980.

Hansen, 1993
Hansen, Henny Harold, *Mongol Costumes*, Thames and Hudson, London, 1993.

Hanyu, 1992
Hanyu, Gau, *Chinese Textile Designs*, transl. by Rosemary Scott and Susan Whitfield, Viking and Penguin Publishers, London, 1992.

Harner, 1972
Harner, Michael J., *The Jivaro*, Doubleday/Natural History Press, Garden City, N.J., 1972.

Hartman, 1980
Hartman, Roland, "Kingfisher Feather Jewelry," *Arts of Asia*, vol. 10, no. 3, 1980, pp. 75–81.

Harvey, 1996
Harvey, Janet, *Traditional Textiles of Central Asia*, Thames and Hudson, London and New York, N.Y., 1996.

Hauser-Schäublin, Nabholz-Kartaschoff, and Ramseyer, 1991
Hauser-Schäublin, Brigitta, Marie-Louise Nabholz-Kartaschoff, and Urs Ramseyer, *Textiles in Bali*, Periplus Editions, Singapore, 1991.

Hays, 1998
Hays, Mary V., Correspondence with Victoria Rivers, May 1998.

Heaven's Embroidered Cloth, 1995
Heaven's Embroidered Cloth: 1,000 Years of Chinese Textiles, Urban Council and Hong Kong Museum of Art, Hong Kong, 1995.

Heissig, 1980
Heissig, Walter, *The Religions of Mongolia*, transl. by Geoffrey Samuel, University of California Press, Berkeley, Calif., 1980.

Hepner, 1935
Hepner, Charles W., *Kurozumi Sect of Shinto*, Meiji Japan Society, Tokyo, 1935.

Herbert, 1984
Herbert, Eugenia W., *Red Gold of Africa*, University of Madison Press, Madison, Wis., 1984.

Higgins, 1993
Higgins, J. P. P., *Cloth of Gold: A History of Metallisized Textiles*, The Lurex Co., Ltd., London, 1993.

Hinton, 1974
Hinton, E. M., "The Dress of the Pwo Karen of North Thailand," *Journal of the Siam Society*, vol. 62, no. 1, 1974.

Hitchcock, 1987
Hitchcock, Michael, "Fabrics for a Sultan," *Hali*, vol. 9, no. 3, 1987, pp. 14–21.

Hitchcock, 1989
Hitchcock, Michael, "Colour Symbolism in Bimanese Textiles," *Indonesia Circle*, vol. 49, 1989, pp. 19–29.

Hitkari, 1980
Hitkari, S. S., *Phulkari: the Folk Art of Punjab*, Phulkari Publications, New Delhi, 1980.

Hodge, 1982
Hodge, Alison, *Nigeria's Traditional Crafts*, Ethnographica, London, 1982.

Hodson, 1921
Hodson, T. C., *Naga Tribes of Manipur*, Macmillan and Co., London, 1921.

Holmberg, 1922
Holmberg, Uno, *The Shaman's Costume and Its Significance*, Turun Suomalaisen Yliopiston Julkaisuja, Sarja B, osa 1, no. 2, Annales Universitatis Fennicae Aboensis, Helsinki, 1922.

Holt, 1966
Holt, Eugene I., *Velvets East and West*, Los Angeles County Museum of Art, Los Angeles, Calif., 1966.

Hope, 1990
Hope, Jonathan, "Cloth of Gold," *Hali*, vol. 12, nos. 1–2, 1990, pp. 38–43.

Hopkirk, 1980
Hopkirk, Peter, *Foreign Devils on the Silk Road*, John Murray, London, 1980.

Hornell, 1918
Hornell, James, "The Chank Bangle Industry," *Memoirs of the Asiatic Society of Bengal*, vol. 3, no. 7, pp. 407–448, 1918.

Hose and McDougall, 1912
Hose, Charles, and William McDougall, *The Pagan Tribes of Borneo*, 2 vols., MacMillan and Co., London, 1912.

Hsi, 1991
Hsi, Ai, "Gems of China's Cultural Relics," *Arts of Asia*, vol. 21, no. 3, 1991, pp. 76–86.

Irwin and Brett, 1970
Irwin, John, and Katherine Brett, *Origins of Chintz*, HMSO, London, 1970.

Irwin and Hall, 1973
Irwin, John, and Margaret Hall, *Indian Embroideries*, vol. 2, Historic Textiles of India at the Calico Museum, Ahmedabad, 1973.

Ivens, 1927
Ivens, W. G., *Melanesians of the South East Solomon Islands*, Kegan, London, 1927.

Ives, 1954
Ives, Herbert E., *The Venetian Gold Ducat and Its Imitations*, in Philip Grierson, ed., *Numismatic Notes and Monographs*, vol. 128, The American Numismatic Society, New York, N.Y., 1954.

Jackson, 1997
Jackson, Beverley, *Splendid Slippers*, Ten Speed Press, Berkeley, Calif., 1997.

Jacobs, 1990
Jacobs, Julian, *The Nagas*, Thames and Hudson, London and New York, N.Y., 1990.

Jacobson, 1995
Jacobson, Esther, *The Art of the Scythians*, E. J. Brill, Leiden, 1995.

Jensen and Sargent, 1993
Jensen, Doreen and Polly Sargent, *Robes of Power: Totem Poles on Cloth*, Museum Note 17, University of British Columbia Press in association with Museum of Anthropology, University of British Columbia, Vancouver, 1993.

Jewellery, 1988
Jewellery: Museum of the Ethnography of the Peoples of the USSR, Aurora Art Publishers, Leningrad, 1988.

Jidai, 1995
Jidai Matsuri: Festival of Ages, Shoin, Kyoto, 1995.

Johnstone, 1985
Johnstone, Pauline, *Turkish Embroidery*, Victoria & Albert Museum, London, 1985.

Juynboll, 1922
Juynboll, H. H., *Katalog des Ethnograpischen Reichsmuseums, Band XVI, Celebes*, E. J. Brill, Leiden, 1922.

Kaeppler, 1978
Kaeppler, Adrienne, *Artificial Curiosities*, Bishop Museum Special Publication 65, Bishop Museum Press, Honolulu, Hawaii, 1978.

Kahlenberg, 1977
Kahlenberg, Mary Hunt, *Textile Traditions of Indonesia*, Los Angeles County Museum of Art, Los Angeles, Calif., 1977.

Kajitani, 1979
Kajitani, Nobuko, "Traditional Dyes in Indonesia," in Mattiebelle Gittinger, ed., *Indonesian Textiles*, Irene Emery Roundtable on Museum Textiles, The Textile Museum, Washington, D.C., 1979, pp. 305–325.

Kalter, Pavaloi, and Zerrnickel, 1993
Kalter, Johannes, Margareta Pavaloi, and Maria Zerrnickel, *The Arts and Crafts of Syria*, Thames and Hudson, London and New York, N.Y., 1993.

Kandalavala, 1982
Kandalavala, Karl, *Pahari Miniature Paintings in the N. C. Mehta Collection*, Gujarat Museum Society, Gujarat, 1982.

Karsten, 1923
Karsten, Rafael, *Blood Revenge: War and Victory Feasts Among the Jibaro Indians of Eastern Ecuador*, Bulletin 79, Smithsonian Institution Bureau of Ethnology, Washington, D.C., 1923.

Karsten, 1935
Karsten, Rafael, *The Headhunters of Western Amazonas*, Societas Scientiarum Sennica, Helsinki, 1935.

Kartiwa, 1986
Kartiwa, Suwati, *Songket Weaving in Indonesia*, Penerbit Djambatan, Jakarta, 1986.

Kaudern, 1944
Kaudern, Walter, "Art in Central Celebes," *Ethnographical Studies in Celebes*, transl. by M. Nijhoff, vol. 6, Elanders Publishing, The Hague, 1944.

Kennedy, 1990
Kennedy, Alan, *Japanese Costume: History and Tradition*, Editions Adam Biro, Paris, 1990.

Koch, 1977
Koch, Ronald P., *Dress Clothing of the Plains Indians*, University of Oklahoma Press, Norman, Okla., 1977.

Kooijman, 1963
Kooijman, Simon, *Ornamented Bark Cloth in Indonesia*, E. J. Brill, Leiden, 1963.

Krishna, 1966
Krishna, Rai Anand, *Banras Brocades*, Crafts Museum, New Delhi, 1966.

Kroeber, 1953
Kroeber, A. L., *Handbook of the Indians of California*, The California Book Co., Berkeley, Calif., 1953.

Kunz and Stevenson, 1908
Kunz, George Frederick, and Charles Hugh Stevenson, *The Book of the Pearl*, The Century Co., New York, N.Y., 1908.

Landini, 1994
Landini, Roberta Orsi, "Luxury and Practicality," in Marinis, 1994, pp. 74–110.

Lang, 1994i
Lang, Julian, "The Embodiment of Wealth," in *Indian Regalia of Northwest California*, Phoebe Apperson Hearst Museum of Anthropology, University of California, Berkeley, Calif., 1994, pp. 5–7.

Lang, 1994ii
Lang, Julian, "The Dances and Regalia," in *Indian Regalia of Northwest California*, Phoebe Apperson Hearst Museum of Anthropology, University of California, Berkeley, Calif., 1994, pp. 14–21.

Laughlin, 1980
Laughlin, William S., *Aleuts: Survivors of the Bering Land Bridge*, University of Connecticut, Storrs, Conn., and Holt, Reinhardt, and Winston, New York, N.Y., 1980.

Lebeuf, 1970
Lebeuf, Jean-Paul, "Broderie et symbolisme chez les Kanouri et les Kotoko," *Objets et Mondes*, vol. 10, no. 4, 1970, pp. 263–282.

Lechtman, 1984
Lechtman, Heather, "Pre-Columbian Surface Metallurgy," *Scientific American*, vol. 250, no. 6, 1984, pp. 6–63.

Le Coq, 1928
Le Coq, Albert von, *Buried Treasure of Chinese Turkestan*, George Allen and Unwin Ltd., London, 1928.

Lefferts, 1988
Lefferts, Jr., H. Leedom, "The Kings as Gods: Textiles in the Thai State," *Proceedings of the First Symposium of the Textile Society of America*, Minneapolis Institute of Art, 16–18 Sept. 1988, pp. 78–85.

Leigh, 1993
Leigh, Barbara, "The Theme of the Heavenly Garden: Gold Thread Embroidery in Aceh," in Marie-Louise Nabholz-Kartaschoff, Ruth Barnes, and David J. Stuart-Fox, eds., *Weaving Patterns of Life: Indonesian Textile Symposium 1991*, Museum of Ethnography, Basel, 1993.

Lekagul and McNeely, 1978
Lekagul, Boonsong, and Jeffrey A. McNeely, *Mammals of Thailand*, Association for the Conservation of Wildlife and Saha Karn Bhaet Co., Bangkok, 1978.

Lewis, 1951
Lewis, Albert B., *The Melanesians*, Chicago Natural History Museum, Chicago, Ill., 1951.

Liu, 1983
Liu, Robert K., "Identification," *Ornament*, vol. 6, no. 4, 1983, p. 59.

Liu, 1995
Liu, Robert K., *Collectible Beads*, Ornament, Vista, Calif., 1995.

Lobacheva, 1989
Lobacheva, Nina P., "Clothing and Personal Adornment," in Vladimir N. Basilov, ed., *Nomads of Eurasia*,

Natural History Museum of Los Angeles County, Los Angeles, Calif., 1989.

Lowry, 1974
Lowry, John, *Burmese Art*, Victoria & Albert Museum, London, 1974.

Lucas, 1948
Lucas, A., *Ancient Egyptian Materials and Industries*, Edward Arnold Publishers Ltd., London, 1948.

Lynton, 1995
Lynton, Linda, *The Sari*, Harry N. Abrams, Inc., New York, N.Y., 1995.

Mack, 1988
Mack, John, *Ethnic Jewelry*, Harry N. Abrams, Inc., New York, N.Y., 1988.

Mackie, 1992
Mackie, Louise W., "New on Old: Handmade Textiles in Fez," *Hali*, vol. 14, no. 6, 1992, pp. 88–93.

Maddin, Wheeler, and Muhly, 1977
Maddin, Robert, Tamara Stech Wheeler, and James D. Muhly, "Tin in the Ancient Near East," *Expedition*, vol. 19, no. 2, 1977, pp. 35–47.

Marazov, 1998
Marazov, Ivan, ed., *Ancient Gold: The Wealth of the Thracians: Treasures from the Republic of Bulgaria*, Harry N. Abrams, Inc., New York, N.Y., in association with the Trust for Museum Exhibitions, and the Ministry of Culture of the Republic of Bulgaria, 1998.

Margolin, 1994
Margolin, Malcolm, "Wealth and Spirit," in *Indian Regalia of Northwest California*, Phoebe Apperson Hearst Museum of Anthropology, University of California, Berkeley, Calif., 1994, pp. 8–13.

Marinis, 1994
de' Marinis, Fabrizio, ed., *Velvets: History, Techniques, Fashions*, Idea Books, Milan, 1994.

Marshall, 1922
Marshall, Rev. Harry Ignatius, *The Karen People of Burma*, Contributions in History and Political Science, The Ohio State University Bulletin, The Ohio State University, Columbus, Ohio, vol. 26, no. 13, 1922.

Marx, 1978
Marx, Jennifer, *The Magic of Gold*, Doubleday & Co., New York, N.Y., 1978.

Mato, 1987
Mato, Daniel, *Clothed in Symbol: The Art of Adinkra Among the Akan of Ghana*, Dissertation, Indiana University, Bloomington, Ind., 1987.

Maxwell, 1990
Maxwell, Robyn, *Textiles of Southeast Asia*, Australian National Gallery and Oxford University Press, Melbourne, 1990.

Maxwell, 1992
Maxwell, Robyn, *Cultures at Crossroads: South East Asian Textiles from the Australian National Gallery*, Australian National Gallery, Melbourne, 1992.

McAlister, 1995
McAlister, Elizabeth, "A Sorcerer's Bottle: The Visual Art of Magic in Haiti," in Cosentino, 1995, pp. 305–321.

McNaughton, 1982
McNaughton, Patrick R., "The Shirts that Mande Hunters Wear," *African Arts*, vol. 15, no. 3, 1982, pp. 54–58, 91.

Mekler, 1992
Mekler, Adam, *Invisible People: Arts of the Amazon*, ex. cat., Fresno Art Museum, California, 1992.

Meng, 1987
Meng, Ho Wing, *Straits Chinese Beadwork and Embroidery*, Times Books International, Singapore, 1987.

Micaud, 1970
Micaud, Ellen, "The Craft Tradition in North Africa," *African Arts*, vol. 3, no. 2, 1970, pp. 33–43, 90–91.

Mills, 1923
Mills, J. P., *The Rengma Nagas*, Macmillan and Co., London, 1923.

Minnich, 1963
Minnich, Helen Benton, *Japanese Costume and the Makers of Its Elegant Tradition*, Charles E. Tuttle Co., Rutland, Vt., and Tokyo, 1963.

Morin-Barde, 1990
Morin-Barde, Mireille, *Coiffures Feminines du Maroc*, Edisud, Aix-en-Provence, 1990.

Moseley and Feldman, 1978
Moseley, Michael E., and Robert A. Feldman, *Peru's Golden Treasures*, Field Museum of Natural History, Chicago, Ill., 1978.

Mozzi, 1987
Mozzi, Carlota Mapelli, *La Tejedora de Vida*, Banca Serfin, Mexico, D. F., 1987.

Munan-Oettli, 1983
Munan-Oettli, Adelheid, "Bead Cap 64/88 in the Sarawak Museum Collection," *The Sarawak Museum Journal*, vol. 32, no. 53, 1983, pp. 93–95.

Myers, 1989
Myers, Myrna, "Silk Furnishings of the Ming and Quing Dynasties," in Krishna Riboud, ed., *In Quest of Themes and Skills: Asian Textiles*, Marg Publishing, Bombay, 1989, pp. 126–140.

Naenna and Perangwatthanakun, 1990i
Naenna, Patricia, and Songsok Perangwatthanakun, *La Na Textiles*, Center for the Promotion for Arts and Culture, Chiang Mai University, Chiang Mai, 1990.

Naenna and Perangwatthanakun, 1990ii
Naenna, Patricia, and Songsok Perangwatthanakun, *Costume and Culture: Vanishing Textiles of Some of the Tai Groups in Laos*, Studio Naenna, Chiang Mai, 1990.

Naenna and Phanichphant, 1993
Naenna, Patricia, and Vithi
Phanichphant, "Thai Lineage in Textile
Art," in Songsok Prangwatthanakun,
ed., *Textiles of Asia: A Common
Heritage*, Office of the National Culture
Commission, Ministry of Education and
Center of Promotion of Arts and
Culture, Chiang Mai University,
Chiang Mai, 1993, pp. 40–50.

Nanavati, Vora, and Dhaky, 1966
Nanavati, J. M., M. P. Vora, and M. A.
Dhaky, *The Embroidery and Beadwork of
Kutch and Saurashtra*, Department of
Archaeology, Gujarat, 1966.

Near East, 1969
The Near East in UCLA Collections,
ex. cat., University of California, Los
Angeles, Calif., 1969.

Needham, 1967
Needham, Rodney, "Percussion and
Transition," *Man: Journal of the Royal
Anthropological Institute*, New Series,
vol. 2, no. 4, 1967, pp. 606–614.

Newark, 1950–1971
*Catalogue of the Tibetan Collection and
Other Lamaist Articles in the Newark
Museum*, 5 vols., Newark Museum,
Newark, N.J., 1950–1971.

Newark, 1961
*Catalogue of the Tibetan Collection and
Other Lamaist Material in the Newark
Museum: Textiles, Rugs, Needlework,
Costume, Jewelry*, vol. 4, Newark
Museum, Newark, N.J., 1961.

Newark, 1983
Valrae Reynolds and Amy Heller, eds.,
*Catalogue of the Newark Museum Tibetan
Collection*, vol. 1, second edition,
Newark Museum, Newark, N.J., 1983.

Nolan-Muzzy, 1989
Nolan-Muzzy, Shelley, "Asyut Shawls,"
Ornament, vol. 13, no. 2, 1989, pp. 66–67.

Nomura, 1914
Nomura, Shojiru, *An Historical Sketch
of Nishiki and Kinran Brocades*,
Shimmonjen, Kyoto, and Boston,
Mass., 1914.

Ogden, 1982
Ogden, Jack, *Jewellery of the Ancient
World*, Trefoil Books, London, 1982.

O'Hanlon, 1993
O'Hanlon, Michael, *Paradise:
Portraying the New Guinea Highlands*,
British Museum Press, London, 1993.

Olson, 1960
Olson, Eleanor, *Tibetan Life and
Culture*, The Museum of
International Folk Art, Santa Fe,
N.Mex., 1960.

Oppenheim, 1949
Oppenheim, A. L., "The Golden
Garments of the Gods," *Journal of
Near Eastern Studies*, vol. 8, 1949,
pp. 172–193.

Orchard, 1975
Orchard, William C., *Beads and
Beadwork of the American Indians*,
Museum of the American Indian,
Hewe Foundation, New York, N.Y.,
1975.

Oro del Peru, 1978
Oro del Peru, Museo del Peru,
Monterrico, Lima, 1978.

Oz, 1950
Oz, Tahsin, *Turkish Textiles and Velvets,
XIV–XVI Centuries*, Turkish Press,
Broadcasting and Tourist Development,
Ankara, 1950.

Paine, 1990
Paine, Sheila, *Embroidered Textiles*,
Thames and Hudson, London and New
York, N.Y., 1990.

Pal, 1991
Pal, Pratapaditya, *Art of the Himalayas:
Treasures from Nepal and Tibet*, with
contribution by Valrae Reynolds,
Hudson Hills Press, New York, N.Y.,
1991.

Pal, 1992
Pal, Pratapaditya, "Tibetan Religious
Textiles," *Hali*, vol. 14, no. 1, 1992,
pp. 106–113, 140.

Parker, 1984
Parker, Rozsika, *The Subversive Stitch*,
The Women's Press, London, 1984.

Pavaloi, 1992
Pavaloi, Margareta, "Textile Stories,"
in Kalter, Pavaloi, and Zerrnickel, 1993,
pp. 211–230.

Pavinskaya, 1989
Pavinskaya, Larisa R., "The Scythians
and Sakians: Eighth to Third Centuries
BC," *Nomads of Eurasia*, Natural History
Museum of Los Angeles County, Los
Angeles, Calif., 1989, pp. 19–40.

Pendergrast, 1987
Pendergrast, Mick, *Te Aho Tapu: The
Sacred Thread*, University of Hawaii
Press, Honolulu, Hawaii, 1987.

Perrins and Middleton, 1985
Perrins, Christopher M., and Alex L.
A. Middleton, eds., *The Encyclopedia of
Birds*, George, Allen, Unwin, London,
1985.

Phelps, 1976
Phelps, Stephen, *Art and Artifacts of
the Pacific, Africa and the Americas: The
James Hooper Collection*, Hutchison and
Co., London, 1976.

Picton and Mack, 1979
Picton, John, and John Mack, *African
Textiles*, British Museum Publications,
London, 1979.

Picton and Mack, 1995
Picton, John, and John Mack, *The Art
of African Textiles: Technology,
Tradition, and Lurex*, Lund Humphries
Publishers and Barbican Art Gallery,
London, 1995.

Polakoff, 1980
Polakoff, Claire, *Into Indigo*, Anchor
Books, Garden City, N.Y., 1980.

Polk, 1995
Polk, Patrick, "Sacred Banners and the
Divine Cavalry Charge," in Cosentino,
1995, pp. 325–347.

Poulsen, 1970
Poulsen, Jens, "Shell Artifacts in

Oceania: Their Distribution and Significance," in R. C. Green and M. Kelly, eds., *Studies in Oceanic Culture History*, vol. 1, Pacific Anthropological Records no. 11, Bishop Museum, Honolulu, Hawaii, 1970, pp. 33–46.

Pramat, 1987
Pramat, V. S., "Sociology of the North Gujarat Urban House," in *Contributions to Indian Sociology*, vol. 21, no. 2, 1987, pp. 331–345.

Pressman, 1991
Pressman, Jon F., "The Mythological Origins of Avian Coloration: Feathers of Blood and Fire," in Reina and Kensinger, 1991.

Pritchard, 1984
Pritchard, Mary J., *Siapo*, Special Publication 1, American Samoa Council on Culture, Arts and Humanities, Samoa, 1984.

Purdy, 1902
Purdy, Carl, *Pomo Indian Baskets and Their Makers*, County Historical Society, Mendocino, Calif., 1902, reprinted 1971.

Quarcoo, 1972
Quarcoo, A. K., *The Language of Adinkra Patterns*, Institute of African Studies, Legon, Ghana, 1972.

Quinn, 1934
Quinn, Vernon, *Seeds: Their Place in Life and Legend*, Frederick A. Stoaks Publishers, New York, N.Y., 1934.

Rabineau, 1979
Rabineau, Phyllis, *Feather Arts: Beauty, Wealth and Spirit from Five Continents*, Field Museum of Natural History, Chicago, Ill., 1979.

Randhawa, 1996
Randhawa, T. S., *The Last Wanderers: Nomads and Gypsies of India*, Mapin, Ahmedabad, 1996.

Rasmussen, 1991
Rasmussen, Susan J., "Veiled Self, Transparent Meanings: Tuareg Headdress as Social Expression," *Ethnology*, vol. 30, no. 2, 1991, pp. 101–117.

Ray, 1981
Ray, Dorothy Jean, *Aleut and Eskimo Art*, University of Washington Press, Seattle, Wash., 1981.

Reid, 1986
Reid, James W., *Textile Masterpieces of Ancient Peru*, Dover Publications, Inc., New York, N.Y., 1986.

Reina and Kensinger, 1991
Reina, Ruben E. and Kenneth M. Kensinger, eds., *The Gift of Birds*, University Museum Monograph 75, University Museum of Archaeology and Anthropology, University of Pennsylvania, Philadelphia, Pa., 1991.

Reina and Pressman, 1991
Reina, Ruben E., and Jon F. Pressman, "Harvesting Feathers," in Reina and Kensinger, 1991, pp. 110–115.

Ribeiro, 1957
Ribeiro, Berta G., "Bases para una classificacao dos adornos plumarios dos Indios do Brasil," *Arquivos do Museu Nacional*, vol. 63, 1957, pp. 59–119.

Richards, 1983
Richards J. F., ed., *Precious Metals in the Later Medieval and Early Modern Worlds*, Carolina Academic Press, Durham, N.C., 1983.

Rivers, 1993i
Rivers, Victoria Z., "Jewel Beetles," *The India Magazine*, vol. 13, no. 2, 1993, pp. 6–17.

Rivers, 1993ii
Rivers, Victoria Z., "Indian Mirror Embroidery from Gujarat," *Ornament*, vol. 16, no. 3, 1993, pp. 66–69.

Rivers, 1994
Rivers, Victoria Z., "An Overview of Beetle Elytra in Textiles and

Ornament," *Cultural Entomology Digest*, no. 2, 1994, pp. 2–9.

Rivers, 1995i
Rivers, Victoria Z., "Recycled Textiles: Culture or Commodity," *Ornament*, vol. 19, no. 1, 1995, pp. 38–41.

Rivers, 1995ii
Rivers, Victoria Z., "Roghan: A Disappearing Textile Tradition from Kutch," *The India Magazine*, vol. 15, no. 10, 1995, pp. 42–57.

Rivers, 1995iii
Rivers, Victoria Z., "Heavy Metal— 'Light Work': Zardozi and Gota Work of India," *Ars Textrina*, Charles Babbage Research Centre, Winnipeg, vol. 23, 1995, pp. 11–33.

Rivers, 1996i
Rivers, Victoria Z., "Torans: Textile Door Hangings of Northwestern India," *Arts of Asia*, vol. 26, no. 3, 1996, pp. 86–97.

Rivers, 1996ii
Rivers, Victoria Z., "Gold Print: All That Glitters…," *Ars Textrina*, Charles Babbage Research Centre, Winnipeg, vol. 26, 1996, pp. 129–153.

Rivers, 1998i
Rivers, Victoria Z., "Splendid Patterns," *Surface Design Journal*, vol. 22, no. 2, 1998, pp. 20–23, 56–57.

Rivers, 1998ii
Rivers, Victoria Z., "Culture Cut Apart? Rural Indian Embroideries and Commoditization," *Marg*, vol. 49, no. 3, 1998, pp. 70–77.

Roche, Courage, and Devinoy, 1985
Roche, Serge, Germain Courage, and Pierre Devinoy, *Mirrors*, Rizzoli, New York, N.Y., 1985.

Rock, 1992
Rock, Joseph, *Lammas, Princes and Brigands: Photographs of the Tibetan Borderlands of China*, intro. by Michael Aris, China House Gallery and China Institute of America, New York, N.Y., 1992.

Rodgers, 1985
Rodgers, Susan, *Power and Gold*,
The Barbier-Müller Museum, Geneva,
1985.

Roe, 1995
Roe, Peter G., see Braun, 1995.

Rolle, 1980
Rolle, Renate, *The World of the
Scythians*, University of California Press,
Berkeley, Calif., 1980.

Rose, 1992
Rose, Clare, "Banjara Embroidery
Techniques," *Embroidery*, vol. 43, no. 3,
1992, pp. 157–159.

Rosen, 1998
Rosen, Norma, correspondence with
Victoria Rivers, May 1998.

Rossi, 1986
Rossi, Gail, "Guizhou Textiles," *Shuttle,
Spindle and Dye Pot*, vol. 18, no. 2,
1986, pp. 38–43.

Rossi, 1988i
Rossi, Gail, "Enduring Dress of the
Miao," *Ornament*, vol. 11, no. 3, 1988,
pp. 26–31.

Rossi, 1988ii
Rossi, Gail, "Chinese Silk Felt,"
Shuttle, Spindle and Dye Pot, vol. 18,
no. 3, 1988, pp. 29–33.

Rossi, 1990
Rossi, Gail, "Enduring Dye
Traditions of China's Miao and
Dong People," in *Dyes From Nature,
Plants and Gardens, Brooklyn Botanic
Garden Record*, vol. 46, no. 2, 1990,
pp. 20–23.

Rossi, 1992
Rossi, Gail, *The Dong People of China:
A Hidden Civilization*, Hagley and
Hoyle, Ltd., Singapore, 1992.

Rudenko, 1970
Rudenko, Sergei I., *Frozen Tombs of
Siberia: The Pazyryk Burials of Iron Age
Horsemen*, transl. by M. W. Thompson,
University of California Press, Berkeley,
Calif., 1970.

Rugh, 1986
Rugh, Andrea B., *Reveal and Conceal:
Dress in Contemporary Egypt*, Syracuse
University Press, New York, N.Y., 1986.

Rusch and Stein, 1988
Rusch, Walter, and Lothar Stein, *Siwa
und die Aulad Ali*, Veröffentlichungen
des Museums für Volkerkunde zu
Leipzig, heft 35, Akademie Verlag,
Berlin, 1988.

Ryder, 1969
Ryder, Alan F. C., *Benin and the
Europeans, 1485–1897*, Longman,
London, 1969.

Ryotaku and Keiji, 1985
Ryotaku, Cho, and Ueno Keiji, eds.,
Taiwan genjumin no fuzoku (*Taiwanese
Native Culture*), transl. by Yubi Koh,
Formosa, Tokyo, 1985.

Safer and Gill, 1982
Safer, Jane Fearer, and Francis
McLaughlin Gill, *Spirals from the Sea*,
Clarkson N. Potter, New York, N.Y.,
1982.

Saint-Aubin, 1983
de Saint-Aubin, Charles Germain,
Art of the Embroiderer, translated and
annotated by Nikki Scheuer, with
additional notes and commentaries by
Edward Maeder, Los Angeles County
Museum of Art, Los Angeles, Calif.,
and David R. Godine, Inc., Boston,
Mass., 1983.

Sandberg, 1989
Sandberg, Gösta, *Indigio Textiles:
Technique and History*, A. & C. Black,
London, 1989.

Scarce, 1987
Scarce, Jennifer, "Vesture and Dress:
Fashion, Function, and Impact," in
Carol Bier, ed., *Woven from the Soul,
Spun from the Heart*, The Textile
Museum, Washington, D.C., 1987,
pp. 33–56.

Schenck and Gifford, 1949–1952
Schenck, Sara M., and E. W. Gifford,

"Karok Ethnobotany," *Anthropological
Records*, vol. 13, no. 6, University of
California Press, Berkeley, Calif.,
1949–1952, pp. 370–392.

Schevill, 1997
Schevill, Margot Blum, "Innovation
and Change in Maya Cloth and
Clothing," in Margot Blum Schevill,
ed., *The Maya Textile Tradition*,
with photographs by Jeffrey J. Fox,
Harry N. Abrams, Inc., New York,
N.Y., 1997.

Schienerl, 1982
Schienerl, Peter W., "The Comparative
Study of Jewelry and Amulets,"
Ornament, vol. 6, no. 1, 1982,
pp. 16–17.

Schienerl, 1983
Schienerl, Peter W., "Amulets in
Modern Egypt," *Ornament*, vol. 6, no. 4,
1983, pp. 16–20.

Schifter, 1983
Schifter, Herbert F., *The Mirror Book*,
Schifter Publications, Exton, Pa., 1983.

Schletzer, 1984
Schletzer, Dieter and Reinhold, *Old
Silver Jewellery of the Turkoman*, transl.
by Paul Knight, Dietrich Reimer
Verlag, Berlin, 1984.

Schmidt, 1971
Schmidt, Max, *Primitive Races of
Mankind: A Study in Ethnology*, transl.
by Alexander K. Dallas, reprint, Kraus,
New York, N.Y., 1971.

Schneider and Weiner, 1989
Schneider, Jane, and Annette B.
Weiner, *Cloth and Human Experience*,
Smithsonian Institution Press,
Washington, D.C., 1989.

Schurz, 1959
Schurz, William Lytle, *The Manila
Galleon*, E. P. Dutton and Co., New
York, N.Y., 1959.

Scott, 1993
Scott, Philippa, *The Book of Silk*,
Thames and Hudson, London and New
York, N.Y., 1993.

Shams, 1987
Shams, Glorianne Pionati, *Some Minor Textiles in Antiquity*, Paul Astrom, Sweden, 1987.

Shaver, 1966
Shaver, Ruth M., *Kabuki Costume*, Charles E. Tuttle Co., Rutland, Vt., and Tokyo, 1966.

Simon, 1969
Simon, Hilda, *Feathers Plain and Fancy*, The Viking Press, New York, N.Y., 1969.

Simon, 1971
Simon, Hilda, *The Splendor of Iridescence*, Dodd Mead and Co., New York, N.Y., 1971.

Singh, 1979
Singh, Chandramani, *Textiles and Costumes from the Maharaja Sawai Man Singh II Museum*, Jaipur City Palace, Jaipur, 1979.

Singh, 1993
Singh, Madanjeet, ed., *The Sun: Symbol of Power and Life*, Harry N. Abrams, Inc., New York, N.Y., 1993.

Solyom, 1984
Solyom, Bronwen and Garrett, *Fabric Traditions of Indonesia*, Washington State University Press, Pullman, Wash., 1984.

Speiser, 1923
Speiser, Felix, *Ethnographische Materialien aus den Neuen Hebriden und den Banks-Inseln*, C. W. Kreidel's Verlag, Berlin, 1923.

Spring and Hudson, 1995
Spring, Christopher, and Julie Hudson, *North African Textiles*, Smithsonian Institution Press, Washington, D.C., 1995.

Stabb, 1998
Stabb, Jo Ann, "Golden Stitches: Unraveling Clues to the Origin of a North African Tunic," *Costume Society of America National Symposium Proceedings*, Pasadena, Calif., 1998.

Stein, 1971
Stein, Sir Aurel, *On Ancient Central Asian Tracks*, AMS Press, New York, N.Y., 1971, reissue of 1933 original.

Stirling, 1938
Stirling, M. W., *Historical and Ethnographical Material on the Jivaro Indians*, Smithsonian Institution Bureau of American Ethnology, Bulletin 117, 1938.

Stone, 1985
Stone, Caroline, *The Embroideries of North Africa*, Longman Group Limited, Burnt Mill, 1985.

Stone, 1987
Stone, Caroline, "Fabrics from the Middle East," *Surface Design Journal*, vol. 11, no. 2, 1987, pp. 33–35.

Strathern, 1971
Strathern, Andrew and Marilyn, *Self Decoration in Mount Hagen*, Gerald Duckworth and Co., London, 1971.

Strathern, 1993
Strathern, Andrew, "Dress, Decoration, and Art in New Guinea," in Malcolm Kirk, *Man as Art*, Chronicle Books, San Francisco, Calif., 1993, pp. 15–40.

Summerfield, 1991
Summerfield, Anne and John, *Fabled Cloths of Minangkabau* with intro. by Merrily Peebles, Santa Barbara Museum of Art, Santa Barbara, Calif., 1991.

Takemura, 1991
Takemura, Akihiko, *Fukusa: Japanese Gift Covers*, foreword by Mary V. and Ralph E. Hayes, Iwasaki Bijutsu-Sha, Tokyo, 1991.

Tansug, 1985
Tansug, Sabiha, *Turkmen Giyimi*, Akabank'in Bir Kultur Hizmeti, Turkey, 1985.

Tarlo, 1991
Tarlo, Emma, "A Stitch in Time Revives an Old Skill," *The India Magazine*, vol. 11, no. 2, 1991, pp. 19–27.

Tarlo, 1996
Tarlo, Emma, *Clothing Matters: Dress and Identity in India*, Viking/ Penguin Books, New Delhi, 1996.

Taylor, 1951
Taylor, Lucy D., *Know Your Fabrics: Standard Decorative Textiles and Their Uses*, John Wiley and Sons, New York, N.Y., 1951.

Taylor and Aragon, 1991
Taylor, Paul Michael, and Lorraine V. Aragon, *Beyond the Java Sea: Art of Indonesia's Outer Islands*, The National Museum of Natural History, Smithsonian Institution, Washington, D.C., and Harry N. Abrams, Inc., New York, N.Y., 1991.

Templeton, 1965
Templeton, Bonnie C., "Poisonous Plants Around Us," *Quarterly*, Los Angeles County Museum, vol. 4, no. 1, 1965, pp. 10–13.

Thompson, 1971
Thompson, Robert Ferris, *Black Gods and Kings: Occasional Papers of the Museum and Laboratories of Ethnic Arts and Technology*, no. 2, UCLA, Los Angeles, Calif., 1971.

Thompson, 1995
Thompson, Robert Ferris, "From the Isle Beneath the Sea: Haiti Africanizing Vodou Art," in Cosentino, 1995, pp. 91–119.

Till and Swart, 1997
Till, Berry, and Paula Swart, "Elegance and Spirituality of Japanese Kesa," *Arts of Asia*, vol. 26, no. 5, 1997, pp. 51–63.

Tselos, 1996
Tselos, Susan Elizabeth, "Threads of Reflection: Costumes of Haitian Rara," *African Arts*, vol. 29, no. 2, 1996, pp. 58–65, 102.

Tucci, 1974
Tucci, Giuseppe, *Transhimalaya*, transl. by James Hogarth, Barrie and Jenkins, London, 1974.

Untracht, 1997
Untracht, Oppi, *Traditional Jewelry of India*, Harry N. Abrams, Inc., New York, N.Y., 1997.

Vanoverberg, 1929
Vanoverberg, Morice, *Dress and Adornment in the Mountain Province of Luzon, Philippine Islands*, Publications of the Catholic Anthropological Conference, Washington, D.C., vol. 1, no. 5, 1929, pp. 181–242.

Varjola, Averkieva, and Liapunova, 1990
Varjola, Pirjo, with Julia P. Averkieva, and Roza G. Liapunova, *The Etholen Collection*, National Board of Antiquities, Helsinki, 1990.

V'avra, 1954
V'avra, Jaroslav Raimund, *Five Hundred Years of Glass-Making*, Artia, Prague, 1954.

Von Hagen, 1937
Von Hagen, Victor Wolfgang, *Off With Their Heads*, Macmillan, New York, N.Y., 1937.

Watt, 1972
Watt, Sir George, *A Dictionary of the Economic Products of India*, Gordhan, Delhi, 1972 (reissue).

Weir, 1989
Weir, Shelagh, *Palestinian Costume*, University of Texas Press, Austin, Tex., 1989.

Wills, 1883
Wills, C. J., *Land of the Lion and Sun*, MacMillan and Co., London, 1883.

Wilson, 1979
Wilson, Kax, *A History of Textiles*, Westview Press, Boulder, Colo., 1979.

Wilson, 1990
Wilson, Verity, *Chinese Dress*, Bamboo Publishing, Ltd., and the Victoria & Albert Museum, London, 1990.

Xun and Chunming, 1987
Xun, Zhou, and Gao Chunming, *5000 Years of Chinese Costume*, China Books and Periodicals Inc., Hong Kong, 1987.

Yacopino, 1977
Yacopino, Feliccia, *Threadlines Pakistan*, Ministry of Pakistan, 1977.

Yohe, 1981i
Yohe, Ralph S., "Al Maghrib al Aqsa: Islam's Far West," in Fiske, Pickering, and Yohe, 1981, pp. 19–30.

Yohe, 1981ii
See Fiske, Pickering, and Yohe, 1981, p. 114.

Yoshimoto, 1988
Yoshimoto, Shinobu, *Kain Perada: Hirayama Collection, the Gold Printed Textiles of Indonesia*, Kodansha Publishers, Tokyo, 1988.

Yoshioka, 1980
Yoshioka, Tsuneo, *Sarasa of the World*, Shoin, Kyoto, 1980.

Yuchi and Shizhao, 1985
Yuchi, Zhao, and Kuang Shizhao, *Clothings and Ornaments of China's Miao People*, The Cultural Palace of Nationalities, Beijing, 1985.

Zung, 1964
Zung, Cecilia S. L., *Secrets of the Chinese Drama*, Benjamin Blom, New York, N.Y., 1964.

Museums and Collections

The Bata Shoe Museum, Toronto: 102, 110, 195

Bishop Museum, Honolulu: 224

Robert Brundage: 109, 215, 268

California State Parks, California State Indian Museum: 9, 12, 216, 262

The Field Museum, Chicago: 244, 247, 260

Dr. Edward Gerber: 19, 20, 21, 23, 53, 86, 138, 147, 148

Patricia Harrison and Ross MacDonald: 152

Phoebe Apperson Hearst Museum of Anthropology, University of California at Berkeley, and The Regents of The University of California: 1, 13, 28, 29, 33, 34, 59, 65, 66, 71, 72, 73, 77, 80, 90, 111, 112, 113, 123, 126, 188, 199, 218, 219, 225, 229, 230, 242, 250, 253, 278, 281, 282, 284

The State Hermitage Museum, St. Petersburg: 161

Beverley Jackson: 266

Lee Kavaljian: 30, 31, 41, 43, 44, 50, 58, 63, 64, 84, 87, 88, 89, 91, 97, 99, 119, 130, 131

T. R. and Linda Lawrence: 133

Mary Jane Leland: 137

Los Angeles County Museum of Art, Costume Council Fund: 2

Maharaja Sawai Man Singh II Museum, City Palace, Jaipur: 196, 275

Adam Mekler: 254

Museo Nacional de Antropologia, Mexico City: 246

The Museum for Textiles, Toronto: 7, 24, 25, 35, 36, 38, 40, 49, 54, 60, 61, 78, 96, 121, 128, 129, 139, 157, 158, 159, 162, 163, 201, 202, 204, 206, 220, 221, 226, 231, 237, 238, 239

The National Museum, New Delhi, India: 5, 32, 67, 74, 76, 125, 241, 276, 277, 280

The National Museum of African Art, Smithsonian Institution, Washington, D.C.: 6, 198, 223; 243 (Gift of Milton F. and Frieda Rosenthal)

The National Museum of Denmark, Department of Anthropology: 168

National Museum of Finland, Helsinki: 212, 258, 271

Department of Anthropology, the National Museum of Natural History, Smithsonian Institution, Washington, D.C.: 10, 11, 48, 52, 62, 75, 81, 82, 83, 94, 100, 105, 106, 107, 108, 149, 164, 165, 166, 167, 194, 197, 200, 213, 227, 228, 232, 234, 240, 251, 252, 255, 256, 257, 259, 261, 263, 265, 267, 269

Pitt Rivers Museum, University of Oxford: 279, 286

Her Highness, the Rajmata of Kutch: 69

Jon Eric Riis: 14, 264

Victoria Z. Rivers: 4, 15, 16, 17, 18, 26, 46, 56, 57, 70, 92, 115, 120, 122, 124, 127, 136, 140, 141, 142, 143, 144, 145, 150, 160, 169, 171, 172, 173, 174, 175, 176, 177, 178, 179, 180, 183, 184, 185, 186, 187, 205, 207, 209, 210, 211, 217, 233, 235, 236, 270, 272, 273, 283

Estate of Sandra Sakata: 42, 116, 117

Thomas K. Seligman: 132, 135

Anne and John Summerfield: 101, 151

University of California Davis Design Teaching Collection: 45, 47, 79, 95, 103, 104, 182

UCLA Fowler Museum of Cultural History: 3, 22, 27, 37, 155, 156, 192, 248, 249, 274; 3, 189, 190, 191, 193 (Gift of Anne and John Summerfield)

Photo Credits

© Dugan Aguilar: 214

Martha Banyas: 39, 118, 146

Courtesy of The Bata Shoe Museum, Toronto: 102, 110, 195

Bishop Museum, Honolulu: 224

Steve Boyajian: 266

Eliot Elisofon Photographic Archives, National Museum of African Art, Smithsonian Institution: 6, 198, 223

Field Museum of Natural History, Chicago: 244, 260

© Nora Fisher: 170

© Takeshi Fujimori: 85

R. K. Datta Gupta: 5, 32, 67, 74, 76, 125, 241, 276, 277, 280

Matti Huuhka: 212, 258, 271

© Phyllis Galembo: 222

The State Hermitage Museum, St Petersburg: 161

Bart Kasten: 14, 264

Larry Kirkland: 10, 11, 48, 52, 62, 75, 81, 82, 83, 94, 100, 105, 106, 107, 108, 149, 164, 165, 166, 167, 194, 200, 213, 227, 232, 234, 251, 259, 261, 263, 267

Franko Khoury: 243

T. R. Lawrence: 114, 134

John Lee: 168

Courtesy of the Los Angeles County Museum of Art: 2

Barbara Robin Molloy: 1, 3, 4, 9, 12, 13, 15, 16, 17, 18, 19, 20, 21, 22, 23, 26, 27, 28, 29, 30, 31, 33, 34, 37, 41, 42, 43, 44, 45, 46, 47, 50, 53, 56, 57, 58, 59, 63, 64, 65, 66, 70, 71, 72, 73, 77, 79, 80, 84, 86, 87, 88, 89, 90, 91, 92, 95, 97, 99, 101, 103, 104, 111, 112, 113, 115, 116, 117, 119, 120, 122, 123, 124, 126, 127, 130, 131, 132, 133, 135, 136, 137, 138, 140, 141, 142, 143, 144, 145, 147, 148, 150, 151, 152, 155, 156, 160, 169, 171, 172, 173, 174, 175, 176, 177, 178, 179, 180, 182, 183, 184, 185, 186, 187, 188, 189,

190, 191, 192, 193, 199, 205, 207, 209, 210, 211, 215, 216, 217, 218, 219, 225, 229, 230, 233, 235, 236, 242, 248, 249, 250, 253, 262, 268, 270, 272, 273, 274, 278, 281, 282, 283, 284

Thomas Moore: 7, 24, 25, 35, 36, 38, 40, 49, 54, 60, 61, 78, 96, 121, 128, 129, 139, 157, 158, 159, 162, 163, 201, 202, 204, 206, 220, 221, 226, 231, 237, 238, 239

Museo Nacional de Antropologia, Mexico City: 246

Department of Anthropology, the National Museum of Natural History, Smithsonian Institution, Washington, D.C. Photo Archives: 197, 228, 252, 255, 256, 257, 265, 269

Peter Nelson: 8, 51

Pitt Rivers Museum, University of Oxford: 279, 286

Victoria Z. Rivers: 68, 69, 93, 181, 287

Don Russel: 109

© Thomas K. Seligman: 55

E. Z. Smith: 254

Dr. Sumahendra: 196, 275

Mitch Swanson: 240

© Susan Tselos: 153, 154

© Marie Turner: 98, 203

John Weinstein: 247

© Susan York: 208, 245, 285

Acknowledgments

Accumulating the images and research for this book has required a great deal of assistance and cooperation from many people without whose help I would never have succeeded.

I am most grateful to my husband, John Salkin, for his constant support, patience, and word-smithing skills. Margot Schevill has been my mentor throughout, and Jasleen Dhamija inspired me at the outset and assisted me in India. I am indebted, too, to Martha Banyas and Lee Kavaljian for sharing their knowledge and providing endless encouragement. My gratitude is extended to Gordon Hunting, whose generous gift of a trip to Bali in 1985 started me thinking about shining cloth. My treasured friends in India— Gauri and Sanat Shodhan; Rajendra Kunverba, the Rajmata of Kutch; Haku and Vilu Shah; A. A. Wazir; and Jagruti Pulin Shah—have given much of themselves to benefit my research.

At the University of California at Davis, Jo Ann Stabb must be recognized for the sacrifice she made to help me finish this book. Laura Mills unfailingly located hundreds of obscure research citations. I also wish to acknowledge the major contribution made by Barbara Molloy, who has photographed numerous artifacts with me over the past ten years; many of her images are included in this book. At the Phoebe Hearst Museum of Anthropology, University of California at Berkeley, Joan Knudsen has been most helpful in facilitating my access to the collections there.

I am grateful to Larry Kirkland and Thomas Moore for their photographic skills and their enthusiastic support of this project, as well as to Marion John-Postlewaite, Susan Warner Keene, and Peter Newman for their support in Toronto. Without Megan Langley's help, I would still be typing, and without the generosity of lenders such as Edward Gerber, T. R. and Linda Lawrence, Peter Nelson, and Anne and John Summerfield, this book would lack key artifacts representing certain regions. And without the wonderful people at Thames & Hudson, and the loving support of my parents, Ruth and Kenneth Zellich, there would have been no book at all.

Others to whom I wish to express my heartfelt thanks and gratitude include: Dan and Linda K. Abbot, Guy Bellinkx; Sinasi Cellakol; Rita Kapur Chisti; Katie Crum; Gopal Das; Dr. Kalpana Desai; Brendan Doyle; Nora Fisher; Kate Fitz-Gibbon; Aruna Ghose; Charu Smita Gupta; Andrew Hale; Patricia Harrison; Mary V. Hays; Beverley Jackson; M. Jafarali; Mina Jacobs; Jyontindra Jain; O. P. Jain; Ram Jethmalani; Mary Hunt Kahlenberg; Nobuko Kajitani; Linda Bartlet Keys; Vijay Lakshmi Kotak; Robert Liu and Carolyn Benesch at *Ornament*; Ross MacDonald; Patricia Malarcher at *Surface Design Journal*; Stephen Markbreiter and *Arts of Asia*; Adam Mekler; Thomas Moore; Pratapaditya Pal; Vaishali Parikh; Maharao Pragmalji III and the Maharani of Kutch; Ram Singh Rathod; Fran Reed; Norma Rosen; Gail Rossi; Toru Sanefuji; Kim Saunders; Chandramani Singh; Frieda Sorber; Dipak Sutaria; Mitch and Michelle Swanson; Susan Tselos; and Yoshiko Wada.

Bata Shoe Museum, Toronto: Jonathon Walford

California State Indian Museum, Sacramento: Bruce Stiny

Field Museum of Natural History, Chicago: Nina Cummings

Fowler Museum of Cultural History, Los Angeles: Don Cole; Fran Krystock; Barbara Sloan

Los Angeles County Museum of Art, Los Angeles: Kimberly Kostas; Cheryle Robertson; Kay Spilker; Naomi Weiss

Maharaja Sawai Man Singh II Museum, Jaipur: Yaduendra Sahai

The Museum for Textiles, Toronto: Sarah Holland; Sarah Quinton; Roxanne Shaughnessy

National Museum of Finland, Helsinki: Marja-Leena Kaasalainen; Dr. Pirjo Varjola

National Museum of Natural History, Smithsonian Institution, Washington, D.C.: David Burgevin; Dr. William Crockett; William Fitzhugh; Deb Hull-Walski; Andrew Klefter; Felicia Pickering; Gail Solomon; Deborah Wood

National Museum, New Delhi: Dr. Daljeet; R. K. Datta Gupta; Krishna Lal; Anamika Patak

Phoebe Hearst Museum of Anthropology, Berkeley: Dr. Frank Norick; Barbara Takiguchi

Pitt Rivers Museum, Oxford University: Julia Nicholson; Kate White

The State Hermitage Museum, St. Petersburg: Dr. Vladimir Matveyev

University of California Davis: Gayle Bondurant and Rob Brower in the Department of Environmental Design; Graduate Research Assistants in Textile Arts and Costume Design: Martha Brundin, Annie Farley, Laura Reyes, Kathy Rousso, Linda Welch, and Mary Yaeger; Sue Blair in Business and Contracts, and the Regents of the University of California

This book was prepared with assistance from a US Subcommission on Education and Culture Indo-American Fellowship; University of California Faculty Research Grants and Seed Grant; and University of California Davis Washington Center Faculty Research Grants.

Glossary and Index of Terms

References in *italics* refer to the illustrations

aba obi, unmarried woman's belt, Admiralty and Solomon Islands *237, 238*

abaca, a type of hemp fiber, *Musa textilis 48*

abaigho, ritual garment worn by a healer priestess, Nigeria 222

abaye, cloak, Syria 95

abhala bharat, mirror embroidery, India 66–67

abrak, mica, India 61

Abrus precatorius, crab-eye or rosary bean 127, *241, 243*

abu qalamun, a type of ancient textile 26

abugs, silky tags used in Berber weaving, Morocco *132, 135*

Acacia ehrenbergiana, resin-producing tree, Arabia 32

adalil, Tuareg woman's headcloth 55

adat, social custom, Indonesia *101*

ade, crown, Yoruba, Nigeria, *198*

adi, orchid vines, Admiralty or Solomon Islands *237, 238*

adinkra, stamped cloth of the Asante people, Ghana 32, 59

adire, resist-dyed indigo cloth of the Yoruba, Nigeria 31

adras ikat, ikat woven with cotton and silk, Central Asia 41, *18*

aduro, shiny brown-black dye used in *adinkra* 32

aeeweenuk, northwest Pacific coast man's hat *212*

aftek, Tuareg woman's festive upper body garment 55

agbada or *riga*, oversize shirt, West Africa 54

'ahu'ula, Hawaiian feather cape 130

akajik, sideburn ornaments of the Aguaruna/Shuar people of Ecuador *281, 282*

ak-fju-dat, work-bag, Alaskan peoples *164, 167, 263*

Alcedinidae, kingfisher family 132

Aleurites molucanna, candlenut tree 126

altan, Turkic-Mongolian word for gold 51

amiantus, ancient name for asbestos 61

Anadonia or Lucinidae, freshwater clam family *228*

angarakha, man's close-fitting, front-tieing garment with U-shaped neckline, India *122*

Anodorhynchus hyacinthinus, hyacinthe macaw 132

Ara ararauna, blue and yellow macaw 132

Ara chloroptera, red and green macaw 132

Ara macao, scarlet macaw 132

Archaeopteryx lithographica, 140-million-year-old lizard bird with feathers 129

aren, Naga word for soul-force 135

arti, a part of Hindu worship using light *125*

asherah nahuak, Siwa oasis bridal dress *218, 219*

asu-gutsu, Shinto priest's shoes 57

asyut, tulle fabric worked with flat metal strips from Asyut, Egypt *119*

ataderos, ceremonial boots of ancient Peru *110*

atlas ikat, satin-weave ikat with silk warp and weft 41, *37, 39*

ayi-khwo, Naga name for yellow orchid straw 128

babouche, slippers, Persia *195*

bachakadiyo, envelope-shaped bag, India *176, 177*

badla, flattened silver wire 53, 92, *120, 276*

baghmal, cotton velvet ikat woven in Bukhara, Uzbekistan 35, *36*

bak, Admiralty Islands loincloth *225*

Bambusoidea, bamboo family 128

ba'oulam, conus cross-sections, Sarawak *231*

barkalla, north Yemeni woman's robe with embroidered neck 61

Bombyx mori, cultivated silk worm 26

bompo, healers practicing Jhankrism or shamanism 268

Bridelia micranta, or Badie tree, used to make shiny ink, Ghana 32

Buprestidae, jewel beetle family 9, 135, 136, *281, 282*

butti, tiny floral bouquet motif *32, 276*

byssus, silky mollusk fiber from *Pinna marina* 26

Caesalphinia bonduc, molluca beans or nickernuts 126

calabash, gourd used for carving *adinkra* stamps 32, 59

Ceratonia siliqua, locust tree 127

cermuk, mirror, Sumatra 67, 114, *97, 189, 190, 192*

Cetonniinae, a type of beetle used in Papua New Guinea ornament *285*

chab-blug, lama's holy water flask, Tibet *81*

chakla, square textile, India 110, *174, 175*

chalat, robe, Central Asia *118*

chanking, polishing cloth with a chank shell, India 30

china poblana, Mexican women's national costume from rural dress *149*

chintz, printed and polished cloth from south India 30

chkara, leather shoulder bag, Morocco *114, 115*

choli, short cropped blouse, India 112, *170*

chonin, townspeople, merchants, and artisans, Japan 52–53

chowk, square motif woven in *gharchola* saris, Gujarat, India 92

Chrysophora chrysoclora, type of scarab beetle *281, 282*

Coix lacryma-jobi, Job's tears 127, 144

Conus leopardus, type of shell *231*

corypha, palm and vegetable ivory nut 70

Cotingidae, bird species which includes the turquoise cotinga 131

couching, sewing technique where a needle and thread anchors objects in place 50, *71, 78, 120, 147, 148*

Cycas revoluta, sago palm 122

Cypraea annulus, ring cowrie 122

Cypraea moneta, yellow money cowrie 122

dabka, finely coiled wire used in *zardozi*, India 53

darbha, type of dried grass, India 128

Demostachya bipinnata, type of grass, India 128

devoré, pattern process which destroys velvet pile 31

dhavalo, Banjara ritual bridal songs, India 57

dhom, type of palm 127

dharaniyo, dowry quilt cover, Gujarat, India 110, *4, 173*

dohlja, golden tunic, Tunisia *103, 104*

donson dlokiw, West African hunter's shirt *7*

drapo, Haitian sequinned banners used in Vodou 11, 60, 102, *155, 156*

dupatta, shoulder cloth, India 61

eem, Native American female shaman-healer, northern California 260

ejar, drawstring trousers, northwest India 70

elytra, hard outer wing covers of beetles 7, 9, 14, 15, 96, 123, 134–136, 158, *5, 210, 257, 267, 274, 275, 276, 277, 278, 280*

etsemat, toucan feather headband, Shuar people *253*

Euchroma gigantea, type of beetle *281, 282*

faience, heated and glazed quartz sand material developed by Egyptians 10, 71–72, 116

fei-ts'ui, kingfisher feathers, China 132, *265, 266*

fez, hat, Turkey *142, 144, 145, 146, 205*

fukusa, ceremonial gift cover, Japan 86, 89

gahng-ah-mao, felted silk, Miao people, Zhouxi area, southwestern China *21*

gajia, shiny grass ornaments, India 128

Ganesha sthaphana, household shrine, India *178*

Ganga-Jamuna, brocade with gold and silver threads, India 79

garusu or *geris*, polished cloth, Indonesia 30, 44

tintiin, small obsidian shapes attached to
     dress, Native American peoples, northern
     California 62
tiraz, prestige dress given as gift in Persia 52
togo, glossy brown sap from the mangrove
     tree used to print patterns on bark cloth,
     Fiji/Samoa 60
toli, polished bronze and copper mirrors,
     Mongolia 168
toran, doorway hanging, northwest India
     110, 135, *173, 179, 181*
Tridacna gigas, giant clam 124
tritik, stitch-resist patterned fabric 25
Trochilidae, hummingbird family 131
Trogonidae, quetzal family 133
tucum, hard shiny seeds used in Amazon
     Basin 257
tuik, Shuar name for scarab beetle wings *281,*
     282
tumpal, triangular motif, Indonesia *151*
Turbinella, chank shell 30, *215*
Turbo marmoratus, green turban shell 124
turkudi, high-status pounded indigo cloth,
     West Africa 46, 55, 56

ucetek, Turkmen woman's robe often made
     from ikat-patterned fabric 39
uchidashi kanoko, type of simulated tie-dye
     pattern, Japan 30
ukunch, bandolier worn by Shuar chiefs
     240
umpak, Bagobo or Bilaan woman's upper
     garment, Mindanao, Philippine Islands
     229
ush, river sand containing soda ash used to
     make glass, India 65

vatwa, drawstring purse, India *176, 177*
veves, Haitian diagrams of deities 11

wauwau, Shuar name for *Euchroma gigantea*
     beetle wings, Ecuador *281, 282*

yaake, competitive dance performed by
     young Wodaabe men, Niger 56
yafus, woman's ceremonial dance regalia,
     northern California 9, *214, 216*
yafus'iish, backwrap worn with apron
     (*tantaz*), northern California *214, 216*
yagama, bird of paradise, highland Papua
     New Guinea 245
yanakboven, sequin-edged scarves, Turkey
     146
yan bao, indigo-dyed, glossy cloth with
     steamed egg-white and other substances,
     Miao and Dong people, China *51, 52, 53*

zar, Persian for gold 53, 74
zardozi, textures and shapes of metallic
     embroidery 53, 74, 76, 92, 162, *67, 68, 69,*
     70, 71, 124, 277
zari, metallic-thread weaving, India 76, 83,
     84, 94, *82, 91, 92, 94*
zecchino, the Venetian ducat, a term which
     led to the word sequin 59

Index of Peoples and Places

References in *italics* refer to the illustrations